TVEI AND CURRICULUM THEORY

By David Lee

PUBLISHED BY
David Lee & Humberside Education Services 1996
© Copyright David Lee

ISBN 1 85857 096 4

Distributed in the UK by:

Escon Education Support Consultancy Ltd
Bishop Norton, Lincoln, England LN2 3AY

Printed by Albert Gait Ltd.
Castle Press Grimsby, England

DAVID LEE

David was born in 1946 and is married with two grown up children. His teaching career, which lasted over twenty years, included senior management experience in both secondary and adult and continuing education. He also runs his own independent education consultancy. Since 1990 he has been Area Curriculum Development Co-ordinator for North East Lincolnshire. His responsibilities have included management of the TVEI extension project through which he has introduced a number of unique and successful networking strategies for curriculum and staff development.

David has worked closely with teachers, senior managers of schools and colleges, and LEA officers and advisers. In partnership with them, he has initiated and managed a wide range of developments across the whole curriculum, many of which have resulted in the production of high quality teaching and learning materials and substantial improvements in the management of institutional, curriculum, and pedagogical change.

In 1993 he completed a post graduate research degree in curriculum and pedagogy at The University of Hull. It is that research which provides the basis for this book.

Other publications written / edited by David Lee include:

'The Curriculum 14-19: a report and recommendations'
&
'Managing the Learning Process'

Available from:
The Curriculum Development Partnership
North East Lincolnshire Education Department
Grimsby

Forthcoming:
'Thinking Technology' by David Lee, Geoffrey Harrison & Gina White

All the above publications have been produced as a result of the research undertaken for 'TVEI and Curriculum Theory'

CONTENTS

PART TWO   A REVIEW OF CURRICULUM THEORY

PART THREE
TVEI & CURRICULUM THEORY: CONCLUSION

TABLES

Foreword By Denis Lawton - Professor of Curriculum, Institute of Education, University of London.

One of the most interesting episodes in the history of the secondary school curriculum was TVEI. A good deal has been written about various aspects of TVEI, but much of it from a limited point of view and often in a way that ignored the historical context and curriculum theory.

David Lee has now put that right. He has written an excellent account of the origins of TVEI, its impact on schools and on teaching methods. His book illustrates many of the positive features of the initiative and the developments which took place as a result of TVEI - modular structures, experiential learning, student self-assessment and many others.

But the book is not just about TVEI. Part Two is an interesting comprehensive review of curriculum theories which is then used as a basis for discussing the curriculum implications of TVEI. TVEI and Curriculum Theory underlines the point that the changes which have characterised curriculum development in the past - often *ad hoc* and contradictory - were the result of a lack of theoretical underpinning. It is appropriate that, at a time when the 14-19 curriculum is again seen as a key area of development, that the lessons of TVEI are thoroughly scrutinised.

Because TVEI and Curriculum Theory highlights the study of curriculum, it will also be of interest to those who have responsibility for the initial and post-graduate training of teachers. The conclusions drawn are important and challenging for policy makers and teachers.

TVEI and Curriculum Theory: Introduction by David Lee

TVEI (the Technical and Vocational Education Initiative) was introduced in April 1983 following a short period of preparation. Initially it was a limited *pilot* project involving a small cohort of students in schools and colleges in fourteen local education authorities. They were selected on the basis of bids made to the Manpower Services Commission which managed the initiative. The projects were intended to test the feasibility of providing a technical and vocational element within the curriculum of fourteen to sixteen year-olds, with the opportunity to extend it post sixteen. The pilot phase was extended the following year and the nation-wide TVEI *extension* which involves all students in the fourteen to eighteen age range began in 1987.

The principal purpose of this book, (which focuses on the 14-16 curriculum), is to analyse the development of TVEI in the light of existing curriculum theory. This has involved analysing both published and unpublished material, and synthesising it for the first time. The analysis also highlights the extent to which TVEI has been innovative.

A great deal has already been written about TVEI. There are numerous evaluation reports, case-studies and a significant quantity of published material. However, much of that which is currently available is relatively ephemeral, and even that which is not tends to concentrate on micro philosophical aspects of the programme. There has to date been no systematic analysis of TVEI in terms of the great body of curriculum theory which exists and which stretches from Plato to contemporary writers. In the relatively few instances where the relationship between TVEI and curriculum theory has been explored, it has tended to concentrate on *one* aspect rather than to address epistemological, sociological and psychological aspects of curriculum theory.

There does not appear to have been any serious questioning of the extent to which the aims and objectives of TVEI have a basis in curriculum theory. Perhaps this reflects a generally 'pragmatic' or problem driven approach to curriculum development in the United Kingdom. However no development entirely escapes from theory, since theory emanates from the systematic analysis of the choices and decisions which are open to the curriculum planner who faces the basic questions: What *is* taught? What *should* be taught? How should it be taught? "Teachers are in the grip of some educational theory whether they realise it or not". (Moore in Lawton et al 1978: 16)

Part One: The Characteristics of TVEI

Part one has four chapters, the first of which examines the background to TVEI. In particular, it identifies and explores the principal curriculum issues, pertinent to TVEI, which arose out of the so-called 'great debate'. It draws on evidence from the relevant DES and HMI publications, and involves analysis of published material relating directly to the aims and objectives of TVEI.

The second chapter consists of a detailed analysis of TVEI curricula in terms of 'breadth' and 'balance'. The research material, as in the case of chapters three and four, is based on primary sources, principally national reviews and case-studies. Chapter three focuses on work-related aspects of TVEI curricula, and chapter four is concerned with TVEI developments in teaching and learning. This section is perhaps the most extensive and comprehensive survey of published and unpublished TVEI material undertaken to date.

Part Two: A Review of Curriculum Theory

This part also has four chapters beginning with an introduction which outlines the rationale for part two, its structure, and brief outlines of the three principal curriculum paradigms which are explored: knowledge, society and student centred curricula, and the three main educational ideologies - classical humanism, reconstructionism and progressivism - which underpin them. Chapters six, seven and eight explore, in some depth, literature relating to aspects of knowledge, society and student centred curricula. Part two provides a basis for the analysis and conclusions concerning the relationship between the characteristics of TVEI identified in part one, and those of the curriculum paradigms identified in this part.

Part Three: TVEI and Curriculum Theory - Conclusions

The third and final part involves both analysis and synthesis of the outcomes of parts one and two and sets out conclusions concerning the relationship between TVEI and existing curriculum theory. In this concluding section I attempt to: 1) determine whether there is evidence to suggest that TVEI was consciously based on or related to established curriculum theory; 2) determine whether TVEI would have benefited from the application of such theory to clarify and provide a more sustainable basis for the aspects of curriculum development it supported; and 3) determine to what extent TVEI developments in practice embody some aspects of such theory.

PART ONE

THE CHARACTERISTICS OF TVEI

Chapter One

Introduction and background to TVEI

Prime Minister Callaghan's Ruskin College speech on the 18th of October 1976 began a public debate which created a backwash of conferences, investigations and reports notably from the DES and HMI which continued under the aegis of the Thatcher government culminating in the 1988 Education Reform Act and the National Curriculum. There were many significant outcomes along the way, notably, *'Education in Schools: A Consultative Document'*, (DES 1977) which marked the beginning of the consultative process. That publication highlighted the problems of existing curricula, made recommendations and began to clarify the responsibilities of the DES, the LEA's and schools, in working towards a broad framework for the curriculum. It is an important document in the study of TVEI because despite the fact that it pre-dates the first TVEI pilot projects by six years, it identified many educationally significant changes in society and highlighted some of the 'gaps' in curriculum provision which TVEI may have been intended to fill. Particularly important are sections 2.9 which underlines the importance of science, mathematics, and modern languages and the need for new teaching and learning methods and sections 2.14, 2.15, 2.16 and 2.17, which deal with breadth and balance and the importance of studies which relate to working life. It also explores some of the problems and benefits of a 'core curriculum' up to the end of compulsory schooling and could be argued to provide a rationale for both TVEI and the National Curriculum. Together with other DES and HMI publications it highlighted a number of key issues.

There was the issue of how to establish a productive and on-going dialogue between education and industry, and re-establish industry's confidence in education (Jamieson in Dale et al 1985: 26). TVEI was conceived in a time of national crisis brought about by socio-economic change and sustained criticism of the existing curriculum, particularly the 14-16 phase of the secondary curriculum. The British economy had become increasingly uncompetitive and was losing world markets to the newly industrialised countries. (Roderick and Stephens 1982: 122; Worswick 1985: 1; Rajan 1992: 256 fig.18.3; *'Education Research vol. 22*': 1; see also Hopkins et al 1990: ch.13, regarding TVEI's role). High youth unemployment was a problem, especially in areas which suffered from the contraction of heavy manufacturing industry in the early nineteen-eighties (Watson et al 1983: 4; see Worswick 1985: 6,8; Rajan 1992: 30. 92. fig.7.1 tables B1, B2). The following extract from a memorandum submitted by Cleveland County Council to the 'House of Commons Education Science and Arts Committee' on 27th January 1983 testifies to the problems facing those areas of the country which traditionally relied on heavy manufacturing industry for employment.

"The employment position has traditionally been dominated by heavy industry, and the chemical industry and steel remain the two largest employment groups. Unemployment levels in the county are the highest on the mainland of the United Kingdom with a corresponding level of unemployment amongst young people." (*House of Commons Education Science & Arts Committee, 27th January 1983:* 49 para. 1)

Employment patterns in Britain were changing rapidly in the early nineteen-eighties. As the need for unskilled labour reduced, that for a more skilled and mobile work-force increased (see Russell in Worswick 1985: 68-69). Consequently the need for education to become more responsive to industry's needs became more urgent. (Richardson 1992: 13-14). In general terms, compared with competitor countries, the United Kingdom in the 1980's had a poorly qualified work-force, and an educational system in which vocational education had low status (Wiener 1981; Roderick and Stephens 1982). The numbers of young people continuing with their education post-sixteen were also lower than in many other countries (Hayes, Anderson, Fonda 1984: 82; Rajan in, 'National Targets for Education and Training - The Case for Targets' 1992).

"......a major barrier to up-grading and even to sustaining competitive advantage in industry [has been the way] the British educational system has badly lagged behind that of virtually all the nations we studied. Access to top quality education has been limited to a few, and a smaller percentage of students go on to higher education than in most other advanced nations." (Porter in Rajan 1992: 2)

In the United Kingdom in the nineteen-eighties, too many students left secondary education without attaining a satisfactory level in the basic skills and without any real understanding of the economy and the world of work (DES 1977; 1983; 1985; Hayes, Anderson, Fonda 1984; Rajan 1991: fig 16.1; Rajan 1992: 27 fig. 3.1; 175 table 12.2). There was a need to increase opportunity in schools for young people to become familiar with, and acquire competence in using, the new technologies particularly information technology (OECD 1983: 42-45; Ainley 1990; Thatcher, Barbican Speech Dec. 1982).

Criticism that education did not encourage the most able students to seek careers in industry also increased in the early nineteen-eighties (Richardson 1992; Roderick and Stephens 1982: 65-71). Perhaps the most disturbing criticism which surfaced during that period of time emanated from studies of the relationship between education and industry. Wiener (1981) drew attention to the fact that not only were the problems of the economy and education inter-related, but also that they were deeply rooted in the culture of our society, which he argued is essentially anti-industrial. In 'English Culture and the Decline of the Industrial Spirit' 1850 -1980, he wrote:

"If the argument of this book is valid, the outcome of Thatcher's crusade may turn on how successful methods like lowering marginal tax rates and restricting the money supply will be in altering cultural attitudes formed over many years, The least tractable obstacle to British economic "redevelopment" may well be the continuing resistance of cultural values and attitudes." (ibid 1981: 163; see also Taylor in Worswick 1985; Jamieson & Lightfoot 1982: ch.2; Parry 1971: 51)

In the nineteenth century the role of education was to train the children of the working class for employment in industry and to prepare the sons of the upper class as gentlemen and to fulfil their role of helping to rule the empire. (Wiener 1981: 11-24; Roderick & Stephens 1982: 12; see also Simon 1960: ch.3, regarding 19th century instrumentalism, and Thompson 1967 for a perspective on the 18th century workhouse ethic of 'work discipline'). Those values Wiener argued, still persisted in the second half of the twentieth century. The government recognised the need to restore industry's faith in education. In *'Education in Schools: a consultative document'* DES (1977) for example, there is a complete section (section 7), that deals with school and working life and which calls for the involvement of commerce and industry in curriculum planning. It underlines the economic necessity of ensuring that the curriculum is congruent with the needs of industry, particularly manufacturing industry (ibid: 7. 4.vi). During the early 1980's, in order to achieve those ends the Department of Employment and the Department of Trade and Industry became involved in a whole range of initiatives aimed at improving the quality of education and training, and engaging industry in the process (Richardson 1992: 13-14). TVEI was part of the strategy (Department of Employment 1991: 17) and was regarded by some observers as being a challenge to education traditionalism (see Munroe in *'Times Scottish Educational Supplement'*, 9th Feb. 1990: 48; Dale et al 1990: ch.1). It was through the MSC, an arm of the Employment Department, that TVEI was introduced. The role of TVEI in developing a working relationship between education and industry will be explored in greater detail in chapter three which deals with the work-related curriculum.

A second issue which arose from DES and HMI investigations was the issue of how to establish some sort of balance between general and vocational education and ensure that students had the opportunity to develop a wide range of skills (see McCulloch in Gleeson 1987: 19, 26). By the nineteen-seventies, most of the vocational courses which had been developed in the nineteen-fifties and nineteen-sixties had disappeared (Watts 1982: 13). In some schools there had been a brief attempt at providing some form of vocational education when the school leaving age was raised (Lightfoot and Jamieson 1982: 78), but generally there were few vocational opportunities available to students pre-sixteen. In England the introduction of comprehensive education had not been accompanied by curriculum reform as it had for example in Sweden (McClure in Worswick 1985: 116). The secondary curriculum had become increasingly like that of the grammar schools with the emphasis on academic studies and cognitive-intellectual skills (Watts 1982: 5-6; Hargreaves 1982). There was growing concern that the curriculum had become over-loaded and that some of the essential elements were not receiving sufficient attention (DES 1977). In addition, criticism of the options system for fourteen to sixteen year olds was mounting (DES 1977). The main concern was that it did not ensure breadth and balance in students' programmes, indeed in some instances it reduced their progression and career opportunities (Lawton 1980: 47).

'Curriculum 11-16: towards a statement of entitlement', recommended methods of teaching and learning which would ensure the acquisition of essential skills, attitudes, concepts and knowledge (DES 1983: 27. 2.v). It also accepted the need for improved assessment to monitor pupils' progress and for accessible reporting procedures (ibid: 27. 2.vii). *'Curriculum 11-16'* also outlines a methodology for developing the curriculum, and for assessment and recording of achievement through cross-curricular mapping of essential skills, concepts,

attitudes and knowledge. Students' achievement in those areas, the report recommended, should be reported to parents and employers through a single system of recording and reporting (ibid: 34-41). The HMI proposals have importance to TVEI because they underpin the curriculum policy described in *'Better Schools'* (DES 1983) and much of the work of the LEA's in preparing their TVEI proposals (Employment Dept 1991: 28). The issue of balance between vocational and general education will be explored in greater detail in chapter two which examines TVEI strategies for achieving breadth and balance in the curriculum.

A further complex series of issues which arose from DES and HMI investigations was how to meet the challenges presented by new technologies and changing patterns of employment. Associated issues included: how to equip young people with positive attitudes towards business, industry and employment, and with the personal and social skills needed to make them effective employees and members of society (see Hughes in *'Education Research vol. 22'* Nov. 1989: 3; Stafford, Jackson, Banks in *'Education Research vol. 24'* 1982: 243; see also Jamieson in Dale 1985: 24-26).

The need to improve education and training was a world-wide issue (OECD 1983). The new technologies which were being used increasingly in business and industry, required new skills and competencies, particularly in the use of information technology (Employment Department 1991: 17; see also Watson et al 1993: 4,5; Ford in Worswick et al 1985: 70; see Watts 1983: ch1; FEU 1985, for summaries of training developments from 1972 to the introduction of YTS). Many people in industry were voicing concern over the extent to which education and training were in tune with their needs (DES 1977: section 7, esp. 7.1; see also 1.12, 1.3) and there were others in government and education who were concerned that, in the context of the changes which were taking place in industry and in society, the needs of many students were also not being met (DES 1977; DES 1983; McCulloch in Gleeson 1987: 21, 24-26). As a consequence, the successful economies of competitor countries attracted attention to their educational provision (see Hayes, Anderson, Fonda 1984; HMI 1986; 1991; Praise in Worswick 1985: 40-41). Some critics of the increased emphasis on vocationalism saw TVEI as the means of imposing the German system on British education (see Holt & Reid in Pollard Purvis, Walford 1988: 25).

The concern of the British government expressed in the 1977 DES report reflected an international concern with bridge-building between school and work (*OECD Paris Conference Report* 1970; OECD 1983; ch.6; Watson 1983). In Britain there had been concern over careers education provision since both a House of Commons Expenditure Committee report in 1977, and a survey carried out by The Institute of Careers Officers (1976) indicated that careers education and work experience in schools was unsatisfactory (see Jamieson & Lightfoot 1982: 22-23). One of the principal aims of TVEI has been to improve the bridge between school and work through effective careers education and guidance, work experience, and by developing in particular, the work - related aspects of the curriculum. *'Better Schools'* (DES 1985) reiterated the call for higher standards which would in turn strengthen the economic and social fabric of society (ibid: 88 para. 295). It reinforced the need for a broad, balanced and relevant curriculum, and outlined the way in which it was intended that the TVEI would develop the practical, technical and vocational aspects (ibid: 16-17 paras. 50-51). It stated the responsibility of LEA's not only to respond to the 'DES Circular 8/83', but also to translate their proposals into effective policies (ibid: 12-13). In addition it underlined the importance to students, of developing a range of skills, competencies and personal qualities, which representatives of employers' organisations had identified as important (ibid: 15-16). These issues will also be explored in chapters two and three which deal with curriculum breadth and balance and the work-related curriculum.

A further issue was that of how to ensure a broad, balanced, and relevant general education for all students up to the end of compulsory school attendance (DES: 1978; 1981; 1983; 1987) which was highlighted in 'Curriculum 11-16: towards a statement of entitlement' (DES 1983). This is an important document in TVEI terms and one which articulated the outcomes of the HMI inquiry which began in 1976 and which was punctuated by a number of conferences and publications, the most important of which are arguably; "The Red Book 1" ('Curriculum 11-16: working papers by HM Inspectorate: a contribution to current debate', published in 1978), and "The Red Book 2" ('Curriculum 11-16: a review of progress', published in 1981). The third in the series, 'Curriculum 11 - 16 towards a statement of entitlement' (1983), analysed the outcomes of the inquiry and picked up the positive aspects and the implications for curriculum planning. It provided a contextual background against which a number of key questions were posed to do with the relationship between education and contemporary society (DES 1983: 25-26). It also provided a framework for an entitlement curriculum for students up to the age of sixteen, which included the following requirements of curriculum planners and managers: a statement of objectives in terms of skills, attitudes, concepts and knowledge (ibid: 26. 2.ii) and a balanced allocation of time for all eight areas of experience (the aesthetic and creative, the ethical, the linguistic, the mathematical, the physical, the scientific, the social and political, and the spiritual); which reflects the importance of each (ibid: 26, 27. 2.iii). It strongly recommended provision of an entitlement curriculum in all five years of secondary education, which would occupy 70-80 per cent of the time available, with the remaining time being used to accommodate "individual talents and interests" (ibid: 27: 2.iv).

'Better Schools' (DES 1985) which is particularly relevant to TVEI Extension, also articulated the outcomes of the education debate and spelt out what the broad objectives of the curriculum should be. It also went into specific details regarding the problems that needed to be addressed and set out government policy and the particular responsibilities of the DES, the LEA's, and schools. It made specific, the need to address balance in the curriculum for fourteen to sixteen year olds whose choices of courses through the options system did not always ensure that they would continue with a balanced curriculum in the sense of that described in 'Curriculum 11-16' (para: 69). It recommended a 'core' curriculum to account for 80%-85% of the time, with 15%-20% of time for free-choice options. The intention of the proposal was to provide a core of 'essential' studies with personal interests and vocational aspirations being encouraged through the optional elements, a pattern which it pointed out was emerging through TVEI (ibid: 23).

"This approach is reflected in the evolving pattern of provision for 14-16 year olds within the TVEI, since the practical and technological aspects within TVEI courses are elements of a kind which should be in every pupil's programme." (ibid: 23.69)

'Better Schools' also advocated a more holistic view of the curriculum (ibid: 18.56; 19.59) and was important to TVEI in so far as it recommended that the curriculum should be described in terms of 'outcomes' as well as content, a feature of many TVEI courses (ibid: 17.52, 17.53). The anomalies of imbalance in some of the pilot schemes were, in the main, addressed successfully as a result of the more precise specification for TVEI which was published in 'Better Schools' (HMI 1991: xii; 8). TVEI implemented much of the policy enshrined in 'Better Schools' through the requirements it placed on LEA's in the extension, when it became a contractual obligation to provide a balanced curriculum (Employment Dept. 1991: 28, 31). Extension project LEA's and schools were required to provide development plans on an annual basis to ensure that the national criteria are addressed. The emphasis on curriculum balance and student entitlement in TVEI Extension provided a basis for the introduction of the National Curriculum. This issue will be explored further in chapter two which deals with TVEI and curriculum breadth and balance.

The high post-sixteen drop-out rate and the problems of gender and other forms of stereotyping, made motivation of young people during compulsory education another important issue, particularly in light of the growing need to prepare them for life-long education and training (*House of Commons Education Committee 20th Dec. 1982:* para 72). The comparatively low 'staying on' rates post-sixteen provided another area of government concern. The low take-up of post-sixteen education and training was perceived as wastage of skills and potential and was brought about by several factors. The first was the drop-out rate of students at sixteen caused in part by low value being attached to education by students whose parents were unskilled or semi-skilled. Even after the introduction of comprehensive education, raising the school leaving age, and the introduction of the CSE, it was still substantially less likely for the children of parents in the lowest skilled occupations to continue in education post-sixteen as is evident from table 1.

Table 1 Participation rates in full-time education of 16-19 year olds by socio-economic group of father, Great Britain 1981

socio-economic group of father	% participation rates
semi-skilled and unskilled manual	18
skilled manual and own account non-professional	25
intermediate and junior non-manual	43
employers and managers	45
professional	66

General Household Survey, 1981, OPCS, HMSO, 1983: 125 (in Worswick 1985: 20).

Often in families in the lower socio-economic groups, the pattern had been to leave school at the earliest opportunity to enter a lifetime's occupation in industry (Magnussen 1977: 2-3). The recession of the early nineteen-eighties had hit the areas of heavy industry, traditionally the largest employers of unskilled and semi-skilled labour, very hard.

The other factors in the problem of 'wastage' were gender stereotyping and racial discrimination (DES 1977: 41 *'Swann Report'* 1985) both of which had been addressed by legislation, i.e. the Equal Opportunities Act 1976 and the Race Relations Act 1976. *'The Schools Council Survey'* (1968) had shown that eighty-seven per cent of fifteen-year-old leavers thought that relevance to employment was the most important consideration in determining the 'value' of subjects. However it had also provided evidence of gender stereotyping in terms of male and female values. Housecraft was seen as most useful by eighty-seven per cent of girls, commercial subjects were seen as useful by sixty-eight per cent and needlework by fifty-nine per cent of girls. All of these were considered more 'useful' than science and mathematics. Boys rated the traditional craft subjects and science most 'useful', with metalwork, engineering and woodwork the most popular. Modern languages was rated as useful by only twenty-seven per cent of boys. These values were probably reflected in fourth and fifth year options and post school progression (ibid: 33, 34).

'The School Curriculum' (DES 1977) addressed the issue of equal opportunities and girls' access to science and technology (ibid: 2.17.ii; 1.19-1.20) and set the criteria for LEA reviews of existing practice. Section five dealt with equal opportunities and the special needs of ethnic minority groups, students with learning difficulties and those with physical and mental handicaps. *'Better Schools'* also raised the issues of equality of opportunity and equal access in respect of gender, special needs and minority groups, and highlighted problems caused by stereotyping. It was critical of insufficient variety of teaching approaches, inadequate knowledge of individual pupil's aptitudes and difficulties, and the failure of some teachers to have sufficiently high expectations of pupils' capabilities (ibid: 6.20). TVEI's impact on motivation and equality of opportunity will be explored in more detail in chapter two which deals curriculum breadth and balance.

The "New Technical and Vocational Education Initiative" was launched on 12th November 1982 by the Prime Minister, Margaret Thatcher. The main aim was to provide full-time four-year courses, leading to recognised qualifications, for 14-18 year-olds in general and vocational education. Participation was to be voluntary (Employment Dept. 1991: 6). Courses were to be locally managed by LEA's operating within national guidelines. Curricula had to be broad and balanced and provide equal opportunity and access across the full range of abilities. Subjects encouraged were those which were 'work-related' or enhanced. The popular courses were in technology, business and IT (see Bridgwood in, *'Transition'* (September 1988: 18) for retrospective views of students) and all courses had to include work experience. Curriculum development was to involve colleagues from industry, and the TVEI curricula were expected to reflect local circumstances and needs. The TVEI curriculum was to account for approximately 30% of time in the first year increasing to up to 70% over the four years (Employment Dept. 1991; 9). The criteria for pilot projects placed emphasis on relating what was learned and how it was learned to employment.

The MSC set the following objectives for TVEI projects:

"In conjunction with the LEA's, to explore and test ways of organising and managing the education of 14-18 year old young people across the ability range so that;

(i)   more of them are attracted to seek the qualifications / skills which will be of direct value to them at work and more of them achieve these qualifications and skills;

(ii)   they are better equipped to enter the world of employment which will await them;

(iii)   they acquire a more direct appreciation of the practical application of the qualifications for which they are working;

(iv)   they become accustomed to using their skills and knowledge to solve real-world problems they will meet at work;

(v)   more emphasis is placed on developing initiative, motivation and enterprise as well as problem-solving skills other aspects of personal development;

(vi)   the construction of the bridge from education to work is begun earlier by giving these young people the opportunity to have direct contact and training / planned work experience with a number of local employers in the relevant specialisms;

(vii)   there is close collaboration between local education authorities and industry / commerce / public services etc. so that the curriculum has industry's confidence." (Employment Dept. 1991: 25).

The projects were expected to achieve their aims in a quick and cost-effective way, to be capable of application to other areas of the country, and to have clear and specific objectives. They were also required to provide opportunities for progression into, and be congruent with, other developments in education and training. The vocational strands were expected to reflect local employment trends (op cit: 8).

There was a requirement to vary the general education / vocational education balance according to the needs and abilities of the students and the stages of the programme (ibid: 25-26). The key aims were to develop initiative, problem solving, and personal and social skills (see *House of Commons Education Science and Arts Committee 20th Dec 1982*: for the original NTVEI specification; see also *Education Science and Arts Committee Monday 18 April 1983*: paras; 680, 688, 696-699, 700-702, 703-705, 707; and MSC 1984).

The aim of part one of this book is to explore the various strategies employed in TVEI pilot and extension projects, which address all of the issues set out above. There are several reasons why this is a particularly difficult task. Firstly, not only were the TVEI pilot projects all very individual, they were also very different to the subsequent TVEI extension phase. The Employment Department's full-scale review of pilot and extension projects provides a comparison of objectives and outcomes (Employment Dept. 1991: 12-13). The HMI report 'TVEI 1983 - 1990' states that: "TVEI is not a course of study nor is it concerned solely with technical and vocational skills." (HMI 1991: ix) The irony is that even in government documents such as 'Better Schools' and MSC, Training Agency and Employment Department publications, TVEI pilot projects are often referred to as courses. The difficulty of providing a detailed analysis of the Initiative is also made clear in the HMI statement that: "..there was no single picture at any point in time." (HMI 1991: ix)

However, in both the pilot and extension phases, TVEI sought to address a core of common objectives which are stated in the national criteria (Employment Dept 1991: 25, 26, 28, 31, 34, 35). TVEI has been an agent of change, particularly in the development of practical and vocational courses, other work-related aspects of the curriculum, equal opportunities, special needs, institutional collaboration and teaching and learning (HMI 1991: ix-x). TVEI has constantly changed, and the aims have been 're-focused' (Employment Dept 1991: 34; Finch 1992: 3). TVEI's relationship with the National Curriculum was one of the reasons why it was felt necessary to re-focus and to re-state some of the principal aims of TVEI (Jones in 'Education vol. 173': 14th April 1989: 351-352). Although there have been a huge number of reports and reviews of TVEI there is very little information available on certain crucial aspects such as subject and course content. An additional problem is that of conflicting information since the qualitative data available from for example, case studies, is often not reflected in statistical information: use of information technology across the curriculum is a case in point. This is not surprising since much of the case study material reflects pilot practice, while extension data is gathered from a wider source (e.g. the "TVEI National Database").

There are also some important differences between the pilot and extension projects, the first of which is their size and scope. Pilot projects were confined to a small number of institutions, a small cohort of students, and a relatively small number of teachers and careers officers, also, in most cases, they sought to influence only a small part of the curriculum. In the TVEI extension, all students in the fourteen to eighteen age range were involved, as were all teachers of that age range and most careers officers. TVEI extension sought to influence the whole curriculum whereas the pilot projects were concerned with experimental curriculum models. As a result many new courses, principally vocational courses, were introduced. In the extension projects, change was aimed at influencing LEA curriculum policy and management and supporting the introduction of GCSE and the National Curriculum (Employment Dept 1991; HMI 1991). Consequently many of the vocational courses were phased out with their principal benefits, such as core skills and personal and social education, being absorbed into the work- related aspects of the National Curriculum. Work experience, careers education and guidance, and records of achievement, have become compulsory elements in extension programmes, as is consortium collaboration (Employment Dept. 1991: 12-13). The next chapter will begin the exploration of the TVEI influence on breadth and balance in the fourteen to sixteen curriculum.

Chapter Two

TVEI and curriculum breadth and balance

It interesting to keep the following quotation in mind when exploring the aims of TVEI.

"The aim of the technical secondary school is to provide a sound secondary education by means of a broadly based general course combined with certain specialised studies which have vocational significance and which are used to capture the imagination of pupils in order to maintain their interest and so prolong and further their general education". (Edwards (1960) *'The Secondary Technical School'*; see also Young in *'House of Commons 20th Dec 1982':* paras 22-23 and Young in *'Education 19th Nov. 1982':* 385-386).

One of the principal concerns of government in the mid-nineteen-seventies, was the breadth and balance of the curriculum studied by pupils during the last two years of compulsory schooling. The following extract serves as an indication of that concern:

"Options begin to shape the curriculum significantly in the fourth and fifth years. English and religious education are in most schools a standard part of the curriculum for all pupils up to the age of 16, and it is not true that many pupils drop mathematics at an early stage. But the offer of options and the freedom to choose do lead some boys and girls to abandon certain areas of study at an early age. This is questionable in a society like ours where the rapidity of change puts a premium on the sound acquisition of certain basic skills developed in up-to-date terms to the limit of the pupil's ability and understanding." (*Education in Schools A Consultative Document* DES 1977: 11. para. 2.13)

The DES *'Circular 14/77'* asked LEA's the following question:

"What contribution *has* the authority made to the consideration of the problem faced by secondary schools, of providing suitable subject options for older pupils while avoiding the premature dropping of curricular elements regarded as essential for all pupils?" (Para. B.3 italics - my correction of original).

The first of the HMI red books *'Curriculum 11-16: working papers by HM Inspectorate - a contribution to current debate'* (1978), also concluded that the existing situation regarding options was unsatisfactory and proposed a 'common curriculum' for pupils up to the age of 16. (section 1) *'Better Schools'* (1987: 22-23) talks about 'balancing' pupils' interests and aptitudes whilst: "..retaining breadth and balance so that no pupil can drop subjects or other elements whose continued study may be essential foundation for subsequent learning, training or work." (See also White 1973: chapter 3 for an 'exploration of which subjects might be regarded as essential in this sense). It goes on to describe a subject-based common curriculum post fourteen. Even as recently as 1987 the DES in its rationale for the National Curriculum stated the first aim as:

> "...ensuring that all pupils study a broad and balanced range of subjects throughout their compulsory schooling and do not drop too early studies which may stand them in good stead later, and which will help to develop their capacity to adapt and respond flexibly to a changing world." (*The National Curriculum 5-16: A Consultation Document* DES 1987: 3)

The advent of large comprehensive schools with the capacity to offer a wider range of options from which students could choose, in certain circumstances, made curriculum breadth and balance post fourteen even more difficult to achieve.

> "In the 1960s there was great excitement associated with the development of large comprehensive schools, particularly about the range of curriculum choice which such schools could offer. It seemed that such schools would be able to meet the demands of both able and less able students through the scale and richness of their curriculum design. Regrettably, these aspirations were not fulfilled. As the curriculum explosion of the 70's proceeded and new subjects like information technology or personal and social education pressed their claims for inclusion, the 'option box' component of school timetables became swollen, amid growing concern about balance and continuity. There was reluctance about genuinely reforming the curriculum and hesitation when it came to questioning the established subject disciplines. Yet the need for some considered synthesis was becoming increasingly clear." (Harrison et al 1988: 11)

The problem of ensuring breadth was also a problem of time, specifically the question of how to squeeze into a two year curriculum all the essential experiences a young person might need, particularly when, as was highlighted by the great debate, the curriculum was already perceived to be 'overcrowded'.

> "Unease about the curriculum is expressed in many forms but the principal points of concern appear to be: ..the curriculum has become overcrowded; the timetable is overloaded and the essentials are at risk;" (DES 1977: 11 para. 2.14).

'Better Schools' also addressed the issue of time constraints and suggested that curriculum breadth and balance could be achieved through the redistribution of time for each of the curriculum elements, to provide a minimum period of time for each subject. This would be determined by the discipline, the extent to which it relates to other elements, and by concentrating on improving delivery of the essential aspects of subjects. There is a recognition in 'Better Schools' of the danger of overloading the curriculum in the pursuit of breadth and balance and it recommended the elimination of materials and processes which did not use time to good effect:

".. by avoiding repetition dropping work which is out of date so that new concepts and technological developments can be incorporated, and by improving planning and adopting an holistic view of the curriculum." (ibid: 18.56; 19 paras 57-59)

'Better Schools' was published two years after the launch of TVEI as a limited pilot, and refers to the innovative nature of the project and notes that it was designed to: "explore curriculum organisation and development, teaching approaches and learning styles" and to "test the feasibility of sustaining a broad vocational commitment in full-time education for 14-18 year olds." (ibid: 16-17 para 50) It appeared two years before the national extension was announced, but paragraph fifty-one makes it clear that even then, the Government saw TVEI as a vehicle for promoting the aim of providing a broad, balanced, relevant and differentiated curriculum for all students (ibid: 17.51).

Breadth and balance and TVEI pilot projects

In the early pilots breadth and balance were widely interpreted as the provision of vocational elements to complement general education. One of the minutes of evidence to the Select Committee on the 18th of April 1983 refers to TVEI as being intended to 'widen and enrich' the curriculum (18th April 1983: 159 para. 679). Subjects encouraged were those which were work-related or enhanced. Many of the new courses were in technology, business and IT, and all courses had to include work experience. The vocational courses which schools offered were also expected to reflect local circumstances and needs (Ibid: para. 688).

The summaries of the first fourteen pilot projects make no direct reference to breadth. In fact the proposals contain so many 'new vocationally oriented courses', that achieving a broad general education would not seem to have been a consideration in the selection of the first pilots (*House of Commons Education Science and Arts Committee April 18th 1983*). The MSC review (*MSC 1985*) reported that in some of the early pilots the curriculum had to be restructured to ensure breadth and balance for all students (see ibid 1987: 14; Lines & Stoney 1989: 4).

Perhaps surprisingly, there is no explicit reference to curriculum breadth and balance in the original aims of TVEI or in the original criteria, nor is there any inference that the Initiative was intended to address the problem of curriculum overload (House of Commons 20th Dec. 1982: para. 3; MSC 1984; Employment Dept. 1991: 25). There are four statements in the original aims which might be interpreted as implying breadth and balance. They are: section (a) paragraph 1, which states that students should be encouraged to acquire skills and qualifications which will be of direct value to them at work; paragraph 4 which deals with application of skills and knowledge to solve 'real' problems, and paragraph 5 which calls for greater emphasis on initiative, motivation, enterprise, and the development of personal and problem solving skills. These aspects are made explicit in the criteria for pilot projects, section 2 paragraph 4. The fourth is in section (b) paragraph 3 which states that:

"The educational structures/schemes established to further the aims of the initiative should be consistent with progressive developments in skill and vocational training outside the school environment, existing vocational education for under 16 year old young people, and higher education."

This aspect is also made explicit in the criteria, section two paragraph seven (Employment Dept. 1991: 26). The first statement seems to imply the need for breadth and balance in terms of skills and qualifications and therefore in the scope of the curriculum. The second two statements might be seen as addressing the need to balance theoretical and practical knowledge and the development of personal and social skills. The fourth seems to deal implicitly with the structural aspects of curriculum breadth and balance to ensure that there is provision for progression to both vocational and academic routes post-sixteen. This aspect is expanded in section three of the criteria for pilot projects which states that, a wide range of academic and vocational qualifications should be aimed at including: TEC and BEC (at non advanced levels), RSA and CGLI certificates, GCE 'A' - levels and 'O' - levels, CSE and when available the CPVE.

The extension phase of TVEI was much more concerned with the whole curriculum and this was reflected in the criteria for submissions. The TVEI extension statement on curriculum breadth and balance takes a whole section and reflects the continuing concern over this aspect of curriculum provision: "..the proposals for the curriculum for students to whom the extension applies will be assessed for their consistency with the government's policies for the curriculum as expressed in *Better Schools*". Paragraph 3 of the criteria goes on to state that students' programmes should consist of: "a common core" and "option choices", and be "broad, balanced and relevant" (Employment Dept. 1991: 28; see Jones in NUT *'Education Review'* 1983:(3)1; 50, regarding the special emphasis on science and technology).

Paragraph 4 spells out more precisely what is meant by breadth and balance, stating that as well as consisting of "technical and practical elements," studies should also include English, mathematics and science, plus: "..elements drawn from the humanities and the arts, practical and technological work, and access to modern foreign languages" (Employment Dept. 1991: 28). The 14-16 element of the TVEI Extension curriculum is therefore to be composed of elements from the eight areas of experience identified by HMI.

Disentangling statements in the criteria which refer to breadth and balance from those which refer to other aspects of the TVEI curriculum is difficult, particularly when trying to avoid duplicating information. In the case of the TVEI extension criteria it is a real problem since issues of breadth and balance are also implicit in, for example, paragraph 5 which deals with relevance, and paragraph 7 which deals with differentiation, both of which are dealt with in later chapters.

The 'post National Curriculum phase' of TVEI Extension firmed up the need for breadth in terms of the subject elements of the curriculum. The following joint statement from the Training Agency and the National Curriculum Council makes this clear:

"...schools and LEA's will need to:
co-ordinate planning for TVEI with planning for the National Curriculum;
consider how TVEI can help to promote effective learning in each of the subjects of the National Curriculum (beginning with the three core subjects which have to be taught to pupils in year 10 for a reasonable time from 1990)"
(A joint statement by the Training Agency and the National Curriculum Council: *Insight No 16* Summer 1989: 3)

Changes introduced by TVEI pilot

Data from the TVEI database (1982-1987) which measured all curricular changes in institutions against the curricular provision in the year prior to the commencement of TVEI, revealed that in all schools TVEI had involved introducing 'new' subjects and in many instances the structure and organisation of the curriculum had also changed (Harrison 1989: 9). The curriculum areas which recorded the greatest changes prior to the commencement of TVEI were: English, mathematics, physical education, humanities, and social sciences. The smallest changes occurred in: home economics-commercial, information technology, business studies, vocational and pre-vocational training, and CDT technology, with chemical science, physical science, and integrated and other sciences, all showing some changes (Harrison 1989: 37). The TVEI Review 1990 makes it clear that as a result of TVEI there were further changes in curriculum content (Employment Dept. 1991: 9).

HMI (1983) recommended the provision of an entitlement curriculum in all five years for 70-80 per cent of the time available, with the remaining time to be allocated for various other components which would be chosen by pupils according to their individual talents and interests. The problem with that model was that it was based on the eight areas of experience, which meant that within a subject based curriculum there remained a problem of time. For example, the aesthetic area of experience might cover subjects such as art, music, drama and media studies. Science coverage, if it is to be comprehensive and provide a basis for progression, would cover physical, chemical and biological science (Michell: *Better Science: Key Proposals* 1987: 4; DES 1991 *National Curriculum Order for Science*) which, even in the new 'balanced science' courses, absorbs approximately 20% of curriculum time (Michell 1987: 4; see also NFER 1992: 13).

Re-packaged content

One way of improving curriculum breadth and balance is to re-package the content. This would involve identifying the essentials within existing subjects and adding to them those elements which are not currently being delivered. This particular strategy may or may not be implicit in solutions such as that evident in the following extract which clearly implies that breadth means increasing the range of courses and programmes.

"As a result of the TVEI pilots, the curriculum is being broadened; new opportunities, choices and possibilities are being opened up for young people and teachers involved are responding enthusiastically,

while new courses and programmes are proving popular with students."
(*Working Together* - Education and Training DES 1986)

There is no guarantee however, that curricula broadened in this way contain the 'essential elements' which provide a basis for a wide range of progression routes and occupations, but it would seem to provide a mechanism through which progress towards breadth and balance might be more effectively addressed. In such courses it is perfectly possible to include content which would otherwise be delivered through discrete subjects. It is also possible that other 'areas of experience' not included in the "general core" could also be delivered through 'broad courses' (see Cross et al 1988a: 82; Harrison et al 1989: 11-21).

Additional options
A less pragmatic way of going about the task of ensuring breadth and balance of content might be to simply introduce a range of new 'subjects' which are designed to give students greater choice and either pass to them responsibility for breadth and balance in their courses, or provide 'guidance' on the basis of the individual tutor's interpretation of breadth and balance. This was clearly a concern of HMI in respect of some of the TVEI pilot project curricula.

"New optional subjects did not alone guarantee a coherent, broad programme; guidance for students was essential. Students' programmes were not always broad and balanced before the initiative, but the need to devote time and accommodation to courses introduced or extended in the early developments initially reduced the breadth and balance of some students programmes." (HMI 1991: 8 para. 20).

The introduction of 'new' subjects or courses such as technology, did stimulate a 'weeding out' process as recommended in DES (1987: paras 56-59).

"......in many schools, certain subjects, including commerce, woodwork, and metalwork, either disappeared or attracted fewer students (although not necessarily wholly because of TVEI) to make way for the new and enhanced courses." (Employment Dept. 1991: 9)

The 'TVEI effect' on curriculum subjects
A review of the influence of TVEI pilot projects on the curriculum of students in S4 (Scotland), based on a survey of thirty schools which compared the curriculum of the 'average' pupil' is S4 in the year 1987-88 (the year prior to the projects) with that of the same ability and age grouping of students in the same schools in the year 1988-89 (Lyon Black & Thorpe 1990: 3). In terms of the average time spent on subjects the survey revealed that there were 'winners' and 'losers'. Subjects which gained in average time were: computing, social and vocational skills, business studies, personal and social development, social education, technology, science (in the case of boys at the expense of separate sciences) and French. The authors suggest that some gains such as in science, computing, and social and vocational skills, may have been

attributable to the increased use of Standard Grades rather than to TVEI. Subjects which showed small decreases in average time were: English, geography, history, modern studies, economics, and social and environmental studies. Some 'vocationally oriented' subjects such as accounting and secretarial studies, also decreased in time allocation, as did careers and guidance. Other subjects which decreased in time were: craft and design, technical drawing, home economics (domestic) art, music, physical education, and religious education. (ibid 1990: 2 fig.1; 3).

The Trent Polytechnic report which compared the time spent on subjects by TVEI students with that of the whole student population, showed that the biggest increase in time spent on individual subjects by TVEI students were in: CDT technology (which also records the biggest gain for all students), information technology and business studies, which also showed a general increase in time for all students. Preparation for life, home economics commercial, vocational and pre-vocational training, (which also recorded a general increase) and computer studies, also showed increases in time allocation. In terms of the whole student population, the subjects above recorded gains of between 0.25% and 1% of curriculum time. TVEI time gains for the same subjects were substantially larger ranging from approximately 0.75%, to approximately 4.25%. Pre TVEI, the greatest effects were felt by the humanities subjects which also suffered a loss in general terms of just under 1% of time, however post TVEI, this rose to just over 2.5%. In general, home economics (domestic) languages, biological science, CDT craft (which recorded the largest loss of just under 2.5% of time), chemical science, social sciences, and English all showed losses post TVEI, of between approximately 0.75% and 1% of time. In schools operating TVEI curricula, losses for the same subjects were between approximately 0.75% and 2.75% of time. Creative and aesthetic subjects initially decreased in time post TVEI by approximately 1.25%, but showed a slight increase for all students later, possibly because of the introduction of the GCSE (Harrison 1989: 40 fig.16, 41).

The criteria for the analysis of changes in curriculum balance which was, according to the authors of the SCRE report (Lyon, Black and Thorpe 1990) much closer to the real picture of the over-all curriculum diet which students met, was that recommended for the implementation of the SCCC modes. These are the equivalent of the HMI eight areas of experience* upon which, many English and Welsh LEA's structured their curricula. The SCCC modes are: language, mathematical studies, scientific studies, social and environmental, technological activities, creative and aesthetic, physical education, religious and moral.

The TVEI curricula of the schools which were reviewed had both a 'core' element drawn from the modes, and enrichment elements (the TVEI added value) which were the TVEI extensions of the modes. The survey showed that when both elements of the curriculum were taken together, the time spent by

----

*NB There are some significant differences between the SCCC modes and the "eight areas of experience", notably the exclusion of the ethical and the inclusion of the technological in the Scottish modes.

the average pupil in each mode, both before and after the introduction of TVEI, met or exceeded the required minimum amount of time in all modes except language and communications, where the shortfall was approximately four per cent. The curriculum of TVEI students did show a greater emphasis on technological activities. The two most significant outcomes from this part of the survey were that firstly, it did appear possible to increase the amount of curriculum time that students spend on the technological activities mode without unbalancing the curriculum, and secondly, the average pupil was spending well above the minimum amount of time in that mode before the introduction of TVEI (Lyon Black & Thorpe 1990: 4 Fig. 2 charts 1, 2; see also ibid: 5).

The emphasis on technological subjects

In some instances, because of the emphasis on "technologically based subjects," even the proportion of time that students spent in taking science decreased as a result of TVEI (HMI 1991: xii, 8). The MSC review (MSC 1985) stated that schools taking part in TVEI would develop new curriculum content (ibid: 6). Several TVEI reviews have commented on the difficulty of identifying genuinely new subjects which have been in introduced through TVEI, because of the plethora of titles used by the various schools and projects. The *'Report on Curricular Changes 1982-1987'* based on the Trent Polytechnic TVEI database (Harrison 1989) points out the difficulty of categorising subjects on the basis of subject titles, and the even greater problem of attempting to define whether or not a subject is genuinely 'new' without knowing the content of that subject (Harrison 1989: 23). The same report has attempted to categorise subject titles using thirty-six 'generic subject groups' produced by subdividing the DES 'Proposed Seventeen Categories of Secondary Subjects' (DES 1982 in Harrison 1989: 59). Some indication of the size of the task can be gained from my own trawl of the Training Agency's Developments series case studies, which revealed the following lengthy list of 'new subject titles' (see table 2).

Technical and vocational emphasis

The vocational emphasis of many of the 'new' TVEI subjects and courses is indicated in the titles. The MSC (1985: 5) noted that all projects offered technology, craft and design and business studies, or 'a related area', and that most of the projects had responded to the TVEI requirement to offer courses which were of "particular local interest". The report gives an idea of the range of courses offered. They include some with a strong vocational orientation such as: biotechnology, electronics, engineering, information technology, commercial languages, retail distribution, fashion and textiles, agriculture, horticulture, land-based industries, nautical studies, construction industries, food science and community care (ibid: 1985: 7). The HMI review (1991), while pointing out the value of vocational studies, questioned the long term future of such subjects given the constraints of the National Curriculum (ibid: 31).

Many of the new courses drew on content from a number of discrete subjects and reflected a new emphasis in terms of the type of knowledge which was to be acquired. This aspect of TVEI will be explored in more detail later in the chapter. The TVEI database report (Harrison 1989) concludes that schools did introduce genuinely new subjects into the curriculum, as well as enhancing existing ones (Harrison 1989: 52). The pilot evaluation report (Cross et al 1988c) noted that many new subjects had been introduced through TVEI

Table 2 'New TVEI subjects' as identified by analysis of TVEI pilot project case studies

Subject title	Date	Issue No.	Page
		3	
Biotechnology	1988	3	35-43
Business education	1988	1	45-51
Business management	1988	3/4	31-41
Business studies	1988	3	71-82/v-viii
Caring services	1988	3	1-8
Commerce & business studies	1988	4	2
Commerce business studies & IT	1988	1	23-41
Commercial & industrial language	1988	3/4	7-20
Communication studies	1988	4	35-43/43-62
Community studies	1988	1	43-62
Computer studies	1988	3	63
Computing	1988	9	35-43
Design & technology (modular)	1989	13	41-54
Design & creative arts	1990	1	63
Design & graphics	1988	3	63
Design technology	1988	1	36, 35-43
Electrical instrumentation	1988	1/3	63
Electronics	1988		31-41/35-43
Enterprise technology & business systems			
Food management	1988	7	57
Industry in microcosm	1988	1	16
Industry technology & society modular	1988	1	82
Information & office technology			
Information technology	1989	9	41-45
Integrated science	1988	1	63
Manufacturing technology	1988	3	20, 71-82
Media studies	1988	3	71
Modular technology	1988	1	63
Personal & community services	1988	1	63
Place studies	1988	1	63
Practical business processes	1988	4	1-21
Product design technology	1988	1	7-20
Project technology	1988	7	17
Shared business experience	1988	7	17
Social & life skills	1988	4	23-41
Social & vocational skills	1988	1	7-20
Technology	1988	1	7-20
	1988	1	1-6
	1988	3/4	29-33/71-82/ v-viii
Technology & communications	1988	1	63
Technology & computer studies	1988	1	63
Technology & electronics	1988	1	63
Technology at work	1988	4	1-21
The work of business	1988	4	1-21
Vocational drama	1988	4	43-62
Vocational music	1988	4	43-62

including technology, information technology, business studies and integrated science (ibid: 71).

The TVEI database review took the academic year 1986-87 in order to include the maximum number of schools with a fourth year TVEI cohort. Three hundred and sixty schools returned data on curriculum innovation (Harrison: 27). The frequency table of 'new subjects' (including non-TVEI subjects) which could be grouped under the DES subject fields, showed the greatest increases in technological, creative and vocational subjects, sciences and social sciences. CDT had the largest increase in frequency. Subjects which showed the smallest increases were English, mathematics, languages and humanities (ibid: 28). The frequency table of new subjects for TVEI also indicated that the greatest increases where in 'technological subjects', with business studies recording the largest individual increase followed by information technology, electronics, technology and modular technology (ibid: 29). The HMI report on TVEI (1983 - 1990) also makes the point that in the early days of TVEI pilot projects, new subjects which were introduced into the curriculum tended to be mainly technological. Later the range of new subjects increased to include subjects such as horticulture, agriculture, and electronics, with innovations in other subjects such as home economics and expressive arts, tending to take on a more vocational and applied form (HMI 1991: 8-9).

The enhanced status of technological courses
The Leeds University interim survey (Barnes et al 1987) confirms that TVEI resources had facilitated the introduction of technological courses in the schools visited, and these were often made available to non-TVEI students as well as the TVEI cohort (O'Grady in Harrison et al 1988: 11-21). The status of teachers of those subjects was also enhanced, partly because the new technological courses such as electronics and information technology, attracted the most able as well as average and less able students (op cit: 44, 46). Sometimes technology was an important element in more than one course and in the case of information technology it could be genuinely cross-curricular (see Cross 1988a: 31-41; Cross 1988d: 12). However, in the pilot projects it was often delivered as a discrete unit, subject, or course (MSC 1985: 7). The subjects which did not benefit substantially from TVEI pilot projects were, in the main, those which had traditionally been regarded as the mainstays of general education (Lines & Stoney 1989: 32). Barnes in Preedy et al (1989: 160-161) considers that TVEI has made a major contribution to reducing the subordination of some subjects.

The specialist backgrounds of teachers of the new courses
An important outcome of the increase in technological courses was the transfer of teachers into new subject fields. The varied specialist backgrounds of teachers of the new technological courses highlighted in Barnes et al (1987) was reflected in Harrison (1989) and shows that computer studies drew largely on teachers of business studies and mathematics, and that only 7% had CDT backgrounds. Information technology, perhaps because of its cross-curricular nature, had the greatest variety of teacher backgrounds with business studies providing 17%, mathematics 18%, information technology 13%, science 11%, computer studies 19%, and other subjects 17% (Harrison 1989: 52-53, see fig. 21). The survey showed that 23% of teachers of modular technology came

from science backgrounds, 73% came from CDT backgrounds and 4% came from other subject backgrounds. Control technology drew 37% of its teachers from science and 59% from CDT. Electronics drew mainly on science teachers, with CDT providing only 12% and teachers with specialist electronics backgrounds comprising 10% of the total (see Harrison 1989: 52). This data highlights the fact that the new 'technological' courses drew heavily on mathematics (see also HMI 1991: 32) and science. The transfer of teachers to 'new' subjects also raises the question of the extent to which the content was genuinely new or simply re-packaged. This is an issue which will be addressed later in the chapter.

Breadth and balance and TVEI extension projects
Black in the SCRE review (1990b) makes the following point:

> "Moving from the optional TVEI curriculum of the pilot project to the entitlement curriculum of the extension means that all pupils can benefit from TVEI. But all pupils will only benefit if the curriculum they are offered meets their needs." (Black et al 1990b: 23)

It was perhaps with this in mind that the Training Agency wisely made it clear to LEA's preparing extension proposals, that the extension was a 'different animal' to pilot and that it was the needs of all students which should be addressed (Employment Dept. 1991: 12 para. f). There are examples from the case-studies which indicate that teachers were aware of the strengths and weaknesses of the changes introduced into the curriculum as a result of TVEI pilot projects. In a study of one of the Cambridge pilot schools (Harrison et al 1988: 11-21) the limitations of the 'options models' of TVEI curricula were clearly recognised. The vast array of new subject titles and new examinations syllabuses, which emerged as a result of the pilot developments, also caused the examining boards concern. The NFER report (Wardman 1989) underlines the difficulties faced by the boards, particularly in terms of standardisation of modular schemes and applied subjects such as agriculture, business studies and technology, and the limited use that could be made of such syllabuses under the mode three regulations (Wardman 1989: 3). The same review concluded however, that TVEI had brought about some rethinking of assessment purposes on the part of the academic examining boards particularly in respect of the value of the learning *'process'* (Wardman 1989: 6-7).

Lessons from the pilot projects
Clearly there were lessons to be learned from the pilots concerning what sorts of curriculum change should be avoided as well as included in the extension. The lessons varied from authority to authority, but there were some general lessons which applied to most projects. These will be explored more fully in the following sections of this chapter, but it is worth noting at this point, some which were identified by HMI (1991; see also Employment Dept. 1991). They included an awareness that the "cohort system" and the 'exclusion' of subjects from involvement in pilot projects, was not compatible with the 'entitlement curriculum' concept of the extension. The "bolt-on course" approach which characterised some of the early pilots also raised concerns (HMI 1991: xiv, 9).

Some of the new vocational courses divided time between subjects and tutorials resulting in discontinuity (HMI 1991: xiii).

It has been suggested that the abandonment of many of the new TVEI courses was due to the side-lining of TVEI courses in favour of the National Curriculum subjects (see Lawton & Chitty 1988: 44-45). There may be some truth in that, but cost and difficulties of accreditation as well as incompatibility with the National Curriculum, probably ruled out the implementation of some of the new courses on the scale required by the extension. However the outcomes of pilot projects did indicate that the higher profile which had been given to core skills and themes, such as economic and industrial understanding and the use of "real contexts", were of value, particularly in demonstrating to students the relevance of their studies (HMI 1991: 8). The lessons learned about the increased use of information technology as a cross-curricular skill were also clearly worth building on (ibid: 9, 27). Practical application of knowledge and skills in real contexts, and positive developments in teaching methods were all highlighted as lessons to be learned (ibid: 14-15). Closer collaboration between education and industry and the expansion of work experience, as well as improved careers education and guidance, were all constructive TVEI pilot project developments (ibid: 21-26). The improvement in equality of access and opportunity, particularly in the curriculum areas of science and technology, also provided important strategies which could be used in extension projects (Employment Dept. 1991: 20).

The collaboration between subjects in preparing and delivering new courses had often improved the cohesion of content (HMI 1991: 9). Some of the new "subjects", such as technology and business studies, were clearly capable of expanding to take larger student numbers. The reduction of curriculum time for science in some early pilots had been redressed and new balanced science courses provided a broader foundation for progression (Employment Dept. 1991: 20). The development of balanced science courses and links between science and technology, in particular those which involved activities which were embedded in 'real contexts' and problem solving activities, were welcomed by HMI (1991: 32, Employment Dept. 1991). Some progress had been made in assessment, recording and reporting, particularly in terms of the record of achievement and in approaches to more 'student centred' teaching methods including developments in flexible learning (Employment Dept. 1991, HMI 1991). Lessons were also learned about curriculum organisation and the issues of breadth and balance (HMI 1991: 7-8; Employment Dept. 1991: 28).

Cross-curricular themes and skills
The criteria for extension proposals made explicit reference to learning lessons from the pilot projects. The "Statement of Curricular Criteria" for TVEI Extension in paragraph one, states that: "Authorities will be required to submit development plans... drawing on the experience of the TVEI pilot projects." (Employment Dept. 1991: 28) The criteria also relates to the subjects and areas of experience which should be included in students' programmes 14-16 (ibid: 28). The specification, while not identifying all the individual subjects included in the National Curriculum, does identify the same core subjects: English, mathematics and science, and the same broad areas from which the National Curriculum foundation subjects are drawn. In addition, through the

requirement for LEA submissions for extension funding to be congruent with the government's education policy as set out in *'Better Schools'*, there was an implicit requirement that development plans should also address the 'other elements' of the curriculum. These were specified in the *'NCC Circular 6'* which set out the 'broad context' of the National Curriculum and specified the elements which give it coherence. The circular describes them as: the cross-curricular dimensions of personal and social development, equal opportunities, and attitudes associated with life in a multi-cultural society (paras: 9-11); cross-curricular skills including: communication, problem solving, and study skills (paras: 12-14); and the cross-curricular themes economic and industrial understanding, careers education and guidance, environmental education, health education, and citizenship (paras: 15-18). The Training Agency advised LEA's which were preparing extension proposals that particular attention should be paid to identifying how they intended to relate these elements to their own curriculum policy statements (Training Agency 1989).

Subject emphasis

The "TVEI Focus Statement" (1989) not only re-states the importance of the work-related curriculum, it also makes explicit, the importance attached through it to certain aspects of the curriculum which are identified as: "...skills and qualifications for all; in particular in science, technology, information technology and modern languages." (Employment Dept. 1991: 34)   The work-related emphasis is clear in the focus statement "Priorities for TVEI in the 1990's":

> "The Employment Department's fundamental role is to ensure that the work-force is equipped with the competence needed in a high productivity, high skill, and high technology economy.   Thus the Training Agency's influence is crucial to the economic needs of our society and the training needs of our people." (Employment Dept 1991: 34)

The section of the same document which deals with the Employment Department's role in education (section 2), states that one of the aims is to help education to be: "..practical and enterprising as well as academic." (Employment Dept. 1991: 34)

TVEI and the National Curriculum

TVEI extension and the National Curriculum have brought about a rationalisation of the 'subject-based curriculum' and as Jones (*Insight No 15* 1989: 2) explains, many of the innovations of the pilot projects have either become statutory elements of the National Curriculum, as for example in the case of technology and science, or have become cross-curricular elements. Sometimes, as in the case of economic and industrial understanding, they have been incorporated as themes.   In other instances they have become cross-curricular skills, while in the case of personal and social education and equal opportunities, for example, they have become cross-curricular dimensions (see Hall 1992: 93).

Another important consideration when examining the impact of TVEI extension on the subject elements of the curriculum, is the scope of the project and its influence on the *whole* curriculum of *all* students 14-18, rather than a small cohort within limited pilots (Employment Dept. 1991: 12-13). Taking account of all of these factors, one would anticipate a substantially different pattern of curriculum change even in the earliest extension projects prior the introduction of the National Curriculum at key stage four.

The TVEI extension cohort survey was the first part of a study of year ten and eleven TVEI students over four years, involving 11,445 students in 115 schools. It began in 1991 and it monitored the impact of the project on the curriculum of those students (NFER 1992: 2). In the survey of trends in science and modern languages, it revealed that only 1% of students did little or no science, while 81% had over three hours (ibid: 13 fig. 2.3.1). The TVEI performance indicators progress report also showed that the take-up of balanced science rose from under 70% in 1988-89 to over 90% in 1990-91 (Employment Dept. 1992: 7. fig. 4). In addition, HMI endorse the fact that TVEI helped the implementation of the DES science policy statement and the National Curriculum, by "promoting balanced science" (HMI 1991: 33). Surprisingly the NFER (1992) survey showed that 24% of students spent very little time on, or did not take a modern foreign language, while 51% spent two to three hours a week studying modern languages and 12% had more than three hours study (ibid: 13 fig. 2.1.3). The figures are similar to those in the 1992 TVEI performance indicators report which indicated that in 1989-90 under 70% of all fourteen year-olds studied a modern foreign language, and that by 1990-91 this had risen to over 70% in 1990-91 (Employment Dept. 1992:10. fig. 6).

There was a requirement included in the TVEI extension criteria, for all students to have experience in technology subjects both across the curriculum and through discrete subjects (ibid 1992: 8). Because of difficulties over the definition of 'technology' there are no detailed statistics given for participation given in the NFER survey (1992). However, on the basis of 'individual school definitions of technology', the report suggests that in over half the schools all year eleven students spent at least 10% of their curriculum time on technology studies. There was also evidence to suggest that in some schools, some students spent no time at all on technology (ibid: 15). The TVEI performance indicators report (Employment Dept. 1992: 8-9 Fig. 5) sounds a similar note of caution over the interpretations of 'technology experience', but it provides an indication that the uptake of technology had increased over-all by about 5% between 1988-89 and 1990-91. The introduction of modular technology courses and electronics courses was noted, as were the examination constraints placed on the latter and a lack of coherence and progression in the former (ibid: 28-29)

The content of new subjects and courses
The summary report of three Scottish surveys; Black (1990b; 1990d and Lyon Black & Thorpe 1990) showed that every subject was influenced by TVEI in at least one school. Three-quarters of the teachers surveyed also felt that TVEI had improved the curriculum in their schools (Black et al 1990c: 1). One review indicated that teachers of subjects which involved "technological activities and applications" were more likely than others to feel that involvement in TVEI had impacted on the curriculum in terms of content. However even within this category only about 45% gave positive responses concerning the impact of TVEI (Black 1990b: 12). Very similar outcomes were true in the case of

teachers of aesthetic and creative subjects (ibid: 13 fig. 9), and few teachers of science subjects and mathematics felt that TVEI had influenced course content or development (ibid: 13 fig. 10; 16 fig. 14). The HMI review also considered TVEI to have had little effect on mathematics (1991: 31). The NFER review which included the views of the examining and accrediting boards, revealed that one board in particular felt that the TVEI influence had been substantial and it endorsed the findings of the Leeds University interim review, by indicating that TVEI courses had included new content as they understood it (Wardman 1989: 7).

Developments in business education
Amongst the many new course titles which appeared in the repertoire of pilot projects, was "Enterprise Technology and Business Studies" developed by the Croydon project, which appears to have some similarity with the second category of business studies courses reviewed in Barnes et al (1987). As in the case of so many new courses the content is unclear, but the focus appears to have been on personal and social skills, in particular, group skills. The contexts for study and skills development were mini-company enterprise activities in which a simulated production line was set up by the students who, through role-play activities, dealt with many of the same management problems that would be faced in a real company (Harrison et al 1988: 58, 61-63).

> "Central to the concept of enterprise technology and business studies is that pupils learn by themselves and work together in groups to overcome their problems. ..We have seen the growth of group allegiance and pupil support for each other." (Clarke in ibid: 59)

Obtaining information on the content of new courses has proved to be very difficult. The Leeds University interim survey has provided the most detail but it was limited to a sample of twelve schools and an equally small range of subjects. The survey identified two types of business studies courses. The first, the "office skills model", was primarily concerned with office and secretarial skills. It was often taught out of context and was primarily the choice of girls. The second model, the "business world model", was a broader course aimed at developing economic and industrial understanding and a wide range of personal, social, and business world skills. Of the two types, variations on the first model were the most narrowly vocational. The survey concludes that it is the "business world model" which is closest to fulfilling the aims of TVEI (ibid: 97). It is this model which was also generally welcomed by HMI, particularly in terms of the pedagogical changes associated with it, the use of 'real world contexts' and 'off-site experience' (HMI 1991: 29).

Developments in personal and social education
Personal and social education (PSE) was an important element in most TVEI pilot curricula and often formed part of the "TVEI core". The review of PSE courses in Barnes et al (1987) and Barnes in Preedy et al (1989) identified two main models of organisation. The first was a discrete course with a share of curriculum time allocated to it. The second was a cross-curricular model diffused across the TVEI curriculum (Barnes et al 1989: 98). Most schools surveyed had developed the first model and only three the second (ibid: 99).

The survey also indicated that where the cross-curricular model was in operation, the status of PSE was enhanced and it was seen by teachers as an important element in the course.

The NFER (1992) review also concluded that the special emphasis which TVEI had given to developing personal and social skills had enhanced the value placed on PSE (Lines and Stoney 1989: 32). Although the content of PSE courses or elements vary and cannot be quantified accurately, there appear to be "frames of reference", i.e. social studies, and social and life skilling (Barnes et al 1987: 103). The first of the models described in (Barnes et al 1987) concerned knowledge about society and was "content based" (ibid: 104). The description used in the survey was that it was often: "..nothing more than a watered-down version of academic syllabuses in sociology." (ibid: 104) The 'content' of personal and social education courses varied. For example in the Isle of White Project, Medina High School offered: survival language units, money management, careers guidance, work experience, and current affairs. It sought to develop positive attitudes and values in students and to improve their skills in presenting themselves for employment (Reynolds in Harrison 1988: 53-54).

Developments in technology courses

On the question of the extent to which the content of the 'new' technological courses is new, or simply old content applied in a new context, the following extract which refers to new technology courses, is particularly relevant and suggests that the latter may often be the case.

> "The concepts, theories and explanatory principles may be derived either from one of the sciences, such as physics or biology, or from an area of technological knowledge, such as engineering or ceramics." (Barnes et al 1987: 48)

The same survey concluded that in the modular technology courses which were explored the first year typically concentrated on factual knowledge, i.e. knowledge of cause and principle, drawn mainly from physics, electronics, engineering and control technology. The examples of content which are given in the report are: friction, mechanics, Ohm's Law and AC/DC, theory of structures, linear and rotary motion, and transistors (ibid: 49). Much of the content was high level knowledge, some of it normally associated with advanced examinations and undertaken by post-sixteen students (ibid: 50). In the instances where electronics and control technology courses were observed, both scientific and technological sources of knowledge were included, with emphasis on technological knowledge. However such knowledge was not always acquired in technology (ibid: 48). In one school identified in the report, knowledge acquired elsewhere was applied in a practical 'workshop' situation. In the review conceptual knowledge was identified as being of greater concern to teachers with science backgrounds than to those with CDT backgrounds, and that the latter were more likely to be concerned with applications (ibid: 50). The authors describe electronics and technology courses as being:

> "..driven by the demands of a discipline. ..their underlying principle being that there are established fields of knowledge which need to

be known in themselves, before the question of application in particular environments is addressed." (ibid 51; see also HMI 1991: 28)

Although there was a considerable amount of theoretical knowledge involved in TVEI technology courses, the application of it was minimal. Students often resorted to trial and error methods when research, reflection, and application of knowledge previously gained, might have resulted in a better solution (Medway and Yeomans 1988: 16-24; Barnes et al 1987: 60). One possible reason for this may have been that where there was a 'theoretical element' to the course, as for example in electronics, this was often delivered in the fourth year. In addition the knowledge often required by students in the fifth year was 'procedural' knowledge to support their individual projects. Two reports indicated that the types of knowledge most commonly required by fifth year students were those which informed problem solving activities (Medway and Yeomans 1988: 16-24; Barnes et al 1987: 52; 53).

Pilot project reviews such as those noted above, endorse the accepted view that practical knowledge is particularly important in technology courses and can be subdivided into four kinds of knowledge and skills: The first is the ability to select from a range of practical operations that which is most appropriate; the second is knowledge of systems; the third is knowledge of processes and materials and the fourth is knowledge of what things can do and the extent of their capabilities. These types of knowledge and skills are often acquired through practical activity although they can also be acquired through instruction. However they require different teaching strategies and learning situations to those employed in the teaching of cause and principle (see Dodd in Lawton 1983b: 67-68; Barnes et al 1987: 48).

Information technology can be used as a 'tool', in which case 'operational' knowledge is required, or it can be concerned with control, programming, or research and development, in which cases theoretical knowledge such as that used in electronics or programming may be demanded. In TVEI courses information technology is usually, but not exclusively, concerned with applications rather than principles (Barnes et al 1987: 51; see also HMI 1991: 15). One of the reasons for this may be that in pilot projects information technology was often part of the TVEI compulsory core and in extension it was a statutory element of the National Curriculum, in both instances therefore, it has to be accessible to students with a wide range of abilities.

In all the technology courses seen in operation by Barnes, Medway and Yeomans, process skills played a major part. Technology capability in all instances involved designing and making and required two kinds of skill. The first is concerned with imagination and creative responses to design problems and includes identification of the kinds of materials and processes that such solutions might involve. The second is more 'practical' and involves identifying and attempting to solve problems. It requires the application of strategies such as reflection, review and evaluation, and refinement, in the process of working towards a final solution (Dodd in Lawton 1983b: 67; Barnes et al 1987: 54-55). This particular capability is what Barnes calls "systems competence" (ibid: 57). A third skills area, that of manual and craft skills, was observed in modular technology courses. Craft skills in particular proved to be problematic when students had little previous experience before commencing a course (ibid: 58). In the Exeter pilot a 'problem solving approach' was adopted based on real problems and needs, and to overcome problems of knowledge and skills acquisition on a more 'bespoke' basis, supporting workshops (differentiated into a number of levels) were provided to run alongside assignment work (Harrison in Cross et al 1989: 58-59).

New technology courses featured in several of the TVEI case studies. For example in the Bradford pilot project there was a technology 'core' consisting of two elements; information technology, (including computing, satellite technology, robotics etc.) and "integrating modules," which were intended to provides opportunities to link the curriculum with the outside world. The programme was flexible and related to other parts of the curriculum, particularly business studies and geography, but also to most other curriculum areas (Cross et al 1988a: 63). In the Hertfordshire project students were able to select from "constrained technology options" described as: computer studies, manufacturing technology, modular technology, electrical instrumentation, information and office technology and communications. Each of these courses involved a wide range of technological activities covering the same range of basic skills regardless of the options chosen (ibid: 63). Bedfordshire introduced a system of linked technology options consisting of: technology and electronics, design and graphics, and technology, and computer studies (ibid: 63). In all of these, information technology as opposed to 'design technology', formed a major element.

New courses versus traditional subjects
The Hereford and Worcester project adopted what it called: "the broad skills-based approach". They used a modular scheme to try to get away from 'traditional subjects'. In technology there were compulsory modules in electronics, mechanisms, pneumatics and structures. Each module contained a number of structured assignments and projects and was twenty-four hours in length. Year ten students had to take nine - twenty-four hour compulsory modules and year eleven students had to take three - sixty-hour modules. The emphasis was on skills development with problem solving, communications, and decision making, all encouraged (Cross et al 1988a: 62-63). In the Wirral pilot, clusters of modules were combined to form a core course. In technology the cluster consisted of control technology, electronics, and computer studies modules (Cross et al 1988a: 62).

Developments in science courses
HMI (1991) credits TVEI with having made a major contribution to the teaching of biotechnology and adds that the quality of the work was high where biotechnology was a key element within a balanced science course (HMI 1991: 32). One of the biotechnology 'pioneer schools' which gained support from industry was Wirral County Grammar School (*Insight Digest vol. 3* 1988: 4). At Weatherhead High School, another member of the Wirral project, an "enrichment package" was developed for O-level students in chemistry, physics and computing. It had the following aims:

"To place the students in an experiential learning situation in order to develop further skills in science.

To allow the students to see the relevance of their studies by undertaking appropriate projects.

To help students gain the necessary skills to complete a set task.

To allow the students to develop their own personal skills and initiatives". (Cross et al 1988a; 75-76; see also Versey in *'Education in Science'* 1989: (134)2; 21-23)

In the extension phase TVEI continued to support the introduction of balanced science and the National Curriculum Order for science (NFER 1992: 13).

Developments in creative and expressive arts

The arts have been an area of curriculum change in both pilot and extension projects. In Calderdale inter-school developments resulted in the implementation of a design and creative arts package (Cross et al 1990b: 63). In Wigan there were attempts to integrate students experiences of work placements into the curriculum by 'sharing' them through arts activities (ibid; 46). The use of outside consultants and practising artists in residence also helped to bring real world activities into schools (ibid: 3, 64). Residential experiences were also integrated into the Calderdale arts programmes where possible (ibid: 64). One of the approaches to combined arts included the use of drama as the focus for an extended cross-curricular project. Another approach was to introduce a unifying element (a special project) which required students to respond in more than one of the arts disciplines. Special projects of this sort were often accommodated by collapsing the timetable (ibid: 44). The areas of experience covered included: drama and theatre arts, film, video, sound, art and design, photography and print - making (ibid: 44, 65-66). The use of technology was seen as enhancing the learning experience, providing access (particularly in music making activities) and as motivating for students (ibid 15, 65, 81).

The new integrated arts courses, like other 'new' courses, sought credibility through the award of a nationally recognised qualification. In 'low content' courses examination accreditation problems though difficult, were not insurmountable. Three examining boards offered combined arts syllabuses and the Calderdale project adopted two of them, the "Expressive and Performing Arts" syllabus (piloted by the NEA) and the SEG "Creative Arts" syllabus (ibid: 66-67). The latter was originally available only as a one year course for mature students. The assessment objectives of the Bedfordshire courses covered technical, critical, creative, vocational, co-operative, and communications skills (ibid: 18). Another arts development, the "TVEI Arts Inter-Authority Project", encouraged development of skills which were more specifically related to tasks. These included: adherence to a brief; self-assessment of responses; preparation and delivery of formal presentations; negotiation; organisation and problem solving (ibid: 56). A second group of skills were more specific to media education and included: de-construction, analysis, the reading of symbols and signifiers, framing and exploring ideas by means of story-boards (ibid: 56). In the Dumfries and Galloway theatre arts course two main types of learning outcomes were specified, each of which had a range of performance criteria. The first of them related to the range of personal and group skills exhibited by the student. Examples given are: "expresses ideas in relation to the dramatic activity"; and "puts forward ideas, develops others' ideas". The second group of learning outcomes are connected more directly to the application of theoretical knowledge, for example, one of the learning outcomes is described as: "knows and uses basic theatre terms." (ibid 76)

Content and subject cohesion
The examples above indicate that the content of many of the 'new' subjects was often different to that which students would have encountered at the same age and stage of development pre-TVEI. In the case of technology subjects such as electronics and computer studies, this was almost certainly the case (HMI 1990). In addition, through re-structuring and cross-curricular interaction between subjects, the possibility existed for greater coherence of content across the curriculum (see O'Grady in Harrison et al 1989: 14, 17). Another strategy which encouraged cross-curricular coherence was block time-tabling. The MSC 85 survey identified a number of projects in which a block of time had been identified specifically for cross curricular activity (MSC 1985: 7).

Content: Cross curricular skills
As well as courses which might be described as new, there were numerous new course 'elements' or 'units'. Many of them appear to have been relatively free of 'theoretical' content, placing emphasis instead on transferable skills and personal and social development. This chapter has explored curriculum breadth and balance in terms of subjects, but breadth and balance in TVEI is not achieved by simply ensuring coverage of subjects.

> "Too often schools concentrate on the intellect, for some reason restrict practical skills to the less able, and neglect the education of the emotions and the development of interpersonal skills. Society needs all three legs of this stool". (Jones in NUT Education Review 1989: 49)

TVEI also required that curriculum entitlement included the opportunity to acquire a range of skills, competencies, and experiences which prepare students for the world of work. Cross-curricular elements such as economic and industrial understanding, and the acquisition of skills such as problem solving, were equally important in providing broad and balanced curriculum experiences. In TVEI projects there was also a requirement to provide work experience and careers guidance and counselling. Relating the curriculum to the world of work through the use of real contexts, and enhancing students' skills in using new technologies, were all important elements in a balanced TVEI curriculum (HMI 1991: 7, 8, 15, 16, 38). Indeed, in the extension phase of TVEI post National Curriculum, these aspects arguably became even more important (Employment Dept. 1991: 34-35). In addressing the requirements of submissions to specify cross-curricular development targets, the extension projects sought to embody the spirit of the entitlement curriculum set out in 'Curriculum 11-16: towards a statement of entitlement' (DES 1983).

Information technology as a cross-curricular skill
One element of the curriculum that initially was often introduced as a subject and which increasingly become a cross-curricular skill (particularly after the

introduction of the National Curriculum) is information technology. In the pilot programmes information technology was almost always part of the TVEI 'core', but it was also central to new courses such as business studies and communications (Cross et al 1988c: 46, 49-50; see also 54-55). The Bradford pilot for example, included computing, satellite technology and robotics in one of the two core elements which went under the heading of information technology (Cross et al 1988a: 63). In the arts as in other curriculum areas, the early tendency to use information technology out of context was to some extent replaced by a better understanding of the ways in which it can, when used as a learning 'tool', become a creative extension of the learning activities available to students (Cross et al 1990b; 6, 15, 63). However some of the statistical information which has been gathered on the use of information technology seems to conflict with the impression gained from the more 'qualitative' reports such as HMI (1990) and the case studies documented in Training Agency publications such as *'Developments'* and *'Insight'.*

Survey data indicates that the use of information technology in a wide range of contexts, was not as broad as might be imagined. This is perhaps more surprising given the TVEI emphasis on application of knowledge and skills. The range of skills used in information technology indicated in the TVEI cohort report (NFER 1992) is also quite low. It showed that word processing was an activity experienced by students "quite often", 34% of the cohort total saying they spent time "learning to word process", and 25% saying they spent time 'doing' word processing. The difference might imply that the larger percentage relates to exercises and de-contextual practice of word processing skills. Computer graphics were used "quite often" by 21% of the students and databases by only 17%. Programming activities were undertaken by 8% of students (ibid: 16 fig. 2.3.4). The emphasis on learning rather than applying information technology skills, is also reflected in the section of the report that deals specifically with the cross-curricular application of information technology (ibid: 27 and fig. 3.2.3).

Balance between theory and application of skills

The Wirral project tried to provide a balance as well as a comprehensive range of practical and theoretical skills to support employment aspirations in a variety of technical occupations. Students received counselling at the start of their course to help them decide which "skills areas" they would most like to develop. The areas included analytical chemistry, microbiology, physics, food sciences, electronics and hardware development, and computing and scientific software development (Cross et al 1988a: 75-77). The MSC review (1985) stressed the importance of TVEI in encouraging students to work towards achieving skills and qualifications that would be of value to them in employment, and highlighted the importance of learning activities which involved the practical application of knowledge (ibid: 14).

The flexible learning projects developed through TVEI placed particular emphasis on study skills such as investigation, analysis, research, information gathering, personal organisation, planning and problem solving etc. (see Lyon, Black and Thorpe 1990: 30; Eraut, Nash, Fielding and Attard 1991: 61-67; Trayers et al 1989: 2-3; Employment Dept. 1992b: 16). The work-related aspects of the curriculum emphasised a wide range of personal, social and vocational skills, such as teamwork, initiative, communication skills, taking responsibility, using technology, problem solving, coping, planning and organisation (see Employment Dept 1991b: 22 table 5a; Cross et al: 1991: 113; Cross et al 1988f: 66-69, 94-98; Finch 1992: 14). The importance of cross-curricular elements, particularly work-related skills, will be explored in chapter three.

Curriculum models

Before TVEI schools generally offered either a compulsory core and options, or a core and constrained options; "core fields" is the term used in Harrison (1989). These are groups of subjects within the same 'area of experience' or 'mode', for example sciences, arts, etc. The core varied between 30% and 80% of curriculum time and the average number of option blocks was five (Harrison 1989: 11). The earlier MSC review also noted that most schools addressed the issue of breadth and balance post fourteen prior to TVEI, by requiring students to take certain core subjects and options structured so as to cover the main areas of experience, with some opportunity for free options after individual counselling (MSC 1985: 6).

The examples of curricular patterns in TVEI, identified in MSC (1985) are: a combination of linked, blocked, and free options; options plus a common core element; thematic options and integrated courses, sometimes with a series of taster modules in the fourth year (ibid 1985: 6-7, 8-13). The Inverclyde pilot project required students to undertake compulsory 'core taster modules' in information technology, electronics, computer programming, CAD, computer-aided control, biotechnology and computer graphics (Gardner in Harrison et al 1988: 5; see also Brain in 'Insight No 14', June 1988: 24-25). The 'MSC 85' report (op cit: 6-13) gives examples of TVEI pilot project curricula offered in schools, all of which had a general common core taken by all students. The models follow a similar pattern to those identified in later reviews, i.e. dispersed and constrained options, although there is only one example of the former (ibid: 8, fig. 4).

Other models identified were: a common core plus constrained options (ibid: 9, fig. 5); a common core plus discrete, but linked TVEI options with a compulsory element (ibid: 10, fig. 6); a common core plus a TVEI core and constrained options (ibid: 11, fig. 7); and a common core plus TVEI thematic options (determined by choice of examination), plus compulsory modular technology (ibid: 12, fig. 8). Another version of the thematic or co-ordinated options model is identified in Harrison (1989). Examples of this model are: design technology and physics; office practice, business studies and information technology; dual science, industrial society and technology. The common aim of all models was to provide broad, balanced and coherent programmes of study (ibid: 17 fig. 7, 18).

TVEI - early curriculum models and their purposes

Barnes et al (1987) identified three "patterns of accommodation" for TVEI. The first was what he called the "adaptive extension" which involved reshaping the whole curriculum. The second is "accommodation" in which the TVEI curriculum is contrasted with the existing curriculum. The third model is "containment" in which the TVEI curriculum is integrated into the existing curriculum (see also

Gleeson et al 1987: 4). In Barnes' study of twelve schools, seven used "containment" and five "accommodation". Only one school had restructured its timetable and then only to increase the length of teaching periods in order to accommodate TVEI courses and off-site experience. It should be pointed out however that the report was on the period 1985-86 and the authors emphasise its interim and partial nature (Barnes et al 1987: 12; see also Lines & Stoney 1989: 36-37; Harrison 1989).

The HMI report on TVEI (1983-1990) also identified three main strategies for implementing the pilot projects. These were a TVEI 'core course', extended dispersed options (available to students in about 40% of schools) or modular programmes which were typically a term or half a term in length (HMI 1991:7). The core course normally included technical and / or vocational core skills such as problem solving, group skills, information technology (Cross et al 1988a: 32-37; 1988d: 8-13; 1988h: 6-7; Barnes et al 1987: 22) and personal and social education. Achievement in these areas was recorded through profiling or records of achievement (Cross et al 1988a: 44-47; 1988e: esp. v-viii). Core course elements often also included work experience, recording achievement or skills profiling, residential experience, careers guidance and counselling, and cross-curricular or pre-vocational modules (Cross et al 1988e).

Constrained / co-ordinated options as a strategy for ensuring breadth and balance in TVEI

There are three variations of the 'co-ordinated options' model identified in Harrison (1989). They are "extended courses" (e.g. science and technology) "linked subjects", such as design with technology, and information technology with business studies. The third model is "thematic options" (e.g. business studies, business accounting, typing and information processing (ibid: 17 fig. 7; 60 appendix 4.1). The Bedfordshire pilot project developed a system of linked technology options (e.g. technology and electronics, design and graphics, technology and computer studies (Cross et al 1988a: 63) while in the Wirral pilot, clusters of modules were combined to form a core course. In technology the cluster consisted of control technology, electronics, and computer studies modules.

There are several reasons for the constrained options strategy identified in the TVEI pilot surveys. The first is to provide co-ordinated learning experiences (the word 'coherent' is not used but perhaps could be applied in some instances). A second reason is to provide flexibility while maintaining coherence (Cross et al 1988c: 72). Yet another reason is to provide breadth of experience (Harrison 1989: 9-18). The alternative to the flexible and constrained options models is the modular system (ibid; 21; Cross et al 1988c: 72; MSC 1985). The common objective of all three strategies was the avoidance of curriculum over-load. Duplication of experiences was avoided through co-ordination of content across the groups of subjects or units, while breadth of experience was maintained through the systematic organisation of options or modules, to ensure coverage of the essential areas of experience (Harrison 1989: 9-20; see also Cross et al 1988c: 72). The NFER review (Lines & Stoney 1989) which sought the views of senior managers in education, reported that head teachers and deputy head teachers felt that TVEI had brought about a broader and more relevant curriculum offering a wider variety of learning experiences and cross-curricular approaches (ibid: 29).

The two most common curriculum patterns for accommodating TVEI pilot projects would seem to be the core and constrained options model, a variation of which is the core and 'co-ordinated options' model, in which a particular choice of subject carries with it a requirement to take another related one. Arguably the second most popular structure was the core and dispersed options model, in which the TVEI options are dispersed within the general option blocks. There are numerous examples of these models in TVEI case studies (see Harrison: 1989: 14 fig. 4; Lines & Stoney 1989: 36-37; Harrison in Cross 1988a: 64; Schofield & Tubb in Cross 1988c: 1-4; Gambie in Cross 1988c: 47; Rennard in Cross 1988c: 71-77; Williams in Cross 1988d: 3; Long in Cross 1988d: 28-35; Busher in Cross 1988d: 48-49; Gardner in Harrison 1988: 5-10; Butlin & Pettin ibid: 29-38, 43-44). In some projects, schools co-operated to provide students with access to a greater range of options.

TVEI within an 'entitlement curriculum'
An example of the core fields approach which was used to accommodate TVEI within an 'entitlement curriculum', is that of Bretton Wood a Cambridge pilot project school (O'Grady & Gribble in Harrison 1988: 11-21). Bretton Wood operated an entitlement curriculum before its involvement in TVEI so the aim was to avoid the options model, characteristic of many pilot projects, and ensure a whole school - whole curriculum approach. When TVEI was introduced the objective was to identify ways in which each area of the curriculum could contribute to a technical and vocational education (ibid: 17). The 'core' course, which was called "Industry in Microcosm", was made up of linked modules covering materials testing, electronics, keyboard skills, computers, graphics and reprographics (Chapman in Cross et al 1988a: 82). There were two other broad based courses "practical business processes" and "product design technology" (also described as: "cohesive pathways through a modular curriculum") which were taught by "integrated teaching teams" (op cit: 17). The Bretton Wood approach is particularly interesting because it was a deliberate attempt to break the mould of options which were preserved in many TVEI developments.

"In schools with option model timetables TVEI has characteristically increased the size of the option pools. The benefits of TVEI have been seen in the option box appendages, temporarily enriched but shortly to diminish as funds expire. Often the curriculum remains unreformed." (ibid: 20)

The 'TVEI core'
In each of the case studies in Cross et al (1988d) the 'TVEI core' typically contained elements such as: work experience, recording achievement or skills profiling, residential experience, careers, guidance and counselling, and information technology (see Lines & Stoney 1989: 36; Harrison 1989: 13). In some instances cross-curricular and / or pre-vocational modules were included (Cross 1988d: 4, 7). Lines and Stoney identified work experience, profiling, guidance, information technology and residentials, as typical TVEI core experiences (Lines & Stoney 1989: 36). The core was often combined with

other TVEI elements which may or may not be available to students outside the TVEI cohort (see Barnes in Preedy et al 1989: 32). In the Solihull pilot case study for example, the TVEI consortium core elements were as above (Schofield in Cross et al 1988c: 1,2) and the additional course options included caring services, commerce and business studies, food studies, media studies and manufacturing studies. In some TVEI programmes the effect of having a 'TVEI core' in addition to the 'normal' core programme which all students followed, was to reduce the scope for options.

Some of the curriculum models in pilot TVEI projects were incredibly complex. One TVEI pilot curriculum included a general core and a TVEI core plus 'broad fields' modular courses composed of dispersed options (Cross 1988d: 2-7). The 'general core' which all students followed comprised of: English, mathematics, health and social education, 'world of work', and PE. The second element was the 'TVEI core', consisting of basic skills workshops. The third element was drawn from the TVEI options which were broad-based courses, supplemented by the skills workshops. The courses were: "technology at work", "the work of business", and "personal and community services", and the year four skills workshops included information technology, communications, materials and food technology. In year five the workshops were: communication skills, problem solving and group and individual skills. The year five curriculum was modular (Williams in Cross et al 1988d: 6-7) and the courses were structured so that students had to complete three "project assignments" in year four and five in year five.

Modularisation
The MSC report (1985) made the point that all of the curriculum models described in the survey, could be offered in modular form (MSC 1985: 7). The term 'modular', was used to describe a complete course made up of discrete but related units of study of roughly equal time, often providing a variety of optional routes through a course or programme. It was also used by schools to describe units of study which might vary in length and comprise a single pathway through a subject or course (ibid: 21; Moon 1988).

Modular schemes provided a flexible structure aimed at rationalisation and elimination of course overlap to provide time and space for TVEI core experiences (Moon 1988: 61). The MSC (1985) identified the use of modular structures as a practical way of improving breadth and balance because they could offer flexibility and coverage over a wide range of subjects (see also HMI 1991: 7 para. 18. iii; Moon 1988). The Leicestershire "Business Education Modular Course" for example, covered "six educational areas": economic awareness, consumer competence, numeracy and financial awareness, communication and information skills, enterprise education, and political and legal awareness. Some modules, such as economic awareness, were cross-curricular and involved problem solving activities. Accreditation was through GCSE mode one (Gambie in Cross 1988c: 47; see also Willars in Moon 1988: 55).

In the Cumbrian project the modular core covered: problem-solving and study-skills, computer appreciation, word processing and keyboard skills, electronics, business management, graphics, computer control, biotechnology, creative and performing arts (Wind in Cross et al 1988a: 31-40), and was accredited through NPRA unit accreditation (ibid: 9-17). In the Inverclyde project the TVEI core elements included taster modules covering: information technology, electronics, computer programming, computer-aided draughting, computer control, biotechnology and computer graphics. The second year modular courses were accredited by SCOTVEC, initially on a trial basis (Gardner in Harrison et al 1988: 5-10).

The MSC review seemed to indicate a good level of interest in modular developments but accepted that they had "..posed a particular challenge to the examining boards" (MSC 1985: 18). In some areas a number of LEA's co-operated to produce materials for modular curricula (see Moon: 48-76; 77-92). In the Scottish projects the Standard Grade Social and Vocational Skills course was used, as were the 16+ Action Plan modules which the Scottish Education Department had given schools permission to use with 14-16 year old students (op cit: 19). The Scottish surveys conducted by SCRE between 1985 and 1990, also indicated a high level of involvement in modular courses. One of the Scottish curriculum innovations associated with TVEI, was the introduction of forty-hour modular courses accredited by SCOTVEC, which according to the surveys, more than 80% of pupils in round five schools claimed to have taken. A reason given for the introduction of SCOTVEC modular courses was, 'to provide greater breadth and flexibility in the curriculum'. In the Scottish experience National Certificate modules were often part of a TVEI core curriculum (Black et al 1990c: 5).

Accreditation
Another of the positive features of TVEI, the modular core, was intended to improve the motivation of students through establishing short term goals (Cross 1988c: 13, vi; see Moon 1989: 9; Hitchcock 1988: 153). The NFER evaluation report (Wardman 1989: 5) underlined the importance of modular schemes in TVEI developments although they were not without problems, particularly in terms of standardisation and coherence (see ibid: 5; see also HMI 1991: 7 paras. 18, 19). Projects also frequently made use of mode three examinations through which core skills and cross curricular courses could be accredited (Wardman 1989: 4). The "pilot profile on assessment", a joint initiative between Sheffield LEA and Sheffield University, stressed the value of short term goals and rapid reinforcement on the basis of identifiable learning outcomes (Cross 1988c: 13). The importance of learning objectives and negotiated targets is endorsed in Trayers et al (1989) and in Moon (1988: 9). Informing students of unit or module learning outcomes and assessment criteria (short-term goals) has been a strategy used in TVEI to improve motivation and achievement (Hitchcock 1988: 153; Cousins in Cross et al 1989: 30).

Block time-tabling
Another interesting outcome of TVEI which is picked up in Barnes (1987) is the use of large blocks of time for discrete and / or, co-ordinated courses (ibid: 13). This could provide opportunities for collaboration between curriculum areas. However in certain circumstances it caused friction and provoked criticism from non-TVEI teachers who felt that TVEI was dictating the structure of the time-table (Barnes et al 1987: 73). Block time-tabling was a strategy often employed in TVEI pilot projects since it facilitated 'off-site' activities. An example of the

strategy is documented in (Cross 1988d: 41; see also 23-40) in which the TVEI curriculum consisted of two courses (PT1 and PT2), the first being for the most able students and the latter for the less able. There was also a two- part core programme. The course for the less able provided a choice of a craft-based technology course, including metalwork or engineering, plus off-site link courses.

The 'subject-based' curriculum
In TVEI extension projects the curriculum returned to a more traditional subject-based form (Ainley 1990: 47). This has been reinforced by the introduction of the National Curriculum (ibid: 25). Extension projects placed particular emphasis on modern languages, science and technology, and the principle of a curriculum entitlement for all students featured in TVEI extension submissions, either implicitly or explicitly, through the compulsory endorsement of the policy embedded in 'Better Schools' (Employment Dept. 1991: 28). Some projects such as Humberside and North Tyneside, used the TVEI extension aims of student centred approaches to teaching and learning, real contexts, cross-curricular themes and skills, equal opportunities and records of achievement etc., as "development themes" which run across the whole curriculum (see also Parish in Cross et al 1989: 53).

'Work-related' aspects of the curriculum
The work-related aspects of the curriculum were particularly important in TVEI and for that reason they were often included in the TVEI core. There was a requirement for all extension projects to provide work experience and careers guidance and counselling. Relating the curriculum to the world of work through the use of real contexts and by enhancing students' skills in using new technologies, were all important elements in a balanced TVEI curriculum (HMI 1991: 7, 8, 15,16, 38). It is the third of the criteria specified in 'Better Schools' relating to 'relevance', which is restated in the "TVEI Focus Statement" (Employment Dept. 1991: 34-35) and which will be explored in more detail in chapter three.

Equality of opportunity
Breadth and balance also needs to address the issues of access and equality of opportunity. A broad and balanced curriculum is not necessarily achieved through coverage of subject content. Access, entitlement and differentiation are important concerns to those who see breadth and balance in terms of the individual student. These issues were significant in TVEI programmes (Cross et al 1988b; Trayers et al 1989: 106-108; Employment Dept. 1991: 28, 31, 34; Finch 1992).

TVEI was launched shortly after publication of the 'Swann Report' - 'Education for All' (1982), the introduction of the Sex Discrimination Act, the 'Interim Report of the Committee of Inquiry into the Education of Children from Ethnic Minority Groups' (1981) and the setting up of the Equal Opportunities Commission. The issue of access to practical subjects, and of the relative achievements of the sexes and students from minority ethnic groups in a wide range of curriculum subjects, became one of the main objectives of the projects (House of Commons 20th Dec 1982: paras 2-3; Employment Dept. 1992; Murray et al 1991). The problems of gender stereo-typing and imbalance, particularly in the science disciplines, was also highlighted by the *'Secondary Science Curriculum Review'* (Michell 1987). The review findings showed that three times as many boys took physics as girls, three times as many girls studied 'O' level biology as studied physics and chemistry, and one and a half times as many boys studied 'O' level physics as studied chemistry and biology (Michell 1987: 1). TVEI made a commitment to equality of opportunity, but in the early days of the pilot projects progress was limited. Indeed in some instances the new courses might actually have increased discrimination (Wickham in Dale 1985: 107).

Special needs

Students with special education needs were involved in many of the pilot projects. A number of strategies were employed to improve both curriculum access and opportunity. They included supported integration into mainstream courses, link courses, and participation in activities at specialist TVEI centres with the opportunity in some case, for students to follow a TVEI common core curriculum (MSC 1985: 15). In the extension projects all special schools had the opportunity to become involved in collaborative activities with mainstream schools (Department of Employment 1991: 28; Finch 1992: 25-26). The NFER study (Murray et al 1991: 35-48) also identified strategies employed in TVEI for managing educational entitlement.

An early survey of pilot projects (Underwood in Cross et al 1988c: 64) revealed that a number did not provide access for special needs students. In some projects, core elements including personal and social education and enterprise activities, were made available to special needs students after individual counselling. In one TVEI project, special needs provision was seen very much as a prevocational scheme, and some modular courses including robotics, mountaineering, canoeing, graphics, welding, oral history, community service, computing, word processing and model making, were available to special needs students. In other projects specialist support was provided to encourage mainstream integration.

The joint SCPR - Employment Department report (Finch 1992) provides in much greater detail, the full range of strategies used in TVEI projects to address special education needs. It concludes that TVEI had a major impact on the special needs curriculum. Particularly important were the changes which took place in teaching and learning, the organisation of the curriculum, and access to mainstream education for both staff and students. The report suggests that involvement in TVEI often raised levels of attainment and expectations, as well as providing an impetus for curriculum development (Finch 1992: 13, 16, 17, 24-26).

Gender stereotyping

The MSC review (1985) identified some of the strategies which were used to ensure that projects were avoiding sex stereotyping. These included providing a core technology experience for all students, examination of content, teaching styles and presentation, and review of the organisation of the curriculum to ensure that such factors did not impede equality of opportunity (MSC 1985: 14-15). Other TVEI strategies which were used to reduce gender stereotyping included making traditionally gender stereotyped courses (in addition to technology) part of a 'common core', linking options so that traditional choices were linked with non-traditional ones, providing single-sex starter modules and option groups, and in extension projects by providing an 'entitlement curriculum' in which option choices were minimal (McIntyre 1987: 8; see also Cousins in Cross 1989: 29-30). Another strategy to address gender imbalance in technological subjects was to re-label them (Carr-Archer in Cross 1988b: 13).

Modular courses which offered a short-term commitment and involved less 'risk' on the part of the students than full courses were also effective (McIntyre 1987: 8). This was a strategy used in the Birmingham pilot project (Parker, 'Insight Digest vol. 3' 1988: 18-19). In the Inverclyde project students were encouraged to question career limitations caused by gender stereotyping (Harrison et al 1988; 7). However there has been some criticism that gender stereotyping was not always been addressed as vigorously as it ought to have been in TVEI projects (Cross et al 1988b: 26; & 1988f: 22). It is also important to note that not all the equal opportunities arguments used in TVEI were based on egalitarian principles. It is clear that an instrumentalist rationale, i.e. 'the avoidance of wasted potential', was never far from the surface (see Cross et al 1988b: vii).

There are remarkably few recorded instances of the TVEI curriculum being deliberately restricted to students of a particular level of ability. Barnes (1987) identified one school which had developed courses only for low ability students in a clear breach of the MSC guidelines (Barnes et al 1987: 13). The same report also indicated that in some of the schools certain options were taken predominantly by students of low ability (ibid: 23). The evidence from the SCRE survey (1990) showed that TVEI attracted a good spread of ability and a gender balance (Lyon Black & Thorpe 1990: 28-29). However there is an example of a differentiated curriculum in Cross et al (1988d) which hints strongly of both gender stereotyping and banding. The course (PT2) which was for the less able provided a choice of a craft-based technology course including metalwork or engineering; plus practical drawing and science, or business studies and information technology. A link course, run in conjunction with the college of FE, offered motor mechanics or welding.

By the 1986-87 round of pilot projects, the overall gender balance was 55% boys to 45% girls but in about 20% of the LEA's the proportion of girls per cohort was as high or higher than that of boys (Tenne 1989: i). The ethnic mix of TVEI students was a reflection of the individual school's mix but with about 4% more Asian students than would be expected (ibid: 2). In terms of ability, the range had improved but there was still quite a high proportion of students in the lower to middle ability range and the over-all ability profile of girls was slightly higher than that of boys (ibid: 3). In the high ability bands, i.e. those students with the estimated potential to achieve four or more 'O' levels or two 'A' levels, there were approximately 2% fewer TVEI students than non-TVEI students. The middle band, i.e. those with the estimated potential to achieve one to three 'O' levels, had 4% more TVEI students than non-TVEI students. and in the band assessed as capable of two to five CSE passes there were 3% more TVEI than non-TVEI students. There were also three per cent fewer potentially ungraded students opting for TVEI courses (Tenne 1989: 4 fig. 2).

The patterns of science options for boys and girls still indicated traditional preferences, however the introduction of balanced science did much to improve the science curriculum of both sexes (see Dunkerton in: 'Insight 17' Autumn 1989: 7). The report TVEI Students and Studies: 14-16 Students (1989: 4) showed that in the 1986-1987 intake, 92% of boys and 90% of girls took a science subject. There were still considerably more boys opting for technology courses than girls, with the exception of Information technology which attracted a better balance. Boys appeared to like specialist technology courses while girls preferred broad courses. The (1987) interim review indicated that in business studies both boys and girls showed a preference for the broader 'business world model' (Barnes et al 1987: 76) and that when technology and business studies appeared in the same option box it often reinforced gender bias (ibid: 88). The NFER report (1989) indicated that in terms of examination achievement, those TVEI students at the upper end of the ability range did less well than expected (although 73% achieved four or more GCE or CSE grade one passes) while those in the middle and lower bands did better than had been expected. There appeared to have been little difference in achievement between indigenous and ethnic minority students (Tenne 1989: 14, 15).

From the commencement of TVEI extension onwards there was a considerable improvement in gender balance and in the take-up of traditionally gender stereotyped subjects. Progress towards achieving a better gender balance in science has been good. The statistical evidence indicates that while the gap between boys and girls showed a marginal increase in 1990-91, the over-all percentage of students taking balanced science increased from approximately 65% in 1988-89, to over 80% in 1989-90 and reached over 90% in 1990-91. The difference between boys and girls was proportionately less in 1990-91 than in 1988-89 (Employment Dept. 1992: 7 fig. 4). The take-up of technology subjects by boys remained fairly constant between 1988-89 and 1990-91 (about 75% of the cohort). The take-up by girls was still low but did show an improvement from just under 35% in 1988-89, to just under 45% in 1990-91 (Employment Dept. 1992: 9 fig. 5). The number of girls studying modern languages at fourteen increased by about 5% from approximately 75% in 1989-90, to just over 80% in 1990-91. The number of boys taking a modern foreign language also increased from just under, to just over 60% in the same period. The imbalance between boys and girls in modern languages would seem to be slowly decreasing (ibid: 10 fig. 6). Gender stereotyping disadvantages both boys and girls McIntyre (1987: 8) and despite the high profile given to equality of opportunity by TVEI, responses by gender seem to indicate that there is still work to be done in order to change traditional attitudes to science and modern languages (op cit: 19. fig. 2.5.1; see Millman and Weiner in Gleeson 1987: 173-176).

Access
Student access to TVEI pilot project curricula is an issue which seems to have been neglected in many of the reviews. There would appear to have been three basic methods of cohort selection. The first seems to have been selection based on ability. It should be pointed out that this was probably to ensure a proper spread of ability rather than to 'set' or 'stream'. The second seems to have been by including TVEI as an option choice at fourteen. The third method would appear to be 'self-selection' as a result of choosing

particular subjects or courses from an options pool (see Barnes et al 1987: 19-21).

Access is an important aspect of equality of opportunity and entitlement is closely associated with it. The TVEI extension overview report (NFER 1992) indicated that there were still wide discrepancies between time allocated to science and in particular, to modern foreign languages depending on students' abilities (NFER 1992: 13 fig. 2.3.2; 14 fig. 2.3.3). There also appeared to be problems in terms of gender attitudes to science and modern foreign languages, while technology still drew negative attitudinal responses from both boys and girls. This gave cause for concern and raised questions about the quality of technological experience students were receiving. On the basis of self rating both low and average ability students recorded negative responses to science and modern languages, very negative in the case of the least able. The 'more able' students were positive about both science and modern foreign languages while in technology both low and high ability students recorded slightly negative responses. Students of average ability were slightly more positive about technology (NFER 1992: 19 fig. 2.5.1).

Summary
In this second chapter the range of strategies through which curriculum breadth and balance have been addressed in TVEI have been explored. The TVEI pilot projects were essentially 'experiments' in curriculum organisation, with the explicit aim of testing the possibility of providing a technical and vocational dimension for all 14-16 year old students. It would appear that the early pilot projects were very much concerned with providing a balance between general and vocational education. Strategies included the introduction of innovative curriculum models and new courses which were principally technical and vocational, and which challenged the traditional subject-based curriculum by enhancing the status of such courses.

In some instances the introduction of TVEI actually 'narrowed' the curriculum of some students and excluded some essential aspects of general education. The new courses also effectively 'forced out' of the curriculum, 'old style' craft and gender-stereotyped courses. Many of the new curriculum models were based on the old concept of options, but some of the developments showed that TVEI could also enhance an 'entitlement curriculum', and that in some ways such an approach was more sustainable in the long term than 'bolt-on' courses.

In terms of curriculum time allocation, the principal winners were 'technological courses' which also gained status through the introduction of information technology, business, and 'high-tec' elements such as enterprise activities, electronics and computer programming. The losers were, in the main, elements of the traditional liberal arts curriculum.

The importance of access and equality of opportunity were highlighted as being important issues in any consideration of curriculum breath and balance. It was also noted that TVEI helped to draw attention to the importance of cross-curricular as well as 'subject specific' content. The difficulty in determining the 'newness' of content was noted but it would appear that whereas some subjects were simply 'old content re-packaged', others did include content which while it may not always have been genuinely new, was different to that which students would normally have encountered at the same stage of development. The introduction of modular courses as a strategy to address issues of curriculum breadth, balance and flexibility, and the motivational value of 'short-term goals' were also explored briefly.

Post National Curriculum the subject-based 'entitlement curriculum' shifted the balance away from vocational / general courses back towards general education, but with a requirement to develop opportunities for work-related learning experiences across the curriculum. Another important point raised in this chapter is that concerning the relationship between TVEI and the National Curriculum. The "Focus Statement" which was quoted, made it clear that many of the most important TVEI developments had been 'legislated into the curriculum' of all students, and that TVEI still had an important role to play in enhancing the 'work-related aspects of the National Curriculum.

The 'work-related curriculum' has already been explored briefly in this chapter and will be examined in more detail in chapter three. The aspects which will be highlighted include 'relevance' and the use of 'real contexts' (including problem solving and work experience) the development of links and partnerships between education and business, the 'application of skills and concepts' and the emphasis on the development of 'work-related skills'. The influence of TVEI on the relationship between the 14-16 curriculum and the world of work, and the importance in TVEI of 'extrinsic' or 'instrumental values' will now be explored.

Chapter Three

The 'work-related curriculum'

"Although TVEI can make no claim to introducing the theme of building bridges between education and work, it can claim to have given it greater form and focus". (Cohen in: *International Journal of Education Management vol. 3'*: 13-18; see also Jamieson & Lightfoot 1982: 58; for an indication of similarities between TVEI strategies and those of the Schools Council Industry Project).

In *'Better Schools'* relevance is interpreted in two ways. First there is relevance in terms of the needs of industry, *'Better Schools'* is explicit about the responsibility of educators in this respect (ibid: 14.45.3 - 15.46). Secondly relevance is interpreted in terms of knowledge and skills and their relevance to the world of work.

> "The economic stresses of our time and the pressures of international competition make it more necessary than ever before that Britain's work-force should possess the skills and attitudes, and display the understanding, the enterprise and adaptability that the pervasive impact of technological advance will increasingly demand." (ibid: 15.46)

The TVEI Extension "Statement of Curricular Aims" is very clear about the need for students to acquire skills which will be of use to them in employment. It is equally clear about the need for a shift in curriculum emphasis from acquisition to application of knowledge and skills.

> "Relevance should be sought by making programmes contain a suitable emphasis on personal and social skills, including initiative, and on the practical application of knowledge and skills, including problem solving, all of which are designed to prepare the student for adult working life in a society liable to rapid change." (Employment Dept 1991: 28)

The statement goes on to suggest that vocational contexts related to local and national employment opportunities, can also provide relevance for studies, but warns against narrow vocational specialisation pre-sixteen. It is this second interpretation of relevance as a motivational impulse, that would seem to have caught the imagination of teachers in both pilot and extension projects. The 'new technologies', particularly information technology, have also become an important means of motivating students. Information technology, as Barnes (1987: 51) and HMI (1990) point, out has become a 'learning tool' (Cross et al 1988d: 12) and as such has become increasingly relevant to a wide range of learning situations as well as having vocational applications (see Ainley 1990: 121; Trayers 1889: 10).

The NFER review (Lines & Stoney 1989: 33) also endorses the fact that while vocationalism did increase with the introduction of TVEI, the bulk of a student's programme was made up of general education. The report also states that early fears that TVEI might result in earlier specialisation were unfounded (ibid:

33). Even in the early days of TVEI the MSC was keen to allay concern that it was intended to encourage early vocational specialisation. "The vocational options are not intended to indicate premature specialisation, but are rather a context within which students are better motivated to learn how to learn." (MSC 1985:14)

Relevance and the needs of industry

'Better Schools' refers to the use of new technologies and the economic necessity of equipping students with the skills and competencies required to use them (ibid; 15.46; 23.71). Paragraph seventy-six, while not referring directly to TVEI, does highlight some of its most significant aspects.

> "The Government shares the view of many in the education service and outside it that more emphasis needs to be given to science and technology; to practical application of knowledge and to practical skills throughout the curriculum; and to helping pupils to understand, and to develop positive attitudes towards the demands which industrial and technological changes will increasingly make on all aspects of adult life, notably employment." (ibid: 25,76)

In 1989, in the context of other changes in education, a TVEI Focus Statement was issued. It stressed the continued role of the project in enhancing the link between the school-based experiences of students and the world of work in order to develop 'a more highly skilled and effective work-force.' It made clear the importance of active and practical learning methods, work experience, guidance, and action planning, and the national need to improve skills and qualifications, particularly in science, technology, information technology and modern languages (see Employment Dept 1991). The "Focus Statement", as it is called, restates the need for education to be 'relevant to employment' and it supports the involvement of employers in education and the "involvement of students in the world of work..." (Employment Dept 1991: 34 para. 2). The statement, which accompanied the implementation of the National Curriculum, reiterated the strong link between TVEI and the preparation of students for employment opportunities.

The second "Focus Statement", which was issued in 1990, again stated very clearly that the over-arching aim of TVEI is to improve the quality of the work-force.

> "TVEI's role is to help produce a more highly skilled, competent, effective and enterprising work-force in the 1990's. It is a long term strategy, unique among nations for investing in the skills of all our young people 14-19 in full - time education and equipping them for the demands of working life in a rapidly changing highly technological society. It does this by; relating what is learnt in schools and colleges to the world of work;
> improving the skills and qualifications for all; in particular in science, technology and modern languages;
> providing young people with direct experience of the world of work through real work experience;

enabling young people to be effective, enterprising and capable at work through active and practical learning methods;
providing counselling, guidance, individual action plans, records of achievement and opportunities to progress to higher levels of achievement." (Employment Department in Finch 1992: 3)

Increase in vocational and pre-vocational courses

Between the second and the fourth rounds of TVEI pilot projects, the proportion of TVEI students taking vocational studies increased by 8% to a total across the whole cohort of 11%. The proportion of TVEI students gaining pre-vocational qualifications was 16%, mainly City and Guilds level one (Tenne 1989: III, 18). The take up of electronics, technology and information technology also increased. In the case of information technology this may have been partly due to the increase in cross-curricular applications. Overall there was a good balance of boys and girls taking vocational and pre-vocational courses (Tenne 1989: 9). HMI (1991) endorsed curriculum enhancement brought about by increased use of business and industry contexts and information technology and reported that the best work took place when learning was through practical activities (ibid: 30).

Cross-curricular skills and competencies

Skills development was one of main emphases in TVEI and it formed an important part of the so called, 'work-related curriculum'. There would appear to be a good deal of evidence to suggest that TVEI was effective in this area. A summary of Scottish reports compiled between 1985 and 1990, concluded that TVEI courses had enabled many cross-curricular competencies to be developed. In particular, pupils had developed problem-solving skills and initiative, and had developed their personal and social skills. The education they had received had been, according to teachers, "more vocationally relevant". The report stated that: "The basic TVEI aims of raising technological awareness amongst staff and pupils, and making education more relevant to life outside the school, had been achieved." (Black 1990c: 1, 3. 4)

In the extension phase of TVEI, cross-curricular themes and skills had a high profile and the importance of work-related skills was a major focus. In particular, the development of personal and social skills, and problem solving in 'real contexts' was encouraged, as was the use of information technology. Students also became more aware of their own competencies and achievements through the use of profiles and records of achievement. The application of skills learned in school to world of work contexts was further enhanced by work experience programmes.

> "More than ever before, the aims of TVEI, while supporting the National Curriculum in England and in Wales and curricular developments in Scotland, emphasise the connection between educating for personal effectiveness and work capability, and the need for an adaptable, flexible workforce..." (Employment Dept 1991: 22)

One strategy for involving all curriculum areas in TVEI curriculum enhancement activities, was to map cross-curricular skills in each subject in order to provide a basis for development activities (Lines & Stoney 1989: 36-37). This strategy was used in both pilot and TVEI extension projects, particularly post National Curriculum (Parish in Cross et al 1989: 53; Willars in Moon 1988: 48; Hall 1992: 3).

Enhancement of subjects through work-related activities

One of the major objectives set out in 'Better Schools' was to improve the relationship between education and business and industry and to make each more aware and more responsive to the other. TVEI enabled a good deal of progress to be made on this objective (HMI 1991: 21). There are well documented case studies which are testament to progress made through industrial support and involvement in curriculum enhancement and development activities (Cross et al 1991: 34, 46, 51, 53-63; Cross et al 1988f; Cook 1988: 17-18; 1989: 9-13, 18-19; HMI 1991: x; 'Insight No 25' Autumn 1992: 5-10; 'Insight No 26' February / March 1993: 21).

> "One of the major thrusts of TVEI is to improve and widen the attainment of students in work-related topics, particularly in science, technology, information technology and modern languages. Returns show that significant advances have been made in all these areas." (Employment Department 1992: 7)

The TVEI extension cohort review also made it clear that the aim of improving the quality of the work-force was as central to the extension phase of TVEI as it had been to the pilot projects.

> "The original seven aims of TVEI stressed the development of skills and qualifications of direct value to young people in the workplace, and the encouragement of initiative, motivation and enterprise to enable them to solve real life problems." (NFER: 1992: 1)

The National Curriculum is geared to similar aims. This is particularly evident in the statutory requirements for the teaching of technology and information technology, the latter of which was also a designated cross-curricular skill. Economic and industrial understanding, one of the cross-curricular themes, was embedded within national curriculum subject orders, for example in technology and science (DES Circular 3/90: 7; Statutory Instruments - technology DES 1990: 39; DES science order DES 1991: 22; see also Trainor in Richardson 1992: 18). There would appear to have been some progress made in developing student awareness of industry and the economy. HMI for example, reported an improvement in students' understanding of these aspects of society, due largely to the work-related aspects of the TVEI curriculum (HMI 1991: 15).

Student motivation and self-reliance

Two of the aims of TVEI were to improve self-motivation and to encourage students to take greater responsibility for their own learning. Both the National Curriculum and TVEI placed importance on the acquisition of study skills, records of achievement and individual action planing. In both pilot and extension projects, TVEI encouraged the development of teaching and learning methods that focused on the individual student and encouraged learner autonomy. The flexible learning developments that were undertaken through TVEI are an example of one over-arching strategy (Tomlinson and Kilner 1992). There are other examples, for instance the pilot case study of Greenfield School (Cross et al 1988d: 6) indicates that all courses required students to undertake assignments which were student centred and negotiated with teachers who acted as 'facilitators' or 'enablers' (Williams in Cross et al 1988d: 6; see also Richmond - Dean in Trayers et al 1989: 68; Muse in Trayers 1989: 100-101). When surveyed, a small majority of Scottish teachers, whether involved in TVEI or not, felt that the strategies used in TVEI motivated children to learn and had resulted in more pupils learning on their own (Black et al 1990b: 5). Although the notion of students taking greater responsibility for their own learning was something most teachers said they wished to see increased, the demands of syllabus content meant that they still often used traditional methods (Black et al 1991: 19).

The TVEI cohort survey (1992) reviewed the extent to which students in the survey cohort participated in learning activities that might be classified as, 'individual learning activities requiring personal motivation'. The activity most frequently experienced by students was "project work" or "assignments". This was followed by "using initiative and planning targets". In terms of negotiating learning experiences, "choosing partners" offered most scope for students, followed by "pace of work" and "working methods". Opportunities for negotiation of projects, assignments or units of work, were all very limited (NFER 1992: 26 fig. 3.2.2).

'Real contexts' for learning

> "Classrooms are everywhere, not just in school buildings - so we should view the school as a hub and as a provider of individual learning programmes rather than the source of all learning."
> (Abbott et al 1989: 5-6)

Another strategy encouraged by TVEI which has already been mentioned, was the use of 'real contexts'. In the Exeter pilot technology projects for example, a problem solving approach was adopted based on world of work problems. The introduction to the section in the Leeds University interim review on "the context of learning" (Barnes et al 1987: 32) begins:

> "It makes a good deal of difference to the nature of learning whether skills and knowledge are imparted in isolation or in the context of some broader activity. They may be taught for their own sakes, as exercises and out of context, or they may be taught, learnt and exercised in a context that will attribute a purpose to them, show how they are important and create awareness of the ways in which their use relates to other concerns and priorities." (ibid 1987: 32)

TVEI was not intended to be narrowly vocational (see MSC 1985: 6; Employment Dept. 1991: 6; HMI 1991: ix) and in that sense the contexts used would be expected to enhance learning experiences, rather than to constrain or focus knowledge and skills on specific job training. Business and industry often provided contexts in which learning activities could take place. Sometimes they involved people from industry in school-based activities (Cook 1989: 9-10; Smith & Towsin in Cross et al: 1988f: 46; Hirst in Cross 1988f: 52) while in other instances they engaged students in 'off-site' experiences. In the Sandwell project technology problems were set by local employers and students made study trips industrial premises to seek advice (Harrison in Cross et al 1988a: 59; see also O'Grady & Gribble in Harrison et al 1988: 18; Roebuck in Cross et al 1988f: 34; Hirst in Cross 1988f: 62; Dutton, Mayall in Cross 1988f: 94-95; NFER 1992: 29-30). The HMI review (1991) also makes the point that TVEI encouraged the use of real contexts and notes that: "Students were most positive about any aspect which they considered to be relevant to their future adult life." (Ibid: 8) In "Enterprise Technology and Business Studies", a course developed by the Croydon project, the focus was on group skills. The contexts for study and skills development were mini-company enterprise activities in which a simulated production line was set up by the students who, through role-play activities, dealt with many of the same problems that would be faced in a real company (Harrison et al 1988 57-59). Learning together and peer-group support in new situations was also motivating for students in TVEI.

"Central to the concept of enterprise technology and business studies is that pupils learn by themselves and work together in groups to overcome their problems...We have seen the growth of group allegiance and pupil support for each other." (Clarke in Harrison et al 1988: 59).

In the Wirral pilot project the science course was assignment based and all assignments involved problem solving activities which were intended to be as near as possible to "real world" experience. An "enrichment package" was developed for GCE "O" level students in chemistry, physics and computing. The package was intended to provide opportunities for "experiential learning" to enable students to see the relevance of their studies to real world situations. They were required to apply their knowledge and skills to complete a set task and in the process to develop a range of personal skills and initiative (De Middelear in Cross et al 1988a: 75, 78).

Real contexts have often provided a focus for cross-curricular activities and projects. In Lincolnshire for example, an MLD special school developed a cross curricular enterprise project that included aspects of art, information technology, mathematics and English, and involved activities such as: market research, costing, advertising, production, selling and accounting. The project also included workplace observation (Dutton & Mayall in Cross et al 1988f: 93-100).

Residential, work experience and other 'off-site' experience
Residential experience featured prominently in many of the pilot projects (HMI 1991: 17) and work experience was a major focus in both pilot and extension projects (Cook: 1988; HMI 1991: 22-24; see also NFER 1992: 40-41). In the Borders pilot the social and vocational skills contexts which supplemented the TVEI core of PSE and information technology, were: work experience or community placement or residential; organising and running a community event; making an item or providing a service to show potential for self employment; a leisure activity; and participation in a co-operative activity. These areas of experience map onto the "Scottish Vocational Skills Areas" -

social and communication skills and practical skills - which to begin with were only accredited at the lower and middle levels (Geddes in Cross et al 1988a: 1-5).

The development of problem solving skills was also important in both pilot and extension projects (Employment Dept. 1991: 25, 28). Barnes (1987) gives some examples of problem solving activities in the context of work experience, an activity which provided some apparently scarce opportunities for students to deal with real problems (Barnes et al 1987: 36-37). Business contexts were used in Staffordshire where a tradition of industry links was established before TVEI. The project built on existing practice and the practical business course formed one of four broad curriculum areas, the others being: social and life skills, commercial and industrial language, and place studies (Price in Cross 1988a: 7-20; see also Price and Thompson in *'Insight No 13'* June 1988: 7-10). A broad range of world of work skills were developed through the "Shared Business Experience" which was part of the core curriculum. The skills programme included: enterprise, raising capital, controlling finance, researching, designing, evaluating, manufacturing, marketing and selling. Other generic workplace skills included: group work, using technology, and working in business and industry. In the Wirral project, as in the Staffordshire project, the development of a wide range of generic skills including: design, management, marketing, evaluation, team-work, presentation and communication skills, as well as subject specific skills, were main objectives. The work of students on the science courses involved industrial research and development projects. Close links with industries such as Unilever and with higher education were established to 'tune' courses to developments in industry (De Middelear in Cross et al 1988a: 75,80).

In TVEI extension projects 'real contexts for learning' provided motivation, real problem solving activities, and an opportunity for students to apply knowledge and skills in a wide range of enterprise situations (Cook: 1989: 11). A particularly successful example is given in (*'Insight No 19'* Summer 1990: 4-5). Although the project was science-based, the subject was really a vehicle through which students set about solving a real problem set by a real company, in the process of which, a range of cross-curricular skills and world of work skills were experienced and developed by the students. The project was an integral part of the GCSE science course.

The HMI review (1991) endorsed the view that TVEI had encouraged 'off-site experience' and that it had often enhanced students' studies and improved their understanding of the world of work. Meeting and dealing with adults and real problems would also seem to improve students' self confidence and encourage them to take greater responsibility for their own work (HMI 1991: 17). The TVEI philosophy regarding off-site experience is reflected in the following extract from the Training Agency Publication: *'From Teaching to Learning'* (Abbott et al 1989). "We must build on the fact that young people learn much outside school / college - and enjoy doing so." (ibid 1989: 3)

Technology and Enterprise Centres
Apart from work experience in its various forms, project work, and residential experience, some students had opportunities to spend time in specialist TVEI

centres. Sometimes the problem of small option groups was addressed by collaborative provision of courses involving pairs or groups of schools (Bridgwood 1989; Saunders & Stradling 1991). This in some instances, involved a common TVEI curriculum and shared resources such as a specialist centre. The Wirral schools for example, shared a technology centre which provided specialist facilities for the study of biotechnology, electronics, and other technological courses. Sometimes such centres were staffed by industry tutors or consultants who worked with teachers and students (Price & Thompson: 'Insight No 13' June 1988: 7-10).

In Sunderland, industry involvement began before TVEI but was enhanced by it. An "enterprise centre" was already established in a factory unit on an industrial estate. Enterprise projects for students were planned and provided by teachers, centre staff and industry consultants. The projects were tailored to the needs of individual groups of teachers and students, and were an integral part of the courses that students were following. They were intended to broaden the students' experience, to help them develop skills and competencies related to business and industry, and to provide access to new technology and 'real world problems'. The learning experiences extended to teachers as well as students through the provision of INSET and participation in activities which promoted student centred teaching (Cross et al 1988f:41-49).

Industrial tutors
In many of the case studies of pilot projects, the aims which apply to the use of industry tutors were the same. They were to broaden approaches to teaching and learning, to help students acquire new skills, and encourage closer working between education and industry (Hirst in Cross et al 1988f: 52). Industrial tutors were drawn from a wide range of backgrounds and often played a part in establishing direct and fruitful links between industry and education (Cook 1989: 9-10). The Essex project for example, appointed a tutor in residence on a one year secondment to a school. He was an industrial draughtsman with the Ford Motor Company and had experience in staff assessment (Cross et al 1988f: 51, 56). At the start of the secondment he helped with various aspects of the TVEI curriculum including helping students with technology project work and developing support material to help students plan and chart their progress. He was also involved in working with teachers to develop profiling and records of achievement (ibid: 56).

In Leicestershire six industrial tutors visited a community college regularly as: "friendly adults" (Cross et al 1988f. 51). The students and the industrialists exchanged information about themselves prior to meeting and discussions between them were wide-ranging and not limited to the world of work (ibid: 57-59). In Berkshire a team of tutors from ICI with experience of personnel management, were engaged to teach various life skills aspects of the TVEI curriculum (ibid: 51). A factory based work simulation was also developed and made available to students, and a German link was established through the company involving the provision of a preparatory language course and work experience (ibid: 51, 62-63).

In Wiltshire over 100 workplace-based tutors were visited by students on a one to one basis. Wiltshire was chosen as one of the original areas for the Schools

Council Industry Project and had an Industry Education Liaison Co-ordinator in post prior to TVEI. Students were responsible for approaching industrialists for project support and for making their own travel arrangements (ibid: 51, 52-55).

National targets for education and training
In the extension phase of TVEI, compacts and education business partnerships played an increasingly important part in developing education - industry links (see Nuttall; Romanowska; Hebditch; in Cross et al 1991; see also *'Insight No 21'* Spring 1991: 5-7; and O'Kane: *'Insight No 25'* Autumn 1992: 17). There is now established, a set of national education and training targets which both education and industry need to address. (See Fennell in: *'Insight No 23'* Winter 1991: 8-11 for a review of the CBI publication *'World Class Targets'* which details the Foundation and Lifetime Targets and The case for Targets The National Training Task Force 1992). It is therefore in the interests of both to work together through 'formalised' partnerships.

The White Paper *'Education and Training for the 21st Century'* published in May 1991, made it clear that the government was keen to achieve parity of esteem between academic and vocational qualifications, to encourage schools and colleges to offer students a choice of qualifications, and where it would be of benefit to the individual, to provide a combination of both (Fennell in: *'Insight No 22'* Summer 1991: 6-7).   The government also proposed two new diplomas, ordinary and advanced, which were intended to provide dual accreditation for both academic and vocational qualifications.   As well as endorsing 'A' levels and NVQ's, the government proposed a new vocational qualification - GNVQ - which would not require work-place competence assessment as in the case of NVQ's, but would provide students 16-19 with vocationally specific courses which could be largely school or college based and which were aimed at developing a wide range of generic, as well as vocational skills.   As Fennell points out, many of the core skills in GNVQ have their origins in TVEI developments (*'Insight No 25'* Autumn 1992: 16).

Problems in establishing links with industry
Involving people from industry in projects which are school based has not always been easy.   Industrialists need to be convinced that getting involved is going to be worthwhile (Waddington in Cross et al 1988f: 5).   Using a well known partnership project or scheme has often been a productive way to start but even then success is not guaranteed.   For example, the Somerset project used "Young Enterprise" as a way of integrating a vocational element into the curriculum and to help students relate school subjects to the world of work, but even so, identified the lack of industry involvement as a weakness (see Craggs in Cross et al 1988f: 79; see also Cook 1989: 19).   In attempting to increase and strengthen links with industry, TVEI sought to build on existing links and to utilise, and in some instances co-ordinate, the work of existing agencies in the field for example, SATRO and SCIP (Cook 1989: 6; Fell in Cross et al 1991: 55 Herbart in Cross et al 1989: 15-19).   It also encouraged schemes such as "Neighbourhood Engineers", "Young Enterprise" and the "Primary Enterprise Project", developed by Durham University and sponsored by Marks and Spencers (Stoker in Cross et al 1988f: 81-91; see also Morgan in Cross et al 1991: 115).

Work experience and careers education and guidance as elements of the curriculum

Two of the most important elements of the TVEI curriculum were careers education and guidance, and work experience. The original requirement of pilot projects was to link the work experience with curriculum activities, in particular the vocational options taken by students. This often proved to be difficult (McIntyre & Coombes 1988: 9; Cross et al 1988f: 24). Problems encountered were mainly to do with finding sufficient appropriate placements at the right time for them to be useful in supporting course-work. One strategy employed in an attempt to deal with the problem was to link work experience with elements of the curriculum that are cross-curricular, such as careers or personal and social education (ibid: 25-26). There have also been various pilot schemes to accredit work experience, for example in Scotland, a work experience module was made available through the SCOTVEC scheme (Roebuck in Cross et al 1988f: 33).

The TVEI work experience report, *'Evaluation Working Paper 2'* (McIntyre & Coombes 1988) identified the following forms of work experience: work practice (simulation activities); work creation (the establishment of a job for a work experience placement); work shadowing (observation of a real job in a real work-place); and real work experience, which was found to be the most usual type of experience (ibid: 5 see also Cook 1989: 18). Students who were surveyed for the TVEI extension cohort report, generally felt that work experience had helped them find out about working life and accept responsibility. A substantial proportion of the cohort also felt that work experience had helped them to decide what job to do, to understand how firms work, and what practical skills are required in the job or industry they experienced. The experience had also helped a similar proportion of students make decisions about staying on in education (NFER 1992: 41 fig. 4.3.3). TVEI has made a major impact on the number of students who experience work placements. The TVEI report on performance indicators showed that the proportion of all students experiencing work experience rose from under 35% in 1987-88 to over 55% in 1989-90 (Employment Department 1992: 12 fig. 8).

Some projects, such as that at Haringey, made positive attempts to tackle the problems of work experience and equal opportunities. In that particular project a "work experience charter of good practice" was produced which aimed to give positive guidance on how problems of gender and ethnic stereotyping might be addressed and on how preparation for, and de-briefing after the work experience, might be improved (York in Cross et al 1991: 81-84).

Careers education has also benefited from TVEI through improved resources. This has led to improvements in the quality of experiences which students receive (HMI 1991: 25-26). Careers education is now much broader than it was before TVEI, involving self awareness and the development of transition skills (Sims in Cross et al 1990: 4-5). The developments that have taken place in teaching and learning have also enhanced careers education. It is common for students to be involved in researching information and participating in discussion groups and active tutorials (HMI 1991: 25-26). Industry days and vocational awareness activities which can involve students, teachers, careers officers, people from industry, education business partnership co-ordinators,

SCIP and SATRO co-ordinators, were important features of the Humberside extension project. Students and teachers from several schools worked in teams to research information regarding employment opportunities within a particular vocational area. They had to use a variety of sources - human, technological and literature based. The venues were normally off-site and were often provided by local industry.

The TVEI extension cohort survey (NFER: 1992) examined the extent to which year eleven cohort students found careers and guidance activities useful. The range of activities covered was quite extensive, but students who had direct experience of a job, felt overwhelmingly that it had been the most useful type of experience. Visits to colleges and careers officers were regarded as the next most useful, but talks and careers lessons were thought to be useful by only about 27% of those who had experienced them (ibid: 39 fig. 4.3.1).

Problem solving and personal and social skills
Jones (NUT *'Education Review'* 1989: vol. 3; 50) stated that TVEI was influencing education by:
relating what is learned to the world of work;
teaching students how to be effective and solve problems and to be creative and enterprising;
equipping young people with the skills and competencies needed in a technological society;
providing direct opportunities to learn about the economy and the world of work;
providing them with guidance and counselling and access to continuing education and training (see also Luck in: *'Employment Gazette'* October 1991: 544).

TVEI increased the emphasis on problem solving activities for students. Barnes (1987) provides a "working definition" of what the Leeds University survey team was looking for in terms of problem solving activities. He describes them as tasks that are different to those with which the student is familiar, involve a degree of transformation and generalisation, require analysis of what sort of problem is posed and the identification of the type of solution required, plus the selection of possible solutions (Barnes et al 1987: 38). Two of the main difficulties with open ended problem solving activities are the amount of time taken by students to develop solutions and the temptation of teachers to help them, although in the case of the latter many teachers seen in Barnes' survey were aware of the problem. They also realised the importance of problem solving but were unsure how to ensure that students acquired essential knowledge and skills through such activities (ibid: 41). Some projects, such as the Cambridgeshire pilot, used problem solving activities which involved links with business and industry. At Bretton Wood for example, the "Practical Business Processes" and "Product Design" courses, provided opportunities for enhancing such links. Activities in which industry consultants were used included site visits and simulations (Cross et al 1988a: 82; Harrison et al 1988: 17,18, 20).

Seventy-nine per cent of students consulted in the NFER (1992) survey said they had developed problem solving skills. Seventy nine per cent of teachers consulted during an SCRE survey, thought that TVEI had increased students' opportunities to solve problems, and seventy six per cent thought that it had helped students to improve their social and personal skills (Lyon Black & Thorpe 1990b: 3). Another survey (Black et al 1990) would seem to indicate that students with high academic aspirations were also the most confident in practising skills. They were more competent in taking responsibility for their own learning and in problem solving than students with lower aspirations. This is supported by the findings of the TVEI extension cohort survey (1991) which asked the year ten cohort of students to what extent they thought their personal and study skills had been enhanced. The overview of student responses in all the skills areas indicates that those whose academic self-rating was below average were less likely to feel that their skills had been enhanced than those of higher self rating. The skills associated with taking responsibility were the ones which most students thought had been improved by their courses. The other skills and qualities which were felt by students to have been improved were independence, making decisions, working with others, adaptability, problem solving, managing time and finding information. It would appear therefore that attitudes and personal qualities were the elements which students perceived to have benefited from most as result of TVEI (NFER 1992: 32 fig. 3.4.1 & fig 3.4.2 *NB my correction to error in numbering*). This impression is also reinforced by the views of employers (Employment Dept 1991b: 22 table 5a).

Application of knowledge and skills and use of real contexts
In the skills associated with using technology, there appeared to be a significant difference between the confidence of TVEI and non-TVEI students, with the former appearing substantially more confident (Lyon, Black and Thorpe 1991: 31). However, as the authors of the report point out, one cannot assume that the results are entirely to do with following a TVEI curriculum since such a curriculum might well attract students who are already quite confident in using technology prior to commencing their TVEI courses. However given the improved access to technology which TVEI provided, it may be safe to assume some TVEI influence (ibid: 30-31). The same survey also showed that students enjoyed tasks which were practical and useful (ibid: 15). Another study (Black et al 1990b: 3) indicated that 90% of teachers, whether they were involved in TVEI or not, thought that the Initiative had made the curriculum more vocationally relevant.

The TVEI performance indicators report (Employment Dept. 1992) makes the point that student participation in industry linked activities such as work experience, not only helps young people to see the relevance of their studies but also that the kinds of knowledge and skills they are acquiring are see by employers to be of value (ibid: 12). TVEI encouraged industry involvement in the curriculum by providing materials, tutors, consultants, and support for curriculum development groups, mini enterprise, and teacher secondments (Cross et al 1988f; Cook 1989: 5).

The content of many of the new subjects and courses which were introduced or enhanced by TVEI, reflected an emphasis on the application of knowledge, and skills such as problem solving, and increased the number and scope of learning activities which require application as well as acquisition of knowledge (Employment Dept. 1991: 28; HMI 1991: xi). In the Moray TVEI pilot project for example, a "learning strategy" was made available to students which encouraged transfer of knowledge and the application of skills and competencies to new situations. (McNeil in Trayers et al 1989).

The Employment Department *'Cohort Survey'* (1992) asked students in year ten about the range of 'practical' learning activities they had participated in at least once or twice. The largest responses were for planning surveys, outdoor pursuits, conducting interviews, and producing news sheets (ibid: 28 fig. 3.3.1). Of the students surveyed, 27% claimed to have participated in mini - enterprises, 26% in community work, and 24% in making videos. Other practical activities included working with children, participating in international links and using modern foreign languages outside school. Only 16% of the cohort had been involved in industry or business based projects (ibid: 30 fig. 3.3.2). *'Into Work'*, a study of the recruitment and work performance of school - leavers from the first eleven TVEI extension programmes, found that employers considered that the performance of TVEI recruits was markedly better than that of others. They also agreed that practical ability was as important as examination success (British Market Research Bureau for Employment Dept. 1991b: 4).

The development of teaching and learning situations which encourage and facilitate the application of knowledge and skills will be explored in more detail in the next chapter.

Summary
In this chapter various aspects of TVEI and the work-related curriculum have been explored. It was noted that in TVEI, emphasis was placed on certain personal qualities and abilities which are believed to be important in terms of the individual's 'employability', suggesting a strong instrumental emphasis in the TVEI philosophy. A number of strategies and contexts in which such skills can be developed have been highlighted and some aspects of their influence on teaching and learning experiences and outcomes have been indicated in this chapter.

The inclusion of careers education and guidance and work experience in the mainstream curriculum was highlighted, as was the involvement of industry tutors in curriculum support activities. The use of 'real contexts' such as enterprise activities and problem solving, often involving industry in some way, were shown to be important aspect of TVEI studies. The co-operative involvement of schools in establishing specialist centres for curriculum enhancement activities was also mentioned. Particularly important was the re-statement of the importance of the 'work-related' aspects of the curriculum in the extension of TVEI. The value of 'real contexts' as motivational impulses was another important feature as was the emphasis on the 'application of knowledge and skills'. Many of the generic skills which were important elements in the TVEI pilot 'vocational' courses, became cross-curricular elements in the extension projects, particularly post National Curriculum. TVEI's influence on the expansion of 'vocational courses' was noted as was the gender balance which was achieved in respect of such courses. The role of TVEI in developing and co-ordinating 'education-business partnership' activities and of supporting national projects, was also indicated.

In the final chapter of part one, the focus will be on the impact of TVEI on teaching, learning and assessment, and in particular on the development of "student centred" approaches to these issues. The value of the formative processes which were encouraged by TVEI and the strategies which were employed will all be examined.

Chapter Four

Teaching, learning and assessment

Before TVEI began, many schools had started to develop more student centred approaches to teaching and learning (Harrison 1989: 3). However from the beginning, TVEI placed considerable emphasis on the development of a broad range of teaching strategies and learning activities, aimed at improving student motivation, differentiation, and the management of the learning process.

> "TVEI has always stressed the need to develop a broader range of teaching and learning styles with emphasis on, and success in, developing more practical approaches and increased student autonomy. In many ways this laid the foundation for GCSE projects and assignments." (Employment Dept 1991: 21)

Still, describing her observations of one particular example of active learning in TVEI, identified the following characteristics of lessons:

> The classroom is a base where lessons start and end.
> Students make decisions about what and how they learn.
> Responsibility for learning is delegated to students.
> Group negotiation is part of problem solving activities.
> Students learn through failure as well as success.
> *'Educational Change and Development'* (1988 vol.9 No1. 10-15)

Barnes (1987) identified three styles of teaching employed in the delivery of TVEI courses, which he described as "controlled", "framed" and "negotiated". The "controlled" style is teacher centred, didactic, and is primarily concerned with the learning of de-contextual knowledge. In the "framed" style, the teacher sets the parameters for learning activities but within that framework students can be involved in a range of active, investigative learning experiences. In the "negotiated" style, students share in the determining of learning objectives and methods and the teacher "facilitates" learning (Barnes et al 1987: 24-30; see also Barnes in Gleeson 1987: 143-146).

Problems of mismatch between methods and content

According to an Employment Department survey (1991) seventy-eight per cent of teachers surveyed thought that TVEI had provided an opportunity for them to improve their range of teaching styles (ibid: 24). Perhaps the most worrying criticism of TVEI made by HMI, concerns instances where they identified a mismatch between the type of knowledge being taught and the teaching method employed. However TVEI via the TRIST programme, highlighted the importance of matching content and methods.

> "If objectives are centred on knowledge gain, then didactic methods and terminal examinations may be adequate. If objectives are widened in the ways we have suggested, then they cannot be delivered didactically. Active learning is not, therefore, to be thought of as a set of lively and interesting ways of maintaining the attention of young people, but as the only way of delivering certain objectives,

and therefore as part of an entitlement curriculum." ('*Papers of National Interest 6*' Training Agency 1989: 2).

"..the ardent didactic teacher may need to be challenged. ..Examining the miss-match between objectives and teaching methodology is one way of highlighting the deficiencies of a didactic approach." (ibid: 8)

Factors which inhibited the use of student centred approaches

Perhaps one of the greatest challenges that TVEI faced, was to convince traditionalist teachers of the value of student centred approaches and to provide a supporting framework in which those willing to try new methods could succeed, rather than fail or lose confidence at an early stage. One study unearthed a multiplicity of fears on the part of teachers concerning pupil centred teaching. Many of them were to do with control, noise, and what other teachers might think of pupil-centred classroom activity. There was also a feeling that such approaches might be better suited to some subjects than others (Black et al 1991: 23-25). Some blockages to active learning identified in TRIST training material include:

"Obsession with content.
Departmentalism (subject-centred approach / suspicion of integration).
Dominance of teacher view of knowledge - how to purvey it.
Insecurity about learning outcomes (student / teacher).
Some staff enjoy the didactic role.
Lack of knowledge about techniques and tools of active learning.
Failure to allow learning to take place in a variety of contexts in and out of school.
Fear that assessment is invalid and has no currency." (Training Agency: 1989: 6).

The HMI review (1991) records that there was often little change in teaching methods in the early days of TVEI but later, often as a result of a greater emphasis on vocationally related subjects, more active methods were introduced. Such methods were further encouraged by the introduction of the GCSE. The enhancement of courses through the application of new technologies also supported such developments (ibid: 14-15). HMI point out that practical group work activities, business and community contexts, problem solving and associated activities, and improved assessment and recording methods, all contributed to more active teaching and learning, although there was often insufficient student involvement in assessment and goal setting (ibid: 14-15). In the best examples of active methods, HMI noted well prepared and relevant assignments, often with a real world context, well organised and structured programmes of study which identified appropriate teaching and learning methods and reflected the TVEI criteria. Through supportive teaching, students gained the confidence to take greater responsibility for their own learning (ibid: 14-15). Of the projects seen by HMI many, according to the (1991) survey, "..did extend the range of teaching techniques and often concentrated on the need for differentiation" (ibid: 16).

Problems for students as well as teachers resulted from the introduction of methods which increased student autonomy. Students often had difficulty coping with the new demands that greater personal responsibility created, and the sometimes unrealistic expectations that accompanied such changes. One of the main problems of recording achievement was that students were often expected to perform tasks for which they had not been properly prepared (see Cross et al 1988e: 13, 18, 74). Sometimes the skills of teachers were stretched, resulting in inappropriate structure and sequence of work (ibid: 15). Course organisation also appears to have had an effect on the extent to which particular teaching methods were used. Modular courses for example, were likely to involve individual and group work. In Scotland the introduction of the Standard Grade examination contributed to a move away from didactic teaching (Lyon, Black and Thorpe 1990). Survey data also seems to indicate that some subjects provide greater scope for a variety of teaching styles than others (Black et al 1990: 12-13).

In the SCRE survey (Lyon Black & Thorpe 1990) students were asked to classify subjects under the headings of class, group, and student centred, according to how they thought they were taught. Subjects perceived as class-centred included: English, mathematics, arithmetic, accounting, history, geography and economics. Those subjects perceived as group-based were: PE, RE, social education and guidance, social and vocational skills and most of the SCOTVEC modules, i.e. electronics, living skills, work experience, technological studies, video production etc. Subjects perceived as mainly student-centred were those which involved designing and creativity, or which required individual use of computers, such as computing and secretarial studies (ibid: 12-13; 16-17). However a comparison of the methods employed in teaching the traditional 'O' grade subjects and those of the newly introduced 'Standard Grade' subjects (again using pupil classifications), seems to confirm a significant shift in teaching methods towards more group and pupil centred approaches even in subjects such as mathematics (ibid: 14-15). The survey also included student classifications of SCOTVEC National Certificate Modules. On the methodological map, no modules appear as class-based, most appear as group-based, with some in the pupil centred area and slightly fewer in the mixed area. The evidence seems to show a definite shift in emphasis from class-based teaching methods towards other methods in both 'S' grade courses and SCOTVEC modules (Lyon Black & Thorpe 1990: 16-17). Overall there does seem to be agreement amongst teachers in the Black survey, that TVEI has had an impact on teaching and learning methods (Black 1990c: 5, 6).

TVEI 'innovations' and teaching methods - 'real contexts' and the application of knowledge and skills
The different emphasis which TVEI placed on knowledge, i.e. application of knowledge and skills in 'real world contexts', also made changes in method a major emphasis (Eraut, Nash, Fielding Attard 1991: 25). This is borne out by survey data. For example the SCRE survey (Black 1990b: 5) revealed that not only did 94% of all teachers think that TVEI had brought about a more diversified range of teaching methods, but that slightly more non-TVEI teachers than TVEI teachers, were of that opinion. It also showed that 85% of all teachers surveyed, felt that TVEI curricula encouraged group work (ibid: 5). However the effect that TVEI had on the teaching methods used outside the

project was judged by non-TVEI teachers to have been minimal, although over 60% of TVEI teachers felt that the reverse was true (ibid: 5). TVEI teachers were also more positive about becoming involved in teaching innovation, but a majority of all teachers (just under 80% non-TVEI and just over 80% TVEI) agreed that the Initiative had encouraged innovation in teaching (ibid: 5). The NFER review (Stoney 1989) posed a very open question to head teachers regarding the impact of TVEI on teaching styles. In a high response to the question, over 75% of respondents recorded a positive view of TVEI's influence. Typical responses were that TVEI had "spearheaded" developments in: "..experiential, active, more practically based, negotiated, more open ended or student centred teaching and learning methods." (Lines and Stoney 1989: 30).

One of the most important of the TVEI sponsored national projects was flexible learning. One review of TVEI 1983 to 1990, claimed that 95% of authorities were involved in the flexible learning project (Employment Dept. 1991: 21). Flexible learning is so called because the structure and sequence of content and the methods of learning, are determined by the needs of individual students rather than the preferences of the teacher, or the more general needs of the class. Flexible learning concentrates on the acquisition of learning skills within a framework of support (Eraut, Nash, Fielding, Attard 1991: 11-13, 59; Tomlinson & Kilner 1991; 1992; TEED 1992). This is essential since student centred methods can reduce contact time for some students. The support framework also empowers the learner to change direction or emphasis so as to be able to extend or reinforce his or her knowledge of a subject or topic, or to reflect on earlier learning in order to consolidate and then progress (Trayers et al 1989: 5-6; TEED 1992: 2, 12-13, 16-17).

Black (1991) examined changes taking place in teaching and learning in schools in five LEA's which had begun the extension of TVEI. For the purpose of the study the SCRE team made a distinction between teacher led and pupil centred approaches to learning. They were aware of problems of interpretation of definitions and of over-simplification, but as a baseline, related whole-class activity to teacher led and group work, and individual work to pupil led activity.

> "In every school, most respondents claimed to the use strategies associated with pupil-centred learning more now than in the past, while the reverse was true for teacher-led strategies. In particular teachers claimed to be encouraging pupils to find information for themselves, to be using group strategies and to be individualising pupils' work through allocating tasks according to individual needs and allowing pupils to pace their own work." (Black et al 1991: 6 fig. 1)

Review evidence based on classroom observation suggests a gap between rhetoric and reality. The SCRE review (Black et al 1991) showed that in 70% of lessons observed no time at all was given to group work, in 91% of lessons observed no time was given to individualised work, and in 79% of lessons observed 76-100% of the time was spent in teacher led work (ibid: 9 table 1). However the data was gathered in the period May to June when examination pressures may have had an influence on teaching methods.

Student centred methods - advantages and disadvantages

Amongst the other important findings of the study, were teachers' perceptions that pupil-centred teaching helped develop students' personal, social, and communication skills, and that such methods were on the whole, popular with students. However they were harder for teachers to use and were in general terms, more problematic (ibid: 13; 14-15). The NFER (1989) survey also found that while teachers were very positive about the benefits of student centred teaching and learning activities, they felt that they were: "..the most difficult challenge they had faced within the schemes." (Lines & Stoney 1989: 48)

In Black et al (1991: 16 table 2) teachers' views on which teaching methods were best suited to a variety of learning situations, showed that in terms of problem solving, understanding the world of work, development of personal skills and confidence, team work, acquisition of study skills, and independent thinking, over 60% of teachers questioned thought that non-traditional methods were best (see also Hitchcock 1988: 12.1.6.v). Hitchcock makes the point that didactic methods are not compatible with the aims of increasing student autonomy, or with the development of initiative and enterprise (ibid: 3). The SCRE study (Black et al 1991) revealed that students preferred working in groups and enjoyed doing practical tasks for themselves. It also showed that students liked having things explained to them rather than struggling with a problem or relying on others for help. Students particularly enjoyed tasks which were practical and useful and had relevance either outside school or in other subjects (ibid: 15).

Assessment and student motivation

TVEI has raised a number of important questions concerning both purpose and methods of assessment (see Clough & James in Cross et al 1988c). Firstly, should students be 'partners' in the assessment process and should it be primarily diagnostic? Secondly, should it be positive, i.e. concerned with finding out what the student can do rather than what they can't do? (Cross et al 1988e; NPRA 1989). Thirdly, should it be teacher-centred, i.e. a 'tool for class management' to inform streaming, banding etc. or to inform the organisation of content, sequence, structure and teaching methods? Finally, should it be 'end-user' focused, with emphasis on terminal assessment to inform training providers, colleges, universities and employers etc. of the student's general level of ability? (see Wardman 1989; NPRA 1989). If the emphasis is on the latter of these, as is arguably the case with examinations, one might pose a further question and ask: To what extent should the assessment be allowed to impact on content and teaching methods? It is worth noting that TVEI attached considerable importance to the achievement of "nationally recognised qualifications" throughout the lifetime of the project (Employment Dept. 1991: 31). TVEI students were also encouraged to be positive about their achievements and targets through skills profiles, records of achievement and individual action plans (see Cross et al 1988e; Muse in Trayers et al 1989). The formative record of achievement process can be used to place emphasis on positive and diagnostic assessment and might be described as being primarily 'student centred'. The summative documentation is a means by which to inform 'end-users' about the student's skills, competencies and other achievements.

Student motivation: inhibiting factors - examinations

> "..since the examination syllabus has a stranglehold on the curriculum for those of average and above average ability in year four and above, we must find ways of reconciling process with content." (*'Papers of National Interest 6'* Training Agency 1989: 2)

Student motivation has a good deal to do with the way in which learning and course content is managed (see Sykes and Taylor in Gleeson 1987: 66). Moon makes the important point that for many students the terminal examination is too long term to provide a high level of motivation (Moon 1989: 9). TVEI has shown that short term goals and subject based curricula are compatible (Hitchcock 1987: 11-12). This being the case, there would seem to be no reason why examination courses should not have short term as well as long term goals.

Problems of accrediting student achievement in TVEI were considerably more difficult to overcome because of the TVEI emphasis on the application of skills and knowledge. The SCRE study (Black et al 1990c) undertaken between 1985 and 1990, raised a question concerning extent to which the curriculum of TVEI students was determined by the constraints of external examinations. It makes the point that the requirement for TVEI courses to lead to recognised qualifications had posed a dilemma for teachers, who felt that there was often a lack of congruence between existing forms of accreditation and the broader aims of TVEI. This made some aspects of curriculum innovation difficult to implement in ways which they felt were the most appropriate (ibid 1990c: 5).

Another report (Black et al 1991) also highlighted the dilemma of teachers who would like to give students greater responsibility for their own learning but find it difficult to allocate time because of external pressures, or cannot decide when the learner has acquired sufficient content to enable effective self-directed learning to take place (ibid: 21). According to the report, this seems to be a particularly difficult problem in high content, externally examined courses (ibid: 19). Barnes (1987) found that examination syllabuses were felt by a number of teachers to give little or no consideration to examining cross-curricular elements (Barnes et al 1987: 69). Despite the innovative approaches to curriculum organisation which TVEI pilot projects did much to encourage, the lack of a whole curriculum approach by examinations boards to the content of examination courses, continued to influence teaching methods. One of the Scottish reviews highlighted the continuing issue of content over-load in some examination subjects, which could make pupil-centred teaching impractical (op cit: 28).

Student motivation - short-term goals

> "We would suggest that active learning is classroom activity which:
> -stresses the OUTCOME (learning), rather than ACTIVITY (teaching;
> -lays emphasis on the needs and abilities of the students;
> -is appropriate to the learning objectives;
> -attempts to be varied, interesting and stimulating;
> -acknowledges the positive contribution to be made by each student;

-involves students in taking some responsibility for their own learning, and sharing in and influencing the objectives of the lesson; -involves the teacher in a variety of roles, including that of enabler as well as provider of learning; -acknowledges that there are objectives beyond the knowledge / concept / content base of the subject."
(*'Papers of National Interest 6'* Training Agency 1989: 3)

As was highlighted in chapter two, both 'modularisation' and 'unitisation' have been features of content organisation in TVEI. Modular courses combine discrete but related units, which may offer a multiplicity of routes through a course of study. Units on the other hand, normally offer a single pathway through a course, although they may be differentiated (Moon 1988; NPRA 1989). Perhaps the main reason why unit accreditation and modular courses have proved popular with students, is the emphasis they have tended to place on short-term objectives, learning outcomes, and regular diagnostic assessment. In some of the pilot courses, taster modules were offered to students (Gardner in Harrison et al 1988: 5), and in the modular core activities of the Cumbrian pilot project, each module had a 'motivational phase' (Cross et al 1988a: 32). In some of the Scottish pilot projects, modules formed part of "a distinct TVEI block" in the curriculum. Modular courses which were most common were: personal and social development, computing, electronics, and secretarial courses. The typical TVEI curriculum was composed of some enhanced SEB courses and a discrete block composed of SCOTVEC modules. Some of the modules were compulsory, others were optional (Lyon Black & Thorpe 1990: 11). In the Inverclyde project it was considered important that assessment criteria were made known to students at the start of modules. Career opportunities associated with each module were also explored. These strategies along with short-term goals, were found to motivate students of all abilities (Cross et al 1988c: 6-9).

Attitudes of both teachers and students towards modular courses seems to be quite positive. A Scottish review (Black et al 1988) which examined attitudes towards TVEI, discovered that of those heads who had a favourable view of TVEI, there was a feeling that a modular curriculum would provide learners with short term objectives which might improve the performance of less able students (Ibid: 3; see also Moon 1988; Eraut et al 1991). The SCRE survey (Lyon Black and Thorpe 1990) showed that students had very positive attitudes to modular courses with by far the largest majority of those who were doing modules, either wanting more, or feeling that the balance was right (ibid: 20-21).

Learning outcomes in unit accreditation schemes are commonly expressed in terms of knowledge, concepts, skills and experiences (NPRA/Training Agency 1989). An example of this strategy can be seen in the pilot case study of Greenfield School. The TVEI courses were described as modular, with suggested learning objectives and teaching and learning activities (Cross et al 1988d: 7). In terms of vocational qualifications, learning outcomes tend to be task specific and organised as statements of competence. In the original National Curriculum, learning outcomes were written as statements of attainment and included attitudinal objectives. They were the outcomes of learning activities based on the programmes of study (Emerson & Goddard 1989: 23-24). Currently in terms of the GCSE examinations, broad objectives are included in the assessment criteria. In each case they can be used as short-term or long term objectives. In the case of unit accreditation and modular courses, the objectives are short-term rather than long-term (Moon 1988; 9).

Student participation in assessment as a strategy to encourage 'learner autonomy'
Empowering students to participate to a greater extent in the assessment process, has also been a driving force behind records of achievement and individual action planning (Hitchcock 1988: 136-137). Providing students with access to assessment criteria ought, in theory, to provide greater opportunity for self and peer group assessment, but as the 1992 edition of *'Assessment'* (The journal of the North West Record of Achievement Working Group) points out, the process is still often hindered by a lack of clearly identified learning outcomes, and an over emphasis on terminal assessment, the criteria for which often remain a complete mystery to students.

> "There remains a tendency in schools to plan for coverage rather than for particular skill or concept development. One of the reasons why we have such a reliance on written tests is because teachers aren't necessarily clear beforehand concerning the particular skills or concepts they want students to learn. As a result, they don't look out for evidence of these skills and concepts during the learning and so they have to test the students later to find out if they have learned and understood."
> (The North West Record of Achievement Working Group 1992: 10)

To back up this statement the authors use the following quotation from HMI:

> "..pupils produced work of better quality when their teachers explained the criteria used in its assessment. Relatively few teachers did this effectively, and pupils were generally unaware of any assessment criteria that teachers might have been using. Pupils rarely understood the reason for grades and often felt, wrongly, that features such as length and presentation were most important." (ibid 10)

Through TVEI, learning outcomes in various forms have become increasingly important in the management of learning programmes (NPRA 1989; see also Sykes and Taylor in Gleeson 1987: 66). In some instances they also provide an indication of assessment criteria and are made available to students at the start of units or modules. In this sense TVEI addressed the criticism of HMI that one of the inhibitors of good practice has been a lack of communication of assessment objectives to students (HMI 1991: 16).

TVEI was very much to do with encouraging a broader view of the curriculum to include a range of cross-curricular skills and competencies. This became even more important in the extension phase and has been underpinned by the requirements of the National Curriculum (NCC Circular 6 1989; NPRA/Training

Agency 1989: 8). One of the major problems which has arisen as a result of the increased importance TVEI placed on the value of cross-curricular elements, is how to accredit them.

Records of achievement

Recording student achievement in cross-curricular themes and skills in TVEI was approached in a variety of ways, sometimes through the accreditation of new integrated or cross-curricular courses (e.g. modular examination courses) or by use of an existing and accredited profiling system (e.g. City and Guilds 365) or other vocational qualifications, such as BTEC or RSA. Often accreditation was through a TVEI project or school record of achievement, or through a system of unit accreditation such as NPRA. Schemes like the latter were developed in partnerships between TVEI projects, LEA's and examination boards.

The recording process was given added rigour by the development and implementation of unit accreditation schemes (Eraut, Nash, Fielding & Attard 1991: 42). The advantages of such schemes are that they provide short-term goals without necessarily limiting outcomes to those specified in the unit. They also encourage students to take greater responsibility for their own learning. In addition they provide a vehicle for mapping the delivery of themes and skills across the curriculum, and can therefore assist in the implementation of a whole school policy for the teaching of cross-curricular elements (NPRA 1989: 26-28).

The formative recording process has been a very important vehicle through which management of teaching and learning has been developed (Hitchcock 1988: 136). It is through the recording achievement and action planning processes, that the structure and sequence of study units, clarification of concepts, identification of assessment criteria, and greater consideration of teaching methods and learning activities, have been released from a 'secret garden' for both students and teachers. These, together with the development of reviewing and action planning, along with the TVEI emphasis on application of knowledge and skills, has encouraged student centred teaching and active learning (Dowson, Smith, Turns in Cross et al 1988e: 60).

Evidence from TVEI case studies also shows that the record of achievement process has the potential to impact on pedagogy (Macintosh in Cross et al 1988e: 2-3; Parish in Cross et al 1988e: 23; Ball in ibid: 75; Turner in Cross et al 1988e: 32; Muse in Trayers et al 1989: 99-100). This is partly because the record stresses 'student centredness', but also because, by encouraging teachers to think about outcomes as well as content, they are likely to give greater consideration to the methods by which the outcomes might best be achieved (Macintosh in Cross et al 1988e: 3).

Many Projects like the Bedfordshire one, included employers in the development and validation of recording and profiling schemes (see Carr - Archer in Cross et al 1988e: 70-71, 96-101). Several projects indicated that student involvement in the recording process improved self confidence and motivation (Cross et al 1988e; 14, 74, 76). Outside agencies have also noted such improvements, as is indicated by the following careers service comment on students from the Barnsley project: "It is easy to identify a TVEI student during an interview, they are more relaxed, talk more confidently and have more ideas about what they want to do." (Cross et al 1988e: 72)

Summary

This chapter has highlighted the 'student centredness' of the TVEI philosophy. The record of achievement has become an important 'tool' for the management of the learning process, as well as being important in encouraging diagnostic assessment, and positive recording and reporting of achievements. It has also encouraged students to take greater responsibility for their own learning. It is evident that whereas progress has been made in developing teaching and learning approaches, there are still some factors which inhibit student centred methods. These include content 'overload', external examinations, and a fear on the part of some teachers that they might 'lose control'. HMI criticisms concerning 'mismatch' between teaching methods and the type of knowledge being taught, might be seen as further evidence that 'active learning' was not as widespread in TVEI as is often imagined. However there is a good deal of evidence to support the notion that in TVEI the emphasis was on the application of knowledge and skills.

The use of 'real contexts', problem solving activities, and short-term goals, are examples of strategies employed to improve student motivation. Developments in flexible learning have explored new methods of organising course content and accrediting learning outcomes, unit accreditation schemes and modular courses are two examples. Emphasis on vocational courses in the pilot projects, and on cross-curricular skills and competencies in both pilot and extension projects was noted. Teachers and students it is clear, had positive views on the impact of TVEI. However it is also evident that many teachers find student centred developments very challenging.

The first four chapters have explored the main aims, outcomes and characteristics of TVEI. TVEI 'evolved' from a small pilot scheme, concentrating on exploring the feasibility of a vocational element within the 14-16 curriculum, into an important national programme. During the pilot phase the emphasis was on vocational courses, in the early extension projects there was a gradual shift towards curriculum models which could provide a broad work-related curriculum. This developed into the establishment of a 'working relationship' between TVEI and the 'subject-centred' National Curriculum. Consequently the picture which has emerged is complex and multi-faceted, but one which clearly has some relationship with aspects of curriculum theory. Whether the relationship was intended or unintended will be examined in part three.

PART TWO

A REVIEW OF CURRICULUM THEORY

Chapter Five

Introduction to Curriculum Theory

In 'Curriculum Development' Tanner and Tanner write:

> "In the absence of a guiding theoretical base buttressed by
> conceptual research, curricula reforms often are promoted as
> consensual reactions to emerging crises. The consequence of this is
> that the gap between theory and practice grows even wider as
> innovations and reform measures are adopted, modified, discarded,
> and rediscovered so as to be in fashion with whatever socio-political
> tone is most pervasive at any given time."
> (1975: 53)

The main purpose of part two is to provide a framework which can be used to explore the extent to which TVEI curriculum developments have some basis in theory. In part three, I will also examine the extent to which TVEI developments are inclined towards one or more theoretical models and attempt to establish which, if any, aspects of 'TVEI curricula' might be considered innovative. I shall begin by identifying the main paradigms of curriculum theory and the three educational ideologies to which they relate, with brief summaries of the variations in emphasis of knowledge, society and student centred curricula. This will be followed by a more detailed examination of those strands most relevant to contemporary secondary schools and TVEI curricula.

Tyler (1949) suggested the following areas of investigation as a basis for identifying educational objectives:
   1) "Studies of the Learners Themselves...." (ibid: 5-16);
   2) "Studies of Contemporary Life Outside School" (ibid: 16-25);
   3) "Suggestions About Objectives From Subject Specialists".
   (ibid: 25-33)

Taba (1962: 10-11) identified three dimensions of rational curriculum planning:

   1) "the demands and requirements of culture and society";
   2) "the learning process and the nature of learners";
   3) "the nature of knowledge and the specific characteristics and unique contributions of the disciplines from which the content of the curriculum is derived".

Dewey in his various writings also identified three inter-related areas of investigation and interaction:

   1) the school and society; (the social context and democratic values);
   2) the child; (the interests and abilities of the individual);
   3) different types of subject matter.

Lawton writes:

"In curriculum there are at least three popular theories or sets of assumptions held by teachers, sometimes referred to as the child-centred view of education, the subject centred or knowledge centred view, and the society centred view, i.e. education justified in terms of the supposed needs of society." (Lawton et al 1978: 2)

In practice most curriculum planning is more a question of identifying existing inadequacies or problems, or a particular point of departure, or emphasis, rather than one of choosing a particular model. For example, Skilbeck (1984a: 30) described four foci for curriculum analysis:

1) Curriculum as a structure of forms and fields of knowledge.
2) Curriculum as a chart or map of the culture.
3) Curriculum as a pattern of learning activities.
4) Curriculum as learning technology.

It would appear that there is some agreement between education writers and theorists regarding possible starting points, emphases, or dimensions for curriculum study, investigation and planning. However several of those already mentioned also argue that it is emphases we are talking about in respect of such classifications rather than dogma.

Dewey's view of the functions and aspects of the curriculum is arguably one of the most holistic though often and wrongly, as Taba (1962: 404-405) points out, it seems to be reduced to a simplistic stereotype of 'progressivism'. Dewey abhorred "dualism" or divisive thinking, wherever it occurred in education (see *'Democracy and Education'* 1916). Other writers, for example Squires (1987: 46-48) and Taba (1962) also describe 'multi-dimensional' planning models. Taba for example writes:

"An emphasis on a single basis, such as the content, the needs of society, or the needs of the learner, have produced an unnecessary versus thinking with its unfortunate juxtaposition of considerations that should be combined into one comprehensive curriculum theory." (1962: 3)

According to Tyler, educational philosophers see the purpose of education as being to transmit a society's values from generation to generation and use philosophy as the basis for selecting objectives. Sociologists analyse contemporary life as a basis for selecting curriculum objectives, and educational psychologists emphasise the development of the child as the basis for selecting objectives (1949: 4, 5-25). From this argument it may appear that the problem of 'divisiveness' could be due in part to the origin of particular theories, i.e. whether the theory is essentially philosophical, psychological or sociological. Belth writes:

"....education is always engaged in the application of the theories of learning, which it is in the realm of psychology to develop. It also applies the theories of society, social organisation, and social behaviour with which the science of psychology is concerned. Moreover, education is applied philosophy, since it is the means by which we communicate the moral values of a people, a society, a civilisation, to the oncoming generation." (1965: 2)

Indeed Tyler himself, drew on all three strands (op cit: 16-25, 33-37). Lawton, who also advocated an holistic approach, provided a summary of the different contributions to curriculum planning made by philosophy, psychology and sociology (see table 3).

Table 3. The interaction of philosophy, sociology, psychology with education processes

Philosophical criteria:	Sociological considerations:	Psychological theories:
worthwhileness, the structure of knowledge.	social change, technological change, ideological change.	development, learning, instruction, motivation.

(Source: Lawton et al 1978: 5 extracted from fig. 1).

Squires (1987: 3) also described the modern concept of the curriculum as being concerned with outcomes and process as well as content. It is about the ways in which teachers teach and learners learn, as well as what they teach and learn. It has come to have some in-built rationality, not only in terms of structure and process, but also cause and effect. Taylor (1966) proposed a curriculum model which has three dimensions: knowledge, objectives and teaching method. He also argued that there is a macro and micro application of this model, i.e. application to the whole curriculum and to individual curriculum units. Hirst and Peters also seem to endorse a broader view of the curriculum when they write:

"We conclude then that educational processes are those processes of learning, which may be stimulated by teaching, out of which desirable states of mind, involving knowledge and understanding, develop. There are many such processes - learning by experience, from example, from personal instruction, from teaching machines, and so on. In recent times the discussion of these processes has tended to polarise into those favouring a 'traditional' teacher-centred approach and those favouring a 'progressive' pupil-centred approach. It is our belief that both 'models' are one-sided. A fuller analysis suggests that the processes of education are more complex than either side suggests, and that a doctrinaire insistence on any limited range of activities can only be unprofitably restrictive." (Hirst & Peters 1970: 86-87)

Despite the holistic emphasis in the writings of Dewey, Tyler, Taba, and others, there has at times been disagreement between theorists and educators, and educators and policy makers, which has often resulted in doctrinal attitudes and values being embedded in approaches to curriculum planning, e.g. behaviourists versus progressives, liberal educators versus advocates of child-centred approaches, academic versus vocational education etc. Perhaps therefore, it may be appropriate to examine briefly the principal ideologies which, in their pure forms, embody the most extreme belief and value systems in education and society, and the most extreme differences between the main paradigms of curriculum planning.

Ideology and the curriculum

Skilbeck in Horton and Raggatt (1982) and Lawton (1983a) identified three main ideologies, the first of which is Classical - Humanism which emphasises the philosophical dimension and advances the purpose of education as being to impart high status academic knowledge. In pedagogical terms the emphasis is on abstract, de-contextual knowledge structured independently of the learners, with emphasis on the written rather than the spoken word (see Keatinge 'The Great Didactic of Comenius' (1910) and Hutchins: 1952). It is associated with 'high culture'. In terms of process however, the classical - humanist curriculum has been linked with mental discipline or faculty psychology (see Taba 1962: 19-22; 79-80). This has led to curricula ranging from an elitist academic curriculum based on classical studies (liberal arts), to a general subject-based curriculum for all, with a strong emphasis on examinations (see Hirst 1974). The curriculum emphasis is on the acquisition of knowledge and the understanding of concepts.

Reconstructionism emphasises the sociological dimension and supports the purpose of education as being to develop knowledge, skills and competencies which reflect social needs and cultural values, or to bring about social change through education. Utopian reconstructionism is based on the idea of the existence of some 'formulae' which might remedy the problems of society (see Lawton 1983: 10). In terms of process, some aspects of reconstructionism might be argued to have links with social engineering, behavioural psychology, programmed learning, and associationist theory (see Kelly 1980: 15; Bobbitt 1924; Skinner 1968; Taba 1962: 25-27; 83-84; 206-210). It also draws on anthropological analyses of culture (see Lawton 1983: 24-26). Curricula range from a curriculum based on subjects or areas of experience (but with revised content) derived from the outcomes of cultural analysis, to some form of vocational education and training based on 'courses' rather than subjects. The curriculum may emphasise the application of knowledge and skills (see Taba 1962: 24, see also 216-218).

Progressivism emphasises the psychological dimension of child development. The purpose of education is to make the culture accessible to all. It is child-centred rather than content-centred and attention is focused on holistic (individual) development, i.e. development of the 'whole person'. Intellectual and other skills are developed through experiential activities and reflection. In this school of thought the curriculum is the 'stimulus' and the teacher is a 'resource', i.e. the child-centred curriculum (see Rousseau's 'Emile' (Foxley 1911)). In terms of pedagogical process, progressivism has been linked with active learning experiences such as investigation, problem solving and discovery (see Taba 1962: 84). Learning activities may be task or occupation-focused, with the school as a community or a microcosm of society (see Dewey 1915). Sometimes there is no planned curriculum as such, while in other instances the curriculum can be based on subjects or some other structure, with an emphasis on student centred active learning. The curriculum may emphasise the 'integration of knowledge', the interaction of abilities, creativity and individuality and the development of learner autonomy (see Taba 1962: 148-162; 'Froebel' translated by Fletcher and Welton 1912).

What is evident from this brief exploration, is that although a particular educational ideology may draw more strongly on either philosophy, psychology or sociology, as the major influence within that particular ideology, these individual elements (i.e. philosophy, psychology, sociology) are not mutually exclusive. The descriptions above are descriptions of the 'pure forms of the ideologies' and as Lawton (1983: 5), points out, they are forms which are seldom, if ever, seen.

Variations of the main curriculum paradigms

Tanner and Tanner (1975 & 1980) identified a number of variations of the three main curriculum paradigms, each of which reflects various 'diluted' forms of the ideologies and which 'blur the edges' where the various forms of the curriculum merge. I use them hesitantly, being aware of their complexity and interactive nature. They are by no means 'definitive descriptions' of the various forms of curricula. The first group are variations of the classical humanist philosophy and will be explored more fully in chapter six which is concerned with the characteristics of the knowledge-centred curriculum.

The first and arguably the 'purist' form is "perennial studies", in which the curriculum is permanent and universal because it is based on certain 'truths' which are gained through the disciplines of grammar, dialectic, rhetoric, logic and mathematics, music, and astronomy, which are selected for their value in 'training the mind'. The perennialist curriculum does not recognise the importance of the physical sciences or the developing nature of knowledge (see Tanner & Tanner 1975: 10-11; 1980: 104-109; Taba 1962: 19-22; 79-80).

In "essentialist studies" the curriculum again consists of essential knowledge and 'truths' which are a reflection of the 'essence of the society', it has a hierarchical structure and selection of students is on the basis of cognitive-intellectual ability. The programme of studies consists of grammar, literature and writing, mathematics, science, history, and foreign languages. The purpose of education is training in intellectual skills, and non-academic study has low status (see Tanner & Tanner 1975: 11-12; 1980: 109-113; Taba 1962: 19-22: 172-174). In "the curriculum as disciplines", there is an acceptance that knowledge can expand and that the disciplines can therefore also expand. However they are often studied as discrete elements and, as with the previous philosophies, low status may be accorded to the non-academic needs of the student. The work of Phenix and Hirst on the structure and forms of knowledge has provided frameworks which might assist in the selection of content. The traditional disciplines are preferred because they are "logical and progressive" (Tanner & Tanner 1975: 12-13, 42-43; Hirst 1974; see also Phenix 1964).

The next group of curriculum 'types' are all to a greater or lesser extent, variations of reconstructionism, which will be explored further in chapter seven. The "curriculum as experience" would appear to have similarities with Lawton's notion of the curriculum as "a selection from the culture". The curriculum as Lawton describes it, is arrived at by a process of cultural analysis and mapping, based on a comparison between existing education provision and the needs of contemporary society. In one form it may be a reflection of society, in another it might be perceived as a means of changing it. The most extreme form of this approach is Utopianism (see Tanner & Tanner 1975: 15-16; Lawton 1983; 1986; Skilbeck 1984a). The curriculum as "core learning experiences" has several interpretations. In one form it provides "common learnings" which are delivered across the curriculum (see Tanner and Tanner 1975: 501-503; Taba 1962: 300-301). In another, it aims to provide the student with a basic minimum of knowledge and competencies which are regarded as essential for progression as well as personal and career development (see White 1973: Lawton 1983; DES 1976, 1983).

The next two brief descriptions concern curriculum types which could be considered to relate as much to the student centred curriculum (which will be dealt with in chapter eight) as to the society centred curriculum. In the "holistic approach" to curriculum planning, the emphasis is on unifying learning experiences which draw the various elements of content together (see Tanner & Tanner 1975: 33-34). In the case of Dewey, the curriculum was driven by the need to ensure development of the whole person (Dewey 1902;1916). Closely related to it is the curriculum which has as its focus "reflective thinking". Reflection is an active and unifying process which encourages the application of knowledge and skills through activities such as problem solving and investigation (see Tanner & Tanner 1975: 14-15; Dewey 1916: 169-177; Dewey 1915: 147-148). In the curriculum as vocational education, 'relevance' may be the primary concern, in which case the emphasis is on the application of knowledge in 'real contexts'. Alternatively it may be concerned with the acquisition of specialist employment skills (see Tanner & Tanner 1975: 69, 113, 543-544; 'Georg Kirschensteiner' by Simons 1966; Dewey 1916: 362). The "activity analysis curriculum" is arrived at by close observation of occupations (Tanner & Tanner 1975: 27; Bobbitt 1924; Patty 1938). The curriculum as 'behavioural objectives' is concerned with 'measurable' learning outcomes. It owes much to stimulus response theory and is concerned with 'programmed learning' and accountability (see Tanner & Tanner 1975: 28-29; Tyler 1949; Thorndike by Jonich 1962; Bobbitt 1924; Skinner 1968; Popham & Baker 1970).

Each of the curriculum models so far briefly described, has a degree of emphasis that relates to the extent to which it is influenced by the particular ideology or ideologies. However, the common factor which runs through all of them is structure. The curriculum exists as a plan which, in some form or other, organises knowledge skills and concepts into a programme of study. The next two forms of the curriculum are not necessarily formalised at all. The first is the curriculum as "interaction processes", in which the curriculum consists of key issues which may be student or society focused. The processes of teaching and learning are interactive, and student's own interests and development are central to the planning of their course or programme (see Tanner & Tanner

1975: 24-25; Bruner 1966: 6, see also, 13-14, 52-56; Stenhouse 1975). The second form is "guided living" in which the 'curriculum' interacts with, and may be indistinguishable from, everyday living. The 'curriculum' can be a diffuse series of planned and unplanned activities and experiences, and is potentially esoteric (see Tanner & Tanner 1975: 21; Taba 1962: 400-406).

This chapter serves to illustrate that there is no one model for the curriculum which emanates from each of the principal paradigms, and this variety of emphases and complexity will be addressed in the three following chapters. For the purpose of structuring the remainder of the chapter, I shall return to the three main headings under which the three principal paradigms of curriculum theory already outlined will be explored further. Each subsection will relate to the principal variations and emphases of the particular paradigm to be investigated. The chapter headings are:

1.   Knowledge and the curriculum.
2   Society and the curriculum.
3   The student and the curriculum.

Chapter Six

Knowledge and the curriculum

In making a selection from the literature concerned with knowledge and the curriculum, as with the other aspects of curriculum theory, I shall concentrate on those aspects which are likely to be most relevant to the purpose of this study. That is to provide a framework of the principal characteristics of each of the paradigms which will be used to make comparisons with the principal characteristics of TVEI. In this chapter, I do not, therefore, propose to do much more than indicate, in a general way, the characteristics of the more extreme forms of the paradigm, and the psychologies of learning associated with them.

The knowledge centred curriculum as liberal education

Liberal education, the generic description of curricula which are knowledge centred and which reflect the notions and values associated with 'high culture', has its roots in classical Greek philosophy (see Hirst 1974: ch. 3). However, there are many interpretations and contradictory definitions of the paradigm. This causes problems and Hirst for example, finds it easier to define what a liberal education is not. His understanding is that it is not a narrow or specialised education (Hirst 1974; 30). This squares with Peters' (1966 ch.1 1977: 73-84) idea of what constitutes the 'educated man'. Plato's writings are very significant, although not exclusively in terms of the curriculum as knowledge, as I shall indicate in later chapters.

When exploring Plato's rationale it is important to remember that the society which Plato describes is Utopian; everyone has their place, knows their duty and has the good of society as their principal objective (see Taylor 1935: 'The Republic of Plato Book III' 412; 415-417, 'Book IV': 421, and 'Book VII' 540). According to Plato, the purpose of education is to ensure the survival of the culture in its purest form. Those of the highest intellect, 'men of gold', are prepared for their role as the guardians of the culture and are educated in a manner deemed, on philosophical grounds, to be most appropriate, as indeed are the 'lower classes' those of silver, iron, and bronze (ibid: 'Book III' 415). Selection is meritocratic and although the child will generally inherit the qualities of the parent, when the child of a man of gold is of an inferior intellect he will be demoted from the class of his father and vice versa (ibid: 'Book III' 415). Knowledge can justifiably be for its own sake (ibid: 'Book VII' 527). Plato's is a classless society in terms of wealth accumulation but meritocratic, and in that sense divided, in terms of intellect (ibid: 'Book III' 415). In Plato's republic real riches are intellectual riches (ibid: 'Book VII' 521).

Basic education consists, perhaps surprisingly, of disciplines which have both academic and 'practical or vocational' applications. Arithmetic calculation and geometry have dimensions at the higher level, of perception and truth and application to other forms of knowing, while at the lower level they have applications in war. Likewise astronomy at its higher level, informs man's understanding of his place in creation and at the lower level has application in terms of knowledge of night and day and of the seasons which inform farming and husbandry (ibid: 'Book VII' 525-527). The dialectic (the ability to form and communicate reasoned argument) is the key-stone of knowledge and intellect, while philosophy is identified as requiring the very highest intellect. It enables man to not only relate the qualities and needs of society to the ideal, but to use intellectual skills and knowledge in order to preserve and nurture what is good within society and to preserve the purity of the culture. So that even within the highest class there will be those of supreme intellect who are permitted to extend their education in order to become the philosophers (ibid: *'Book VII'* 431-437 and 519). "But let me venture to say this also, that we must make our most perfect guardians the philosophers."

Plato accepted that they will be few in number and that they are the intellectual elite (ibid: *'Book IV'* 503). But even those who are educated in the dialectic and in philosophy, as well as having sufficient education for their tasks in society, must take their turn as politicians and rulers. This embodies the notion of liberal education being a balance between the disciplines of education and liberty (ibid: *'Book VII'* 519-540). Plato explored the arguments for and against an egalitarian approach to the education of the classes, and concluded that the needs of society would be best served by differentiating between them and educating them in the manner most appropriate to their likely future roles (ibid: *'Book IV'* 420-421). I shall explore in chapter seven the work of Bantock (1963, 1968) who also uses a form of 'cultural analysis' to suggest the need for differentiated curricula based on the different needs, experiences and culture of working class and middle class students.

One interpretation of Plato's argument, the one selected by advocates of liberal education, is that it is essential to preserve the culture by selecting the finest minds to transmit it from generation to generation. Only those capable of reaching the highest order of academic discipline are trusted with such responsibility and they must be 'trained' in order to attain the very maximum human intellectual capability. This is the basis of the 'knowledge centred' curriculum. The perennialist, essentialist argument extends from this basic premise to the selection of knowledge on the basis of: (1) knowledge which must be acquired in order for the culture to be transmitted; and (2) types of 'discipline' that best develop and train the mind, so that the knowledge in (1) can be (a) assimilated and passed on; and (b) explained and if necessary defended through logical argument and sound philosophy. In the case of (1) knowledge is truth, and thus might include the disciplines of arithmetic, geometry and the natural sciences, while in (2), knowledge is logic and rhetoric and might include philosophy, language and the fine arts.

The perennialist and essentialist curricula in their 'modern form', the 'typical grammar school curriculum', consist of disciplined study of: language, in particular the systematic study of grammar, literature and writing; mathematics, (algebra and geometry); science, (physics, chemistry and biology); history or geography or both; foreign languages, Latin, Greek or sometimes both, and a modern foreign language. The primary purpose of education is to develop cognitive-intellectual skills. Other aspects of the individual's development are of relatively minor importance and non-academic study has low status, although in the grammar school of the nineteen fifties and sixties, music, art and craft as well as physical education and religious education (or scripture) were normally included as 'additional elements' (see Rée 1956: 27; see also Larkin 1959; see also Burgess 1972: 94, for a 'broader' grammar school curriculum). In terms of the three classes (or schools) described by Comenius (Keatinge 1910: 274) they are most similar to "the Latin class".

For Hutchins (1952) not only is a liberal education the only real education, access to which should be available for all, but it is a life-long process undertaken through the study of classical literature.   Originally a liberal education consisted of the seven liberal arts: grammar, dialectic, rhetoric, arithmetic and geometry, music and astronomy (*'Comenius'* by Keatinge 1910: 274-275). Gordon (1981: 34) describes it as consisting of the trivium: grammar, dialectic (or logic) and rhetoric, and the quadrivium: arithmetic, music, geometry and astronomy. Aristotle described five types of intellectual virtue: art, scientific knowledge, rational intuition, practical intelligence and wisdom. (*'Aristotle translated by Lloyd'* 1968: 224) He also had three classes of disciplines: ethics and politics, logic and metaphysics and the poetics (ibid: ch.10, ch.11). Comenius described three schools: the "Mother School", which is the first school; the "Latin School", for those students destined to progress to higher education; and the "Vernacular School" for those destined for manual labour. Students of the "Latin School" not only studied the seven liberal arts, but also physics, geography, chronology, history, morality and theology (ibid: 295-281). In this sense, although he upheld the principle of universal studies and the great books, his vision of the curriculum was broader than perennialist and essentialist studies.

According to Hutchins, the other disciplines were created by 'breaking away' from philosophy to produce political science, sociology, and psychology, and these, he argued, suffered from a confusion about the nature and scope of scientific method which widened the gap between them and caused misguided changes in philosophical study. These same dark forces are further denounced for their distortion of truth in chapter five since also according to Hutchins, they wrongfully undermined the liberal arts (1952: 27-31). He questioned the value of experimental science in terms of locating truth, maintaining that it is in certain instances, for example. the social sciences, a profoundly unsafe method (ibid: 38-39) and that there are many 'truths', including those to be found in the great books, which do not reveal themselves through experimental science and empirical study (ibid: ch.4). Also, Hutchins argued, there were great thinkers before the 'domination' of experimental science. The great books Hutchins claimed, are concerned with man's best efforts to seek the truth. They examine 'both sides' of all issues and provide us with a sound basis by which to judge the value and appropriateness of experimental methods of inquiry (ibid: 37-38).

Some writers have indicated the limited value of such extreme curricula as are to be found in perennialist and essentialist studies. Taba for example (1962: 19-22) questioned the value of a curriculum which is limited to such a narrow range of knowledge and experiences. It is particularly questionable in the modern world where the application of knowledge and skills is so important, and in which change takes place so rapidly. This applies not only to the kinds of knowledge required, but to the expansion of knowledge itself. She also pointed out that in such hierarchical curricula, there is no place for vocational experience and even the basic skills, such as reading and writing, are placed on a lower level than the academic disciplines. Moreover, they neglect other important aspects of an holistic education, such as the development of personal and inter-personal skills. In terms of the notion of 'mind training', in particular so called 'faculty psychology', one would have to say that despite being 'discredited as a theory' (see Thorndike in Jonich 1962; Taba 1962: 80; Peters 1966; Hirst 1974; Bantock 1963: 136) there are still vestiges of it to be found in comprehensive education today. It can be seen particularly in the hierarchical structures, for example in 'high and low status subjects', and the 'streaming' of pupils on the basis of their levels of ability in only a few subjects. The implication perhaps being, that if students can 'do well' in those, they will automatically have 'developed a desirable range of intellectual skills' enabling them to master other 'lesser' subjects (see Bantock 1963: 136-137; Gordon in Lawton et al 1978: 148; see also Lym in Cox & Dyson eds. 1971: ch.6, on the essential need for streaming).

Hutchins would probably have supported such arguments since he regarded the development of the intellect as being of greatest importance, as is indicated in the following extract: "The purpose of education is to develop a good mind. Everybody should have access to the kind of education most likely to develop such a mind." (Hutchins 1952: 16). It would also appear that he disapproved of student choice, believing that all students are capable of acquiring a liberal education and should not be given the opportunity to 'opt out'. He believed that when students follow other types of education it is the fault of teachers, who avoid the difficulties of enforcing a liberal education on the grounds that it is too difficult or not appropriate (ibid: 46). For Hutchins 'difficult is good' (ibid: 47). Hirst on the other hand rejects the notion of the mind as something that can be trained, filled or set in motion.

"What we see or understand about any situation is not a simple given. It is dependent on those concepts and categories, those basic units of intelligibility, which the mind brings to the situation....To be without any knowledge at all is to be without mind in any significant sense. ..The acquisition of knowledge is itself a development of mind and new knowledge means a new development of mind in some sense....In the third place we must, I suggest, reject the notion that the mind naturally carries out certain mental activities according to the canons of valid reasoning, as if logical principles were laws of psychological functioning." (Hirst in Hooper 1971: 240-241).

There are of course those, both in education and politics, who nurture a desire for elitism in education and in various forms, for example, public schools, grammar schools, streamed comprehensive schools and more recently, city technology colleges, it has been, and to some extent still is, a part of the education scene. With the current emphasis on terminal assessment and the notion of a GCSE 'threshold' level in the National Curriculum at key stage four, elitism might be described as making a strong comeback. However, in terms of access to a broad and balanced curriculum some contemporary developments, including TVEI, have been concerned with equality of opportunity and breadth of experience. That 'right of access' is echoed in the writings of Hirst and Peters (1966).

"In brief, education is not simply for the intelligent. It is not a question of some being capable of it and others not. It is a matter, rather, of how far individuals can progress along the same avenues of exploration".... "A quality of life is not the prerogative of an intellectual elite." (Peters 1966: 178)

The curriculum as knowledge raises three very significant questions: (1) What knowledge should be included? (2) For what purposes? (3) How should we teach whatever it is that we can justify as being of most worth and appropriateness?

Hirst, writing about cognitive objectives, makes it clear that it is important that they should range across all the forms of knowledge, arguing that if there is a logical and unique conceptual structure to the discrete forms of knowledge we must take care not to exclude students from access to the whole range of 'uniqueness', i.e. all the forms of knowledge (Hirst 1974: ch.1).

There are, as I have already indicated, some historical arguments for the inclusion of particular types of knowledge (see Hirst 1974) and there are a number of 'ready-made' classifications of disciplines. For example that of Broudy, who suggests that in terms of what it is desirable to know one might well argue: "Everything,.." (Broudy 1954: 183). In fact he proposes three groups of disciplines: natural sciences, social sciences and self science and a heading - guidance (ibid ch. 7). Broudy also amplifies the benefits of a liberal education from the perspective of the curriculum planner: "The faith in the Classics has certain advantages for the curriculum maker, the chief of which is economy of effort and simplicity of form." (Ibid: 198)

Phenix's six realms of meaning or Hirst's seven forms of knowledge provide other models. The latter in particular, has been influential in terms of education policy in England and Wales in recent times (see Lawton in Gordon 1981: 44) and is based on a particular view of the nature and structure of knowledge. The methods employed by Hirst and to some extent by Phenix, would appear to be a sound basis for selecting knowledge. However we need to ask whether knowledge should be the only consideration of curriculum planners. If not, perhaps we need to ask if curriculum content can it be justified through other forms of reasoning. To attempt to find an answer to this latter point, I will begin the next section by examining briefly the work of Peters, the essence of whose philosophy is that the only sound basis for deciding the worthwhileness of curriculum activities is ethics. I shall examine both the rationale for a curriculum which is based on the notion of a 'liberal education', and the values and limitations which are associated with it. I shall also explore the notion of general education and the extent to which it might or might not include elements other than knowledge.

Knowledge and general education
Peters (1977: 19) argued that the basis of curriculum making should begin with conceptual analysis which, while it may not provide the answers regarding what kinds of knowledge and activities are most worthwhile, has value in terms of shaping questions which are precise enough to provide a basis for debate (ibid: 19-20). The issues which arise from such analysis are, according to Peters,

mainly ethical. Addressing such issues through an analytical process can, he argued, provide a framework of logic by which types of knowledge are selected for inclusion in the curriculum, and for helping to determine the value of particular objectives in terms of curriculum structure, for example in terms of breadth as opposed to depth of knowledge (Peters et al 1973: 240, 243). The judgements are also influenced by our own and others' values concerning the extent to which certain elements of content are regarded as 'intrinsically good', or by the extent to which they are considered essential in terms of the types of knowledge which can only be accessed or gained through them. (See White (1973) for a particular interpretation of this line of reasoning). Peters argued that if criteria for selection of curriculum content are to be based on value judgements concerning what is "worthwhile", we must first decide what other values, apart from the intrinsic value of knowledge, we ought to consider (1966: ch.2). There are for example, values associated with personal qualities such as autonomy, integrity, courage, and others associated with an ordered and democratic society, such as justice and equality (Peters 1977: 39-40). There are also those values associated with work and material prosperity. These are what Peters calls "extrinsic" or "instrumental" values and are often the ones which most concern economists and politicians (ibid: 35). Because extrinsic values address economic, as well as personal and other social values, they are instrumental to the well-being of the society and the economy and therefore must be considered by curriculum planners and reformers. As Peters pointed out, extrinsic values can sometimes appear to conflict with intrinsic values, or personal and social values, for example in terms of choice or equality of opportunity (1977: 42). In curriculum terms, some subjects, such as science and mathematics, are central in terms of both intrinsic and extrinsic values (ibid: 38).

The case for a 'core of essential studies'

White (1973) pursued the argument that because the modern curriculum is overcrowded, we need to decide what is a basic minimum education and a basic minimum curriculum. The problem is how to decide what the basic minimum might consist of. He like Peters, explored the notion of selecting content on the basis of the 'intrinsic' value of subjects. He also considered the notion of a criterion based on traditional 'values'. The third basis for a criterion by which curriculum content could be selected might, he suggested, be approached on the basis of which kinds of experiences are good and which are harmful. None of these, White considers, provide satisfactory or complete criteria.

White suggests that educators have a responsibility to provide opportunities for students to have experiences and gain knowledge which the individual may find worthwhile for their intrinsic value, as well as those which they might want or need for their extrinsic or vocational value, or in order to prepare for a particular life-style. He advocates that other personal needs which potentially enhance the quality of life for the individual, such as the opportunity to play a musical instrument or other personal aspirations, should also be provided for. White also considers it essential that educators and curriculum planners ensure as far as possible, that opportunities and needs which may occur in the long-term are not rendered inaccessible by short term choices that are the result of insufficient information or experience, or the inability of the student to reflect on needs and aspirations (ibid: 22-24, 25-37). The problem is how to ensure that students are provided with opportunities to acquire the kinds of knowledge and experience which are essential as a basis for coping with needs which may materialise at some future time.

White suggests that it may be an idea to have two categories of activities and experiences. In the first category, in order for the individual to be able to participate in a meaningful way, there is a pre-requisite for a knowledge base. The second of White's categories contains the types of experience which do not necessarily require any formal preparation in order for the participant to derive some benefit from them (ibid: 27-29). The criteria he suggests can become, in simple terms, the curriculum content test. White used the rationale for "type one" activities in a way which it might be argued suggests a "core of essential experiences" which all students should have. Moreover, his argument that to exclude an individual from such experiences could disadvantage them in the future, would seem to be a basis for developing an argument in favour of an 'entitlement curriculum'. On the other hand his warning that it would be unwise to impose certain kinds of experience on the student unless there is a sustainable argument, suggests that there should be at least some element of student choice (ibid: 37).

Since the mid nineteen seventies there has been considerable debate about the merit or otherwise, of a 'common' or 'core' curriculum in the context of what might be regarded as a 'basic education'. The terms themselves are often confusing and open to interpretation. An article by Brian Holley in Elliot et al (1980) is helpful in clarifying the issues and in pointing out that a 'common curriculum' should not necessarily be thought of as a 'general education'.

Problems of identifying criteria for selecting curriculum content
Peters describes education as initiation into the culture of the society to enable the individual to identify with its systems of values and beliefs (1966: 49, 74-75). It should also provide a breadth of knowledge and understanding and an awareness of both its intrinsic and extrinsic value. He argues that education should also provide a "conceptual framework" which enables the individual to understand the ways in which things relate to one another, and to develop and use 'cognitive skills' and 'modes of thinking' (1966: 30-31, 50). Education according to Peters, should also support the development of a range of other personal and interpersonal skills as well as and the acquisition of knowledge (1966: 55-60). He proposes what he calls: "the product criteria of being educated" (1977: 27-32), but points out that there is no one definitive description of the qualities that are the hallmark of being educated. However he does provide some aims which might form a basis for action these are: "1. Commitment to what is regarded as valuable in itself. "2 .Knowledge and understanding (together with the appropriate effect)." "3. Wholeness." (1977: 28-30)

It is interesting to examine the extent to which Peters' aims square with the notion of a liberal education. Peters suggests that there are at least three interpretations of what constitutes a liberal education. The first is "knowledge for its own sake", i.e. intrinsic worth (1966: 154; 1977: 47, 73-79). This would seem to correspond with the first of his 'aims'. Peters considers this an incomplete basis for selecting curriculum content since it addresses only some of the needs of the student, and because of problems in establishing precise selection criteria (1977: 28, 32, Peters et al 1973: 247-248). Similarly he considers a curriculum based entirely on practical activities to be inadequate since it may involve limited conceptual knowledge (1966: 176-177). Hirst's rationale concerning the structure of conceptual knowledge is important in this respect (Hirst 1974). The second interpretation of what constitutes a liberal education is related to the notion of a 'general education' and deliberations concerning breadth and purpose, and the extent to which it can be regarded as a complete education (1977: 47, 69-73). These deliberations address the issue of the breadth and depth of knowledge (1977: 69-72; Peters et al 1973: 256-258). As a result, they pose the question: How broad does an education need to be in order for it to be considered general? They also raise again, the question: By what definition do we regard a person as 'being educated'? (1966: 27-34;1977; 27-30).

In considering the 'value' of procedural knowledge and skills, Peters suggests that (vocational) training alone is not sufficient to be considered an education. However it is possible to be both educated and trained if the training builds on, or extends a general education. He also rejects the notion that the mere acquisition of factual knowledge provides what might be considered a complete education, and proposes the notion of "cognitive perspective" as a guide to what might constitute "being educated". In other words the education a person has, needs to be broad and deep enough for all issues to be considered in a variety of possible contexts. He needs to be able to 'think things through' and see the possible consequences of his decisions and choices (1966: 31-32). Arguably this also reflects the third of Peters' aims. The third interpretation of a liberal education is that of "a stance against dogmatic teaching" (1977: 47-48) and raises questions concerning the purpose and methods of teaching. It is rather more difficult to square this interpretation with the third of Peters' aims. It is however, a particularly interesting and important aspect which concerns congruence between content (the type of knowledge being taught) and the method by which it is taught (Peters et al 1973: 241; Hirst 1974: ch. 8). It also raises the question of the extent to which the type of knowledge content is limited by the method of instruction. If for example, a curriculum is determined on the basis that all the knowledge has to be imparted through 'the great books' (see Hutchins 1952), is all practical knowledge to be excluded?

Peters' analysis suggests that a strong instrumental case can be made for a general education because knowledge and understanding are essential to the well-being and prosperity of societies (1966: 159, Peters et al 1973: 243-244; 1977: 28-29, 35-38; see also Holt 1979: ch.2). Not only does knowledge help us to control our environment, but by providing us with "cognitive perspectives", it goes some way towards enabling us to understand the probable consequences of our actions (1977: 112-114; Peters et al 1973: 240-243, 261). Secondly, societies rely on effective communication which requires not only language, but also a universal acceptance that there are certain 'truths' which are based on 'accepted evidence'. Such knowledge is therefore essential to our ability to communicate information in ways which make it useful and usable (Peters et al 1973: 243). Thirdly, conceptual knowledge is essential since it provides a framework which enables activities and phenomena to be explained and understood (see Hirst & Peters 1970: 62). Fourthly, it raises doubts about the 'wholeness' of an education which addresses only extrinsic values, particularly when they result in a narrow instrumentalist approach to provision (1977: 30-32 Peters et al 1973: 246-247). His analysis also points up the difficulty of determining criteria by which we can select content or activities for their intrinsic value (1977: 46-47, 48, 58-66).

There are certain kinds of 'activity' which are implicit in some of the processes associated with acquiring knowledge, and which also provide the 'doer' with some kind of reward which is integral to the activity or process itself. The value or reward is therefore in the doing rather than in some additional 'pay off'. In other words the "activity" is worth doing for its own sake (Peters et al 1973: 18; 245; 1977: 28, 74-75). The problem with intrinsic rewards is that to be achieved, they often require perseverance and toil which may only be accepted by the individual until such time as the activity becomes too difficult or simply 'boring' (1977: 78; Peters et al 1973: 258). By contrast, instrumentalist criteria are likely to be based on the expectation of some kind of reward or pay-off, which is external to the activity and which might benefit either the individual who is directly involved in the activity, or some other person or group in the society. Peters warned of the dangers of such a narrow interpretation of the purpose of education (Peters et al 1973: 240-247, see also, 266-267).

The forms of knowledge as a possible framework for planning the curriculum
In the continuing search for a selection criterion, it might be argued that Hirst's work on the forms of knowledge, which provides a logical framework to locate the essential forms of knowledge, is potentially immensely useful as a basis for rational planning (see Hirst 1974: 5). However the philosophical approach to planning curricula is not without critical observers. Young (1971: 23) for example, warns of the dangers of unquestioning acceptance of philosophical arguments. It is important when considering Hirst's work on the structure of knowledge, to remember that for Hirst, the methods by which students learn and develop into mature and intelligent individuals, are also of great importance. For Hirst there are three elements of rational curriculum planning:

> Objectives: learning outcomes;
> Content: that which is to be learned;
> Method: teaching strategies & learning activities.
> (Hirst 1974: 3).

Hirst proposes that there is a basic philosophical truth that all knowledge is capable of differentiation "...into a number of logically distinct forms or disciplines." (ibid: 5) These distinct forms provide a framework through which curriculum objectives can be specifically defined and within which items of knowledge are inter-related, as are the concepts on which knowledge is built. It is these relationships which give each of the "disciplines" its own unique and rational conceptual structure (ibid: 25-27, 96). These structures are important in the development of cognition, and influence the pedagogical process. In Hirst's classification there are seven disciplines: mathematics, physical sciences, human sciences, history, religion, literature and the fine arts, and philosophy (ibid: 46). Hirst acknowledges that although in his view the disciplines provide a logical means of curriculum planning, they are not necessarily to be regarded as the only means by which to organise a curriculum. (ibid: 50, 98,137 see also ch. 9).

Hirst's classification of the forms of knowledge is, as he made clear, a framework by which only a part of the curriculum can be determined since it is exclusively concerned with cognitive-intellectual activities, and therefore does not include experiences, skills or attitudes, however it provides a base which can be expanded to do so (ibid: 51). It follows that in Hirst's terms, an education which is limited to knowledge based on "true propositions" (ibid: 96) possibly acquired through studies of traditional disciplines, should not be considered as providing a complete education (ibid: 51, 96).

Conceptual structure and theoretical and procedural knowledge
Hirst also defines two "types" of knowledge; theoretical and practical (ibid: 46). There is some disagreement between Hirst and Phenix about whether or not knowledge of places, people and things, constitutes a third distinct type of knowledge (ibid: 57-59). Phenix's classification includes it as such, however Hirst disputes this and argues that in philosophical terms this not the case and that if knowledge is other than knowing how (practical knowledge), it is knowing that (theoretical knowledge (ibid: 57). If we accept Hirst's thesis we can indeed describe the broad categories of knowledge as: (1) theoretical knowledge, and (2) practical knowledge (see also Pring in Lawton et al 1978: 19-20). Hirst also points out that all concepts involve elements of both types of knowledge (Ibid: 58). If this is true, an important part of the education process must be to not only initiate the student into these modes of thinking, but also provide opportunities for them to apply knowledge and concepts. As was shown in chapter three, this is an important part of the TVEI philosophy.

Using Hirst's argument regarding the two distinct types of knowledge, one can formulate an argument that certain 'types' of education may place greater or lesser emphasis on one or other of these. It should therefore follow that curricula may be constructed in such a way as to do the same by, for example, providing a greater (or lesser) allocation of time to those 'disciplines' which involve the practical application of knowledge. Teaching strategies and learning activities can also involve a greater or lesser emphasis on one or other of these broad categories. Using Hirst's definition of 'concept' it does not necessarily follow that a curriculum which is designed and taught in such a way as to emphasise the practical application of knowledge is vocational, but it could possibly be argued that such a curriculum might provide a greater range of active learning opportunities than one which is based principally on the notion of liberal education.

Phenix's classification of the objects of knowledge is more complex than that of Hirst's, having compounded as well as singular forms (see table 4). His six realms of meaning are arrived at by analysis of the "..possible distinctive modes of human understanding." There are other important differences between Hirst's (1974) and Phenix's (1964) classification. Phenix's six realms of meaning relate only partially to Hirst's forms. Hirst however, agrees with Phenix on empirics, aesthetics and ethics (ibid: 66).

Table 4 Phenix's Logical Classification of Meaning

Generic classes Quantity	Quality	Realms of meaning	Disciplines
General	form	Symbolics	Ordinary language, mathematics, nondiscursive symbolic forms.
General	fact	Empirics	Physical sciences, life sciences, psychology, social sciences.
Singular	form	Synnoetics	Philosophy, psychology, literature, religion, in their existential aspects.
Singular	norm)		(the varied special areas
	)	Ethics	(of moral and ethical
General	norm)		(concern
Comprehensive	fact)		History
Comprehensive	norm)	Synoptics	Religion
Comprehensive	form)		Philosophy

From Phenix (1964: 28).

Both Hirst's forms of knowledge and Phenix's realms of meaning seem to relate to particular modes of thinking. If this is true, enabling the student to acquire and apply certain modes or ways of thinking must empower him or her to develop a conceptual grasp of the disciplines. Phenix and Hirst both appear to agree that a general education should be broader than the development of purely cognitive intellectual modes of thinking (Hirst 1974; 55, 96; Phenix 1964: 3-4).

Peters, Hirst and Phenix do not provide whole curriculum plans, but they do provide frameworks which have philosophical bases. Such frameworks provide a means by which certain curriculum elements and activities can be justified (see Holt on Hirst 1979: 48-49). Hirst and Peters provide some guidance which can help curriculum makers work towards a rationale by which the inclusion of particular elements might be justified. White seems to go a little further than either Peters or Hirst in pointing to the responsibility of educators to ensure that certain essential experiences are provided for all students. This might be interpreted as an argument for a 'core curriculum'.

What is evident in the writings of Hirst, Peters and White, is a much more holistic view of what constitutes a general education than can be provided by a liberal education alone. Hirst's recognition of the need for learning objectives, contexts which give meaning to content, and the use of these as a means of informing methods, are particularly important in establishing curriculum models which take on board the three dimensions of content, outcomes and methods (see Taylor 1966: 8).

Knowledge and other curriculum elements

Perhaps one of the most significant developments in curriculum planning in recent times, has been the move towards a knowledge based, but not necessarily subject based, curriculum. Perhaps the best known example is the HMI eight areas of experience. There are some similarities between Hirst's forms of knowledge and the 'areas of experience' which were set out in the 1977 and 1983 HMI documents, *'Curriculum 11 - 16'* and *'Curriculum 11-16 towards a statement of entitlement'*. They are the aesthetic / creative, the ethical, the linguistic, the mathematical, the physical, the scientific, the social / political, and the spiritual.

It is important to note however, that HMI also identified a range of cross-curricular skills and attitudes (DES 1983: 29-32) as well as specifying the importance of the relationship between the 'entitlement curriculum' and teaching methods (ibid: 34-37). Lawton (1980: 52-54) makes reference to an article by Brian Kay of the APU, which appeared in *'Trends in Education No. 2'* (1975), in which he stressed the importance of the curriculum being seen not simply as subjects, but in terms of skills and knowledge. In order to look at pupils' performance across the curriculum in a non-subject way, the APU identified six kinds of development: verbal, mathematical, scientific, ethical, aesthetic and physical (ibid 1980: 52). Ethical was later modified to become 'social and personal' (ibid 1980: 54).

As will be seen in the following chapter, there are very distinct similarities between the APU areas of development, the HMI areas of experience and Lawton's eight cultural systems, as well as Hirst's forms of knowledge. The problem is that in each of them there are different interpretations of the ways in which the individual elements relate to each other. The picture is further complicated by Hargreaves' (1982) description of types of ability, which will be highlighted in chapter seven. Squires (1987: 46-49) provided a helpful rationale for a more holistic curriculum plan, which takes on board culture, ability and knowledge as the three 'interactive dimensions' of the curriculum. In a slightly expanded form they are identified as:

Culture	Abilities	Knowledge
social	personal - social	maths
economic	physical - manual	physical sciences
communication	affective - emotional	human sciences and
rationality	aesthetic - creative	history
technology	cognitive - intellectual	literature and fine art
morality		morals
belief		religion
aesthetic		philosophy

There are similarities between Squires' curriculum plan and the HMI notion of an 'entitlement curriculum' as described in *'Curriculum 11-16 towards a statement of entitlement'*. However it could be argued that Squires' model has a greater degree of logic than that of the HMI which in my view has a somewhat arbitrary set of cross-curricular skills.

Summary

In this chapter I began by exploring the more extreme versions of the curriculum as knowledge. I indicated some criticisms of the notion that the purpose of education is to select those individuals of the highest intellect in order to prepare them for the task of protecting and transmitting the culture from each generation to the next, and that therein lies the origin of liberal education. I highlighted the fact that it nurtured and preserved a very academic curriculum, the content of which was originally selected for its value in 'training the mind'.

The work of Hirst, Peters and others supports the notion that in a modern industrialised country such a narrow curriculum would, in all probability, not meet the needs of society in general, or of students in particular. While some criterion for the selection of knowledge content is clearly necessary, it is clear from the work of Taba, Hirst, Peters and others that it requires a more substantial basis than the theory that certain disciplines select themselves because they are best for 'training the mind'.

I indicated in a brief exploration of the work of Hirst and Phenix, that a rationale for a curriculum based on true propositions and the logical structure of knowledge and concepts can provide a basis for an important aspect of the curriculum, i.e. the development of cognitive intellectual skills. The work of Hirst in particular, makes it clear that concepts involve both theoretical and procedural (or practical) knowledge. This has important implications for teaching methods which are informed by both the type of knowledge which is to be acquired and / or applied, and by the context in which it is to be set. The implications for learning objectives were also noted. The work of Peters in particular, illustrates that although the disciplines are both logical and progressive, they are not the only means by which knowledge can be organised. Some of the more recent work on the curriculum, such as that of HMI and the APU, has provided alternative proposals for the organisation of knowledge content.

Another important aspect of the relationship between content and pedagogy was raised by Hirst. It concerns the importance of ensuring that the 'conceptual structure' of the programme of study is made clear to students in order for them to acquire the appropriate 'modes of thinking' which are essential, if real understanding of the particular subject or curriculum area is to be achieved. An example from TVEI might be to present curriculum content in technology for example, in such a way as to encourage students to 'think technology', to ask the: How does it work? What if? questions, as well as to design and make things.

The work of Peters and White has pointed up the dangers of content selection criteria based only on value judgements. White's work in particular, focused on what might be regarded as essential or 'core' experiences and like Peters, on the need to consider both intrinsic and instrumental values in the process of curriculum planning. Peters has pointed out that educators have a duty to consider the various needs of the individual and also those of society. It is society as a focus for the curriculum which I propose to examine in chapter seven.

Chapter Seven

Society and the Curriculum

"If classical humanism is knowledge-centred, and progressivism is child-centred, reconstructionism might be regarded as society-centred. This would, however, be to over-simplify, since an essential aspect of reconstructionism would be to see the individual and society as harmoniously integrated rather than necessarily in opposition."
(Lawton 1983: 9)

The forms of reconstructionism
In much the same way as the academic type of curriculum is associated with classical humanist ideology, so the society focused curriculum is most closely associated with the ideology of reconstructionism. That is not to the total exclusion of the influence of other ideologies, but it is significant in terms of the influences and pressures which are brought to bear on curriculum planners and teachers, as Reynolds and Skilbeck point out (1976: 76-86). There would appear to be three main versions of reconstructionism. The first is 'Utopian reconstructionism' (see Lawton 1983:10; Sockett 1976: 15-16; see also Hirst in Galton 1980), exemplified in Plato's republic. Plato's educational concern was the inculcation and preservation of the culture and values of society. The starting point was an analysis of the needs of the society and the outcome was an elitist curriculum. Plato's purpose was principally instrumentalist, i.e. to shape the society in a particular way. He explored the arguments for and against an egalitarian approach to education and concluded that the needs of society would be best served by differentiating between the classes and educating them in the manner most appropriate to their roles in the society (*Book IV* 420-421).

Durkheim had some difficulty reconciling the needs of the society with individuality. On the one hand he recognised that there is a need for diversity and that it is part of the purpose of education to ensure "the persistence of this necessary diversity, by being itself diversified and specialised." (*'Education and Sociology'* translated by Fox 1956: 70-71) On the other hand, although he recognised that the needs and values of society vary with their various stages of cultural development, he was concerned that the more complex the society becomes, the greater becomes the diversity of need, and that the more specialised education becomes, the more stratified becomes the social order (ibid: 68-70). Durkheim recognised the importance of the role of the state in ensuring that basic principles which are common to all, are imparted by teachers in a clear and objective manner. These he described as: "respect for reason, for science and for ideas and sentiments which are at the base of democratic morality." (ibid: 81) Durkheim's over-riding concern was that education should ensure the preservation of a democratic and orderly society. In other words, as far as he was concerned the principal purpose of education was the inculcation of social and moral values, discipline, and other essential elements of education appropriate to the individual's likely vocation and place in the social structure.

Bantock (1963 & 1968) argued that a common curriculum is impractical and for the majority of students it amounts to the wrong kind of education (1963: 210). Not only did he deplore the concept for causing a waste of ability (1968: 43) which he believed resulted from imposing middle class values on working class children, but he questioned the value of an 'academic' education for most students, including those whose ability might measure up to the demands but whose background and culture might place undue pressure on them (1963: 170-172).

> "If these children have both the 'brains' and the temperament for high learning, they must accept the pains that are the inevitable concomitant of 'spiritual' development; as they achieve the level of consciousness which is in them, as they are helped to realise natures which will make them, to a certain extent, 'different', they must be strengthened in the loneliness which, in some degree, is to become part of their lot; and if they cannot accept that challenge, with all the help we can bring them, they must reluctantly be allowed to slide back." (1963: 171-172)

In his 'plan', Bantock (1963) called for better methods of selection and movement between schools, improved technical education, 'specialist' secondary modern schools, technical schools (for students of average or above average ability who would benefit from such an education) and improved grammar schools (1963: 118).

Bantock (1963, 1968) used cultural needs as an argument for a curriculum based on the particular social circumstances and intellectual abilities of students. As a result, he proposed different curricula for working-class and middle-class students, with some scope for student mobility between them. For working-class students he proposed a curriculum with roots in working class culture. It would place emphasis on the practical and creative aspects of learning, with the focus on learning by doing and investigating (1968: 79). Such curricula would reflect and enhance 'working-class values and culture' and address the likely social and vocational needs of the individual (1968: 85). The other type of curriculum would reflect 'middle-class values and culture', and concentrate on the development of cognitive-intellectual skills. However Bantock points out the weaknesses in the 'traditional grammar school' curriculum, which he believes concentrates too much on the acquisition of knowledge for passing examinations.

> "The culture of the school, then, is geared to the demands of high culture based on literacy but structured not primarily in accordance with the nature of the 'subjects' into which it is inevitably divided to make it manageable but for the purpose of passing examinations;.." (1968: 42).

The second strand of the ideology, could be described as 'social reconstructionism' (see Lawton 1983: 9). Dewey believed in the notion that if harmony and beauty could be achieved within the community of the school, in time society as a whole might be improved and democracy preserved (Dewey 1915; 1916). In Britain in recent times, some educators have seen cultural renewal in areas of urban deprivation as the most important function of education (see Midwinter's *'Patterns of community education'* 1973 esp. 43, 47-48). It has been argued that social reconstructionism is vulnerable to instrumentalist influences, and that it may be seen as social engineering (see Lawton 1983: 9 Taba 1962). It can in such instances, involve a 'systems management' approach to curriculum planning (see Bobbitt 1924 and Popham and Baker 1970).

Dewey was aware of the instrumentalist pressures on the curriculum which could result in education becoming vocational education, which in turn could become 'trade education'. In recent times Peters has articulated similar concerns, and suggests that governments generally have an instrumentalist view of education, i.e. as the source of trained manpower, while the average man sees it as providing "social mobility." (Peters et al 1973: 242-245)

Factors which inhibit reconstructionism - liberal education values
The third form of reconstructionism is what Lawton describes as 'democratic reconstructionism' (1983:11), it is sometimes also described as 'cultural reconstructionism' (see Reynolds & Skilbeck 1976: 86). Such a curriculum might include in its objectives, a common core of experiences which reflect the values, culture and needs of contemporary society (Lawton 1983: esp. chapters 5 & 7). Clearly objectives such as these, cannot be met in total through a curriculum which concentrates exclusively, on the development of cognitive-intellectual skills (see Lawton et al 1978: 3; 1986: 7,13; Hargreaves 1982). Indeed it is extremely doubtful that the needs of any modern industrial society could be met if that was the only criterion for education (see Lawton 1983, 1986; Skilbeck 1984a 1984b Peters et al 1973: 242-245). A rationale based on cultural analysis would therefore appear to lead away from the notion of a curriculum based on purely academic studies (see Lawton 1986; Hemming in Skilbeck 1984b: 305-316; Holt 1979: 49).

There are, however, considerable pressures on educators to preserve the knowledge-based curriculum (see Bantock in Horton & Raggatt 1982; Hargreaves 1982). There would appear to be at least four important reasons why this is so. The first is to do with the fact that reconstructionism is a comparatively young ideology compared with classical humanism (Skilbeck in Horton and Raggatt 1982: 10-15). As a result It has been inhibited by the values and traditions of liberal education (see Young 1971: 36; Skilbeck in Horton and Raggatt 1982: 16), in particular by the long-standing notion that the most important kind of knowledge is factual knowledge, and the emphasis on the written rather than the spoken word (see Hutchins 1952; Young 1971: 37; see also Holt 1979: 3-7, 117).

Hargreaves' book *'The Challenge for the Comprehensive School'* (1982), is particularly interesting in terms of identifying the influence exerted by liberal educational values. It is not only the formal, but also the hidden curriculum which, he argued, is stacked against students from working class backgrounds (see also Apple 1982: 97-100, 110-111). According to Hargreaves, in the majority of comprehensive schools the emphasis is on the development of cognitive-intellectual skills. The school ethos is often based on grammar school values, and high status subjects are those in which the learning can be examined by written tests (op cit: 55; see also Holt 1979: 3-7, 117).

Hargreaves identified four types of skills in addition to the cognitive-intellectual, which he believed are capable of definition and description:

1) the aesthetic-artistic,
2) the effective-emotional,
3) the physical-manual,
4) the personal-social.

The reality is, that although they are generally acknowledged as important, in practice they are often treated as less important than cognitive-intellectual skills and the subjects through which they are addressed have tended to be regarded as 'low status' (see Young 1971: 40).

The low regard for subjects which are concerned with practical, creative, technical, physical and personal and social education, is also reflected in the proportion of curriculum time they receive and the extent of opportunities to progress through them to higher education (op cit: 59-60; see also Young 1971: 40). Hargreaves was concerned that general education is centred around those types of knowledge, skills and abilities associated with academic curricula and with the cognitive-intellectual domain, and that as a result, the ability of the individual is often measured solely in terms of their cognitive-intellectual performance (op cit: 60). For many students however, cognitive-intellectual ability forms only a small part of their overall ability (ibid: 64).

There are external influences, also shaped by liberal education values, which inhibit curriculum change, for example, the "falling standards" argument (ibid: 67; see also Cox & Dyson 1971; Boyson 1975). In the context of TVEI, it is interesting to note that Bobbitt's way around this was to suggest that goals and standards should be set by businessmen (see also Bowmen in Skilbeck 1984: 43). A second factor is the reliance on systems of meritocracy both in education and the world of work (see Hargreaves 1982: 68, 70-71; Apple 1982: 14-15, 41-42; Bowles & Gintis 1976). The third factor is the examinations system, which is geared primarily to examining theoretical knowledge and performing selection procedures, (Peters 1977: 77; see also Bantock 1968: 34) although examinations do not necessarily prevent working-class students from progressing up the 'social ladder' (Hargreaves 1982: 73). Young (1972) provides a further reason by suggesting that it is not in the interests of the ruling class to reform the curriculum, since their dominance is an outcome of the existing system.

Factors which inhibit reconstructionism - 'faculty psychology'
The second major stumbling block to reconstructionism is the importance that is attached to 'faculty psychology' which fostered the notion that the mind could be trained by studying particular (difficult) subjects (see Squires 1987: 15). In criticism of 'faculty psychology' and 'behavioural psychology' Bantock writes:

"...it is feasible to argue that the now discredited psychological theory helped to preserve the notion of a 'liberal' rather than a utilitarian-vocational - which often implied a 'practical' - emphasis in studies. Even the study of the classics,....received a new *raison d' etre* at the hands of the inter-related theories of faculty psychology, mental discipline and the transfer of training.....it was possible to combine both the notions of liberality and utility. By assisting 'general cultivation', the classics, it was argued, were also preparing the grounds for specific understanding; once the mind had been trained it could apply itself to the particular without difficulty." (1963: 136-137)

As long as the parameters of 'essential knowledge' were manageable and 'mental discipline' was the main objective of educators, there was no compulsion to re-examine objectives which aimed at achieving that end (see Tyler 1949: 16; also Jonich 1962: 23-25). However, when studies of training methods revealed the importance of relating school-based experience to real life situations, the whole purpose and structure of the curriculum became open to re-examination. Thorndike's work in the 1920's and 1930's, which did much to undermine the faculty theory of transfer was particularly significant. He advocated a broader curriculum than the traditional perennialist one, and provided a rationale for selecting content which acknowledged the value of acquiring knowledge for reasons other than its intrinsic value (Jonich 1962: 23-25; 144-147). The diminished influence of faculty psychology opened up the question of curriculum content. Thorndike's work raised the question now so familiar to curriculum planners: What content should be included? Relevance became an issue and on that basis vocational studies for example, could seek inclusion. However, as knowledge began to expand rapidly, Thorndike's work also and perhaps more importantly, raised the question: What should be left out?

Thorndike argued for greater importance to be attached to the practical application of knowledge, and for the curriculum to address the interests of society (ibid: 136-137). He provided a rationale for discussions about what content is 'useful' to both the individual and to society and for determining knowledge content (ibid: 145). Thorndike's consideration of what knowledge is of greatest value, concludes that the most 'valuable' forms of knowledge are those which are to do with fundamental truths, with cause and principle, and those which are practical and useful. His guiding measure is that the value of knowledge is proportionate to the number of essential "..situations to which it applies" (Ibid: 145-147). In addition, by raising questions concerning how learning takes place, Thorndike also began to provide a rationale for pedagogical experimentation.

Systematic approaches to curriculum planning and pedagogy
The third of the major obstacles to reconstructionism is that it is, what Skilbeck described as, "an open thought system" (Skilbeck in Horton and Raggatt 1982: 12), and as such the social and Utopian strands may be vulnerable to political pressure and accusations of social engineering (see Lawton 1983: 9-11).

In the United States during the early part of this century, the impact of behavioural psychology and the application of an industrial systems management approach to education had some impact. As a result of a perception that 'the expansion of knowledge' was causing an over-crowding of the curriculum, the Committee for the Economy of Time was established with a brief to examine, and if necessary, reconstruct the curriculum (see Tanner and Tanner 1975). The task they were given was to examine the curriculum to identify and eliminate out of date content, specify what they considered to be the essential elements and make recommendations on content resulting from a programme of "activity-analysis" (Bobbitt 1924: 8). Bobbitt's justification for the application of industrial practices to curriculum planning was that the whole system of education was in need of logical restructuring and, since the purpose of education was to prepare the individual for working life, the nearer learning outcomes could become to occupational competencies, the more useful and relevant they would be. This argument is exemplified in the following extracts from Bobbitt:

"Because of the social changes, education must shift its ground in fundamental ways. It must perform functions which it has not hitherto attempted; and discontinue labours no longer serviceable (1924: 7) .....The plan to be employed is activity-analysis. The first step is to analyse the broad field of human experience into major fields. The lines can be drawn in any number of ways. Each curriculum making group will make the divisions that seem best to it for its purposes." (ibid: 8; see also Bobbitt in Patty 1938)

In 'How to Make a Curriculum' (1924: 1-2), Bobbitt referred to the educationist as "the educational engineer" and suggested that his task was to identify the purpose and outcomes of learning. The plan that Bobbitt formulated, involved analysis of each "field of human experience" so that it could be systematically broken down into specific activities which in turn formed the basis for learning objectives (1924: 8-9; see also Bobbitt in Patty 1938: 13). Charters and Peters advocated a similar form of mechanical curriculum construction (Patty 1938). The rationale for basing the curriculum on these particular activities is the archetypal instrumentalist one. To quote Bobbitt:

"Education is primarily for adult life, not for child life. Its fundamental responsibility is to prepare for the fifty years of adulthood, not for the twenty years of childhood and youth." (Bobbitt 1924: 8)

Advocates of the behavioural objectives method of curriculum structure often use the need for evaluation of student (and teacher) performance as a part of the argument in favour of such an approach. A particular strand of the objectives approach was concerned with systematic teaching programmes and was bound up with notions of the 'teacher or student proof' curriculum. In 'Systematic Instruction' Popham and Baker (1970) the point is made that evaluation should not simply be about the performance of students, it should also be about evaluating the quality of teaching (ibid: 89). This raises questions of accountability and the measurability of outcomes. Popham and Baker's book is intended to provide "a set of tangible competencies that can be employed by the teacher in making instructional decisions," and is organised around five self-instruction programmes (ibid: 2-3).

Popham (1969) argued that objectives which do not include a "clear description" of the intended learner behaviour or outcome, "are of almost no use to the instructor" (Popham in Popham, Eisner, Sullivan & Tyler 1969: 36). Measurability of outcomes can in such circumstances, become the acid test of whether or not certain learning experiences are more or less valid than others. There are obviously great dangers, particularly in terms of maintaining curriculum breadth and balance, if certain kinds of experiences are simply left out because of difficulty in determining the precise behavioural changes which result from a learning activity. The work of Bloom and colleagues (1956) which was influenced by that of Tyler, is potentially useful in this respect. By classifying objectives in terms of the three domains, cognitive, affective and psychomotor, and subdividing them into a more precise classification, e.g. knowledge, comprehension and application, a mechanism is provided which can, potentially at least, give some idea of where 'gaps' might exist in a programme of study.

The behavioural objectives and systems management approaches to curriculum development would seem to lend themselves to the 'centre-periphery' model of diffusion of curriculum innovation, a method popular in the United states in the nineteen sixties and seventies. (See: Glaser in Hooper et al (1971); MacDonald & Walker (1976); House (1974: ch.8); Havelock & Hubberman (1978) in respect of variations on the main models of diffusion; see also, Harland in Gleeson et al (1987: ch.3) in respect of TVEI and the diffusion of innovation).

Value and limitations of learning objectives
There are, as Bloom pointed out (1956: 13) many potential ways of classifying learning outcomes, and in choosing the taxonomy method Bloom worked to particular and precise criteria (ibid: 13-15). But the taxonomy is not simply concerned with classification of outcomes and research into measurability (ibid: 4-5), it also highlights the importance in planning curricula, of questions concerning the sequence and structure of content, so that they match the stages of the student's intellectual development. There are echoes of Tyler and Bruner in Bloom's analysis of the nature of abilities and skills (ibid: 38) and a concern that education should prepare students for change (ibid: 40). There is also a recognition of the importance of ability to apply knowledge and undertake problem solving activities (ibid: 38, 40, 41). It is evident from the extract below, that Bloom's concerns extend (to some extent) to the teaching and learning process in respect of the high level cognitive-intellectual skills, as well as the other aspects already mentioned.

> "It is to be hoped that the taxonomy's analysis of this area (development of abilities and skills) will facilitate the exploration of new methods of teaching for high-level problem solving and assist in evaluating these methods." (Ibid: 43, my brackets)

Bloom's taxonomy may be helpful in raising awareness of breadth and balance issues but it still leaves a number of important questions unanswered. For example, Eisner (1971: 171) asked whether we can assume that, because a student exhibits a certain behaviour in one situation, we can be sure that he or she will behave in precisely the same way in a different situation. He also questioned whether it is desirable or even possible for all objectives to be measurable (Eisner et al 1969: 1-28; see also Stenhouse 1975). One might ask, for example, what 'value' has creativity, imagination, originality, sympathy, empathy, experience, etc. if the criterion for judgement is based on 'measurability'. Even if such outcomes of learning can be broken down into measurable 'micro objectives', what point does the process have if the intrinsic value of the area of experience is sacrificed? (Eisner et al 1969; see also Sockett 1976: 45). Eisner suggests that a distinction needs to be made between "instructional objectives", where the outcomes of learning are precisely identified, and "expressive objectives" which describe the learning activity but are not prescriptive in terms of the desired outcomes. Eisner suggests that it is only by providing a balance of these two types of objective that the purpose of the curriculum as a whole, and of particular teachers, students, and learning situations can be met (Eisner et al 1969).

Tyler (1949) provides some advice on selecting objectives. Firstly, objectives should be concerned with the learning outcomes which are to be demonstrated by the student. Secondly, content is a vehicle through which students learn and coverage of content should not be regarded as an objective, but objectives relating to content (such as understanding and using knowledge, skills and concepts) can be. Thirdly, broad aims can often be broken down into clear objectives. According to Tyler there are two dimensions to a curriculum objective, one concerning content, the other concerning outcomes. These dimensions can be used as the axes in a planning matrix (ibid: 50), and also as an aide to selecting appropriate learning experiences, i.e. by posing the question: Given a particular objective, what would be the most appropriate and effective method of delivering content? The matrix can also be used as a means of identifying 'gaps' in the student's learning experiences (ibid: 55).

Several writers have expressed concern over the 'blanket' application of behavioural objectives in curriculum planning (see Stenhouse 1975; Eisner 1969; Sockett 1976). Sockett (1976: ch. 3) reflects Dewey's thoughts on the value of "an end in view" and the dangers of the notion of an "ultimate goal", but sees the use of objectives as an aide memoire as being useful as long as they are not elevated above that purpose. Stenhouse (1975: ch. 6 esp. 82-83) also warns of the dangers inherent in the objectives model when objectives are regarded as the ultimate goal. Other writers have explored the objectives model and attempted to identify its strengths and weaknesses. Some, like Taba, see objectives in the perspective of an holistic approach to curriculum in which they are an essential part but not the whole (1962: 422-426, 438).

Problem solving as a learning objective
Exploration of stimulus - response theory is a main feature of the work of Skinner, in particular in the development of what Skinner described as "operant conditioning" and "programmed learning" (1968: ch.4). However Skinner, like Bobbitt, had a broader vision of the purposes of education than is often imagined. In particular, some of his thoughts on the application of knowledge in problem solving activities are worthy of note (1968: 131-135). He advised that students need to be taught to recognise types of problems and select appropriate techniques (ibid: 133). He explored the "sink or swim" method of

problem solving and concluded that "students often sink". Another strategy he offered is formal teaching, but he warned that:

> "When teachers turn to direct instruction in problem solving, they are often misled by what may be called the 'Formalistic Fallacy'. To get the student to execute problem-solving behaviour it is tempting simply to show him what to do." (ibid: 133-134)

A third method he identified from the work of Polya, is "first order technique" (or association) in which the student first considers the problem, then identifies a related (similar) problem previously solved which may assist in finding a solution to the existing one. The fourth method involves learning problem solving techniques (ibid: 135). Gagne (1966) also provides one definition of what problem solving as a learning activity involves:

> "Problem solving as a method of learning requires that the learners discover the high-order principle without specific verbal help. (ibid: 164) ....."The key to achievement of a high-order principle does not lie solely in the discovery method. Nevertheless, the evidence strongly suggests that achieving a high-order principle by means of problem solving produces a highly effective capability which is well retained over considerable periods of time." (1966: 164-165)

Problem solving is important, but according to Gagne, some educators place too much emphasis on the discovery method in the belief that students can simply be taught to solve problems (see also Skinner 1966: 132), when the principal pre-requisite of problem solving strategies is the acquisition of "masses of structurally organised knowledge" (op cit: 170) and the understanding of essential principles (ibid: 167). Bantock (1968: 38) points to the value of applying knowledge through problem solving activities. He also makes the important observation that there is no reason why 'studies' and 'life' need always to be treated 'separately'. *Bernstein*

Economic and political pressures
In the previous chapter I made reference to Peters' deliberations concerning what constitutes the 'educated man', and noted above the fact that the work of Thorndike opened the door to vocationalism as much as to other aspects of education. It is probably fair to say that from time to time, governments in both Britain and in the United States, have caused 'alarm bells' to ring by appearing too instrumentalist in their education policy (Tanner & Tanner 1975: 403-409). In terms of the extent to which schools exist to service the labour market, opinions are again divided (see Jamieson in Dale et al 1985: 26-29; Lawton et al 1978: 276; 1983: 56). The conflicting demands of politicians (Young 1971: 20, 22-23), and the instrumentalist demands of industrialists for types of education which maximises investment in expensive new technologies, are increasing. As Bernstein (1971) puts it:

> "Changes in the division of labour are creating a different concept of skill. The inbuilt obsolescence of whole varieties of skills reduces the significance of context-tied operations and increases the significance of general principles from which a range of diverse operations may

be derived. In crude terms, it could be said that the nineteenth century required submissive and inflexible man, whereas the twenty-first century requires conforming but flexible man." (Bernstein 1971: 67; see also Apple 1982: 154-155)

It is arguably the case, that when education is related to productivity, i.e. certain levels of knowledge and skills which are required to ensure economic efficiency, the lack of equality of opportunity is seen only as wasted potential (see Young 1971). According to Bowles and Gintis, equality of opportunity is a myth which schools are unable to deliver (1976: 4, ch. 2; see also Apple 1982: 3, 9). An example of the evidence which supports this belief comes from studies in America which seem to show that there is little connection between schooling and economic success for blacks (ibid: 6, 88). The so-called egalitarian reforms of education have not, they claim, greatly improved real equality of opportunity for students from the lower socio-economic groups. There also appears to be little more connection between ability and economic success than between it and sex or ethnic origin (ibid: 9, 105-106, 142). They also argue that the education system underpins the capitalist economic system in four ways: (1) through a meritocratic system which allocates students a place in the vocational and social hierarchy; (2) by emphasising those aspects of personal development which relate to the hierarchical patterns which will be experienced in the world of work; (3) by reinforcing the stereotyped patterns of sex and social class; and (4) by creating a surplus of skilled labour which provides ammunition for the "..prime weapon of the employer....the power to hire and fire." (ibid: 11) They also maintain that in the search for greater equality it is "capitalism not technology or human nature that is the limiting factor." (ibid: 20; see also Apple 1982: 10, 14-15, 41-42, 44-46, 52)

Apple explored another aspect of control, that of de-skilling and re-skilling, and argued that in education it is manifest in the increased use of pre-packaged curriculum materials. These are often composed of modules with specified content, methods, outcomes, evaluation methods, and pre-determined skills levels (ibid: 144).

Motivation, curriculum relevance and vocationalism
Returning to the notion of vocational contexts in curriculum planning, it is important to note that Bobbitt's particular advocacy for the use of occupations as a basis for the curriculum is in contrast to that of Dewey, whose primary motivation in using occupations within the curriculum was twofold. Firstly, it was to try to avoid what he called the "dualism" between school and the outside world. Dewey believed that education should aim to achieve the cross-fertilisation between the disciplines which exists naturally outside the school (Dewey 1902: 6-7; 1916: 334). Secondly, he proposed the use of occupations to provide stimulus and interest for studies.

"Education *through* occupations consequently combines within itself more of the factors conducive to learning than any other method" (Dewey 1916: 361) ..."The vocation acts as both magnet to attract (information) and as glue to hold it..." (ibid: 362 my brackets) ..."The only adequate training *for* occupations is training *through* occupations." (ibid: 362)

Piaget noted the expansion of vocational elements in secondary curricula and the requirement of "..an internal enrichment of the programmes taught, so that all those who work in skilled trades will have been provided with a broad general culture scarcely different from the wide general education common to all forms of secondary education." (1970: 92)

One of the most influential advocates of vocationalism was Kirschensteiner, whose own early education was one of drudgery and rote learning ('*Georg Kirschensteiner*' Simons 1966: 3-4). To begin with he was concerned with the curriculum of the elementary school and he laid down that the education they provided should consist of three elements: knowledge and skills, physical and practical skills, and moral and religious education (ibid: 14-15). Like Dewey, whose work he came to know later, he strove for unity of experience. He was critical of the compartmentalisation and abstraction of knowledge that he had experienced, and he urged that all the elements of the curriculum should not only be inter-related, but related to real life (ibid: 16). He described two strands of development which he believed all students should experience. These were the vocational or 'pre-vocational' strand, and community education, the most important aspect of which was to provide a moral framework for the vocational element (ibid: 27, 32). He called for co-operation between the continuation schools and the academic schools to provide education for citizenship, which he considered to be the essential purpose of education (ibid: 28-29). Education he believed, should address the individual's needs as family member, and as a member of the economic, industrial and social community (ibid: 30-31).

For Kirschensteiner vocational training was the first step in the process leading towards the state of being educated (ibid: 33). Vocational training he believed, was most conducive to character training (ibid: 39) and it was the task of the educator to utilise and direct in a purposeful way, the student's "functional interests", in order to make him responsive to what was taught (ibid: 40-42). These functional interests, it would appear, are primarily associated with what Peters (1966; 1977) described as extrinsic or instrumental values. Kirschensteiner believed that by harnessing the functional interests of the individual and stressing the essential nature of altruism in productive work, even the potentially socially divisive forces of egoism could be contained (ibid: 44-45). In this regard he was a strong advocate of group activities such as co-operative projects, and of the allocation of particular responsibilities to individual students (ibid: 60-65).

He saw character development as very important and it had, he believed, four aspects: (1) will-power, which he described as having two elements the first relating to attitudes and the second to "activities and deeds" (ibid: 45); (2) judgement and the ability to think logically (3) development of the senses; and (4) the ability to see things through to their conclusion (ibid: 46-47). Kirschensteiner believed that character and skills could only be developed through purposeful activity, hence the need for relevant experiences which combined the need to apply all of the forms of will with physical, practical and intellectual skills (ibid: 48-52). His broad view of the purpose and value of vocational education extended to the belief that the young worker should also understand his rights and responsibilities. The principal purpose of the trade schools which he introduced, was to "produce good and happy workers" (ibid:

55).   Kirschensteiner also introduced a continuation school for general education, but his main concern was the orientation of students towards working life. To this end, he introduced practical work into the final year of elementary school. His influence still pervades the modern German education system (ibid: 87-88).

In more recent times Stenhouse (1967) accepted the need for specialists in a technological society but highlighted the danger of general education being seen simply as a basis for specialism (ibid: 108-110). He identified three strands of culture: (1) "vocational cultures" (2) "specialist leisure cultures", and (3) broader general cultures (ibid: 110).   They relate to: vocational effectiveness, personal development and common culture which are interwoven, and provide a "..basis for self development" (ibid: 113).

Social reconstructionism

The fourth problem for reconstructionism is that it has also been associated with wholesale rather than gradual change (see Lawton 1983).   Dewey, described by Hutchins as a "social reformer," was very clear about the role of education in society, although he is often misrepresented (see Hutchins 1952: 9-11).   Dewey described education as: "..the means of transmitting the resources and achievements of a complex society", and suggested that as the society becomes more complex, the need for formal education becomes greater.   However he also pointed out that there is a danger that formal education can become "..remote and dead" (1916: 8-10).   When Dewey was writing, the impetus for social reconstruction was generated by concern about changes taking place in the social order as a result of the development of democracy, the rapid growth of industry, and the expansion of scientific knowledge. He realised the dangers of social conflict and that reconstruction of social, political, economic and educational philosophy are inter-related (ibid: 381, 386).   Dewey nurtured a belief that a happy and cohesive school community could lead to improvements in society in general (1915: 27). The increase of scientific research into the way in which children learn, resulted in the development of 'active' and 'student centred learning', and was also significant in breaking down the traditional domination of liberal education philosophy.   It was to some extent also, a reaction against behavioural psychology, programmed learning and the Durkheimian brand of sociology.

Durkheim, one of the founding fathers of socio-educational philosophy, was concerned about the apparent breakdown of social values brought about by excessive individualism which he blamed in part on education (Fox 1956: 64, 65-71, 87). Durkheim was sceptical about the extent to which education could be influential in improving society because of the obsession with knowledge and specialism at the expense of socialisation (ibid: 120). However he believed that the teacher's "moral authority", and his ability to interpret "the great moral ideas of his time..", were the potential salvation of a homogenous society, but only if the child could be taught to respect his authority (ibid: 88-90). Durkheim realised that one of the main problems of education was its inability to respond effectively to changes in society.   He also recognised that the need for reconstruction was not a once and for all requisite and that it is not only what is taught, but also the methods of teaching, that need constant revision to ensure, or at least attempt to ensure, that the processes of education are relevant to the contemporary needs of society (ibid: see ch.4).

Democratic Reconstructionism

"Curriculum innovation appears to be a slow, uncertain and difficult process. No truly systematic method of inducing educational change has yet been found, nor, perhaps, could it be. Yet life outside the schools is not subject to these constraints. It moves ahead much more rapidly....In this view, schools become involved in preserving a form of society which has passed, or is passing away, rather than contributing actively to building the future." (Slaughter in Skilbeck 1984b: 291)

Taba (1962: 10-12) argued for a better informed and more scientific approach to curriculum development, and suggested that there are three important strands of analyses which should inform the process: (1) analysis of the society and its culture; (2) studies of learners and analysis of the learning process; (3) analysis of the nature of knowledge. It is the outcomes of such analysis which Taba believed, provide the following criteria for development: diagnosis of needs; formulation of objectives; selection of content; organisation of content; selection of the appropriate learning processes; identification of the outcomes to be evaluated and the methods of evaluation which are to be used. According to Taba: "The school is created by a society for the purpose of reproducing in the learner the knowledge, attitudes, values, and techniques that have cultural relevancy or currency." (ibid: 17) Taba recognised that education needs to be geared up to respond to changes which take place in society, by being proactive and constructive in recognising and supporting them. This she argued, is particularly important in modern industrialised societies in which rapid change is often linked to the introduction of modern technologies (ibid: 25; 231).

As indicated in chapter one, the most acute pressures for change in curriculum provision and in pedagogy in England, particularly in the late nineteen seventies and early nineteen eighties, were also linked with economic and social problems. As a result there have been many attempts by theorists and practitioners to establish new criteria for secondary education which address the perceived needs of society and students. Skilbeck for example, proposed the following aims for a contemporary curriculum. It should aim to provide:

"Highly motivating learning experiences for students of all abilities.
A thorough grounding in, and practice of, basic skills, including practical ability, and social skills.
Broad orientation courses which relate students to all aspects of the human situation and develop a sense of involvement in the affairs of mankind, past, present, local and global, as well as providing opportunities for co-operation, planning and decision making.
Opportunities for a wide range of creative and aesthetic experiences and pursuits.
Courses directed to the attainment of total health: physical, personal, social and moral.

Opportunities for individualised study designed to foster the growth of personal interests and aptitudes, as well as the experience of dedication and application." (1984b: 315)

These aims may be admirable, but three important questions need to be asked: Firstly, can we be certain that these aims are congruent with the needs of students and society? Secondly, to what extent do existing curricula address these aims? Thirdly, how do we go about finding out? Lawton (1983) suggested that cultural analysis is an appropriate starting point in the search for answers. He argues that it is important to be able to justify whatever selection from the culture we decide to make. Again important questions have to be posed such as:

a) What kind of society already exists?
b) In what ways is it developing?
c) How do its members appear to want it to develop?
d) What kind of values and principles will be involved in
    deciding on (c), and on the educational means of achieving (c)?
(Lawton 1983: 28 & Lawton in Skilbeck 1984b: 276-277).

Cultural analysis as a means of planning the curriculum

According to Lawton, the process of cultural analysis involves posing the kinds of questions outlined above. Particular importance is given to establishing the current needs of a society, to examining the existing education provision, and to establishing the extent to which it does or does not, address and provide for those needs. This process should enable identification of objectives and strategies for adjusting the existing curriculum to make it more congruent with the needs of society, while ensuring that it provides a broad range of knowledge and experiences which all students should have access to (1983: 28-29; see also Hemming in Skilbeck 1984b: 276-227). Lawton points out that in societies where change is rapid and frequent, it is easy for the curriculum to be out of step with the needs of the society. He calls this situation "cultural lag" (1983: 28; see also Slaughter in Skilbeck et al 1984b; Taba 1962). Using the cultural analysis method, the first part of the process of curriculum planning involves 'matching and mapping'. That is matching the needs of students in a particular society with the kinds of knowledge and experience required in order to realise their own potential. Any changes to the curriculum should also take account of the changes which are occurring, or are likely to occur in the near future (see Skilbeck et al 1984b). Lawton proposed a five stage model for the curriculum planning process and identified eight cultural sub-systems, described as "cultural invariants," which are characteristic of all societies. They are as follows:

1) social structure/social system;
2) economic system;
3) communication system;
4) rationality system;
5) technology system;
6) morality system;
7) belief system;
8) aesthetic system; (Lawton 1983: 31 see also 30-37).

According to Lawton these sub-systems, although identifiable as discrete elements, are dynamically interactive. The next stage of Lawton's process is to analyse the particular society in order to map its essential characteristics, using the framework of the eight sub-systems. The outcomes, "cultural variables" (ibid: 40-41) vary from society to society and from time to time. The third stage is analysis of the existing curriculum by a process of mapping and matching against the cultural profile produced in stage two. In a balanced curriculum all eight systems should be represented (1983: 38).

Lawton's planning model does not focus simply on content and coverage, it also raises the important issues of why and how, of both teacher and student actions. It addresses philosophical and psychological issues in stages four and five, and underpins them with evaluation of the quality of the education process. His analysis of existing (1983) curricula in England, revealed the following 'gaps and mismatches' in provision: Inadequacies in provision of political and social education; economics (see also Jamieson & Lightfoot 1982: 23) and communications (in the broad sense) and moral education. It also highlighted inadequacies in the provision and methods of teaching of mathematics and science, in the sense that they needed to 'less abstract' (ibid: 55-56, 57-58). He also made the following recommendations: "Technology should be part of the common curriculum; its status as a subject improved and related to other subjects.....'the arts' should be seen ...as an essential part of the curriculum for all pupils" (Ibid: 63).

Lawton recommended that the 'gaps and mismatches' needed to be addressed nationally, but he also recommended that in terms of actions, some might be better dealt with through programmes of "school-based curriculum planning" (ibid: 63). It is not uncommon for there to be a degree of cultural lag in the curricula of modern industrial and technological societies (see Taba 1962: 24, 48-50, 54, 55). However, Lawton's analysis of the technology system would appear to indicate that in England, there may also be "cultural contradictions." We have, it might be argued, developed an educational system riddled with division between for example, arts and science, and between general and vocational education. There also appears to be a deep rooted cultural problem concerning our attitudes to industry (see Wiener: 1981).

It would appear that many, if not all the educational inadequacies that concerned government in the 1970's and 80's, and which were explored briefly in chapter one, are identified in Lawton's analysis (see also Lawton 1980). Lawton suggested that some of them could be addressed through some sort of common core compulsory curriculum, which would be composed mainly of revised forms of existing subjects and the addition of some new elements (op cit: 67). However the eight systems which Lawton identified, do not map neatly onto existing curricula in the sense of a particular system being capable of delivery through one discrete subject (1983: 66-67). This implies a need for an holistic approach to curriculum planning and a broader perception of curriculum than the 'traditional subject based' one.

The new subjects required to provide a balanced curriculum, as identified by Lawton, are: politics, economics, sociology, communication studies, film and television (or media) studies, micro technology, computer studies, comparative religious studies, and ethics (1983: 67). Lawton supported Peters' view that education should not be seen simply in instrumental terms, nor should it exclude students from access through some system of meritocracy. He supported HMI in calling for a common core curriculum, with breadth and balance as an entitlement rather than being dependant on option choice (ibid: 71). He also endorsed the HMI "eight areas of experience" as an interim model pending a reform of the curriculum on the basis of cultural analysis.

Reynolds and Skilbeck (1976) provide an alternative "cultural chart or map" which could be used as a basis for such a task. They also provide a suggested list of "core areas of experience" which are:

1.   Typical work situations and modes of economic operation.
2.   Patterns of social meaning which include rules, norms of conduct, value systems and common social expectations.
3.   Introduction and practical experience of the principal human symbolic systems of language, mathematics, science, history, religion, myth, the arts.
4.   Leisure and recreational interests and opportunities.
5.   Social and political institutions.
6.   Social and political policy.
7.   Styles of interpersonal relationships and ways of handling tension and conflict.
8.   Modes of individual expression and creativity (1976: 124).

Reynolds and Skilbeck point out that this is not a curriculum but a framework of areas of experience which might inform the selection and organisation of content and learning activities (ibid: 124-125).

Curriculum content - context and relevance
Issues of context and relevance which can arise out of curriculum review almost inevitably involve some consideration of 'vocational education', as was indicated earlier. Almost as inevitable, is the argument concerning what vocational education is or is not. There would appear to be at least three schools of thought regarding this issue. On the one hand there are those who believe that education should address the need for trained manpower and a skilled and competitive work-force. Ideally, education would in this case produce students trained in specialist skills and competencies (see Tanner and Tanner 1975: 525-547). In practice, in an advanced industrial society there is, as Peters pointed out, "..a limit to the amount of direct vocational preparation that can go on at school" (Peters 1977: 76). Perhaps Kirschensteiner's work in Munich is most notable as the pioneering influence for vocational education in schools.

In an earlier section of this chapter the work of Kirschensteiner was explored as was his rationale for vocational activities. It had some commonalty with the work of Dewey, who he became aware of some time after embarking on his own programme. Even earlier however, Pestalozzi had attempted to establish one of the few examples of an industrial school. The school at Neuhof was Pestalozzi's dream of a self-supporting school. The idea was to combine learning with occupations, but the intention was more to do with providing revenue to support the school, which was for poor and neglected children, than for vocational training. He did however, recognise the educational value of the occupations and saw them as a means to develop certain generic skills even though, in his early days as a teacher, he had opposed vocationalism ('The Educational Ideas of Pestalozzi' Green 1911). Since, as Peters pointed out, truly vocational courses have until recently been rare in our schools, links with business and industry often take other forms. World of work contexts for learning experiences might be an example. Lawton (1983) agreed that young people in our society should be given the opportunity to understand the economic system and that the curriculum should facilitate students' introduction to, and preparation for, 'the world of work'. He also agreed that the curriculum should "go some way" towards helping them to acquire some of the generic skills which might help them gain employment, but he could not concur with the notion that the principal task of the school is to supply industry with trained manpower (ibid: 55-56).

"However, a distinction needs to be made between the general education of the young which would include developing attitudes and skills which would help in earning a living in a variety of occupations, and narrow vocational training (including attitudes) which would slot school-leavers into specific jobs. There is also a difference between sensibly adjusting the school curriculum to match economic and industrial changes (for example, by developing computer studies or micro-technology), and allowing the curriculum to be dominated by the supposed 'needs of industry'." (Lawton 1983: 56)

Bobbitt (1924), while emphasising that vocational training should be specific, perhaps somewhat surprisingly also maintained that: "Never will a subject be placed in the general training for all persons simply because of its specialised value for certain occupations." (ibid: 67) Dewey was also concerned that, by gearing education too closely to the needs of industry, it may lose its capacity to effect change.

"Put in concrete terms, there is a danger that vocational education will be interpreted in theory and practice as trade education: as a means of securing technical efficiency in specialised future pursuits. Education would then become an instrument of perpetuating unchanged the existing industrial order of our society, instead of operating as a means of its transformation." (Dewey 1916: 369)

Dewey, who believed in the use of occupations, warned that we should avoid a narrow interpretation of the concept of vocation, and the notion of one vocation for each individual. He saw the value of occupations being in their ability to interest and motivate students: "The problem is not that of making the schools an adjunct to manufacture and commerce, but of utilising the factors of industry to make school life more active, more full of immediate meaning, more connected with out-of-school experience." (Dewey 1916: 369; see also Dewey 1902: 6-7).

Another view is that schools can and indeed should, provide a good general education which gives scope for all types of ability to be developed. It should include practical and social skills, with particular emphasis on generic skills such as communications and numeracy. Through this approach the "..specialists select themselves." (Hemming in Skilbeck et al 1984b: 309). Advocates of this kind of broad brush approach to education often argue that all education is vocational (see Dewey 1916 : 364). Dewey was concerned about the danger of 'dualism' through having an academic / vocational divide and saw the need for an holistic approach to education. He advocated "..integration in action of the conflicting various interests in life." (ibid: 381)

Eisner (1971: 171-172) highlighted the need for a curriculum that is seen as relevant by students, and adapts to changes in relationships between students and teachers as the former demand more say in what and how they learn. (see also Eisner *'Learning and Teaching the Ways of Knowing'* 1985: xi). Both parents and students, he suggests, demand the relevance, skills and opportunity for personal development that provide social mobility. Students are "....entitled to encounter educational programmes that result from the application of the most sophisticated tools that we have available" (ibid: 162-164). He suggests that in terms of evaluating student learning, a range of more varied and sophisticated methods need to be employed, some of which would require that both the school curriculum and environment become closer, in terms of contexts, to the situations which the student is likely to encounter in the world outside school (ibid: 171-172).

A third view would be that there is some value in providing different types of curricula for students of differing abilities and aptitudes. Perhaps as in the case of Bantock, for different social groupings. Hargreaves (1982), whilst not endorsing the latter, did suggest that there was some value in the tripartite schools*. The notion of different types of education for students of differing 'abilities' is by no means new or exclusively English. Pestalozzi attached great importance to physical occupations and their value in terms of learning activities, and to the importance of linking the occupations of students with their likely occupations in life, so as to avoid disadvantaging them in terms of employment. This, he believed, was as true of upper- class students as of those from the working-class, and while the former may not need manual skills, they ought to know about them. In fact at Yverdun the children did engage in some manual work (*'The Educational Ideas of Pestalozzi'* Green 1911: 128-129). Comenius also advocated one school for the 'academic' student and another for the potential artisan (Comenius in Keatinge 1910).

There can be little argument that in a modern industrial society, educational institutions and systems need to be examined against extrinsic as well as intrinsic considerations, so that for example, social requirements such as the need for trained manpower, are considered alongside other criteria such as the value of particular forms of knowledge (see Peters 1977: 42). Equally, it could be argued that a purely instrumental approach to education which results in narrow specialisation, could not provide the breadth and balance required for

----

See Pedley (1964) & Passow (1961) for information and comment on the types and roles of schools in the tripartite system of English education, see also Norwood (1929). N.B. Parry (1971) suggests that it was 'two-sided' rather than three.

education to be congruent with all the needs of society as revealed in the kind of cultural analysis undertaken by Lawton and others (Lawton 1983; 1986; Skilbeck 1984b).

Summary

In this chapter I have briefly explored some aspects of the society centred curriculum. In terms of the organisation of content, it might be argued that the 'society centred curriculum' does not lean as heavily on the disciplines as the 'knowledge centred curriculum' (Hargreaves 1982; Lawton 1983; Reynolds & Skilbeck 1976). Using Lawton's classification I highlighted the main curriculum issues associated with reconstructionism. Utopian reconstructionism was mentioned only briefly since it would seem to be at odds with our contemporary society and culture. In terms of education as social reconstruction, the 'authoritarian' approach of Durkheim, the 'cultural values' approach of Bantock, and the 'socialisation / co-operation' approach of Hargreaves, were explored briefly. In the case of the latter, the importance of the community as a focus for the curriculum of all students was noted. Other important aspects of Hargreaves work will be explored in chapter eight.

The holistic approach of Dewey to social reconstruction was also mentioned. The influence of social change was noted in the work of Dewey, and the potential of education to influence such change was highlighted in his philosophy and in the contrasting approach of Durkheim. Also briefly noted, was the notion of curriculum change geared to instrumental values and a 'systems management approach' to the problem of 'curriculum overload', in the context of which, the work of Bobbitt was highlighted.

The third form of reconstructionism, what Lawton described as "democratic reconstructionism," was also examined. Lawton's work addressed the problems of curricula as they existed in the early nineteen eighties. Not only did it provide a framework for curriculum analysis, it made explicit reference to gaps and mismatches in existing provision. Taba and Skilbeck have both suggested that all societies prone to rapid change should ensure that they have education systems which are permanently geared to adapting to change and which are proactive in shaping and supporting cultural change. In exploring the place of vocationalism in the curriculum, the three strands: training, relevance, and motivation were identified. Kirschensteiner's work is particularly significant in these respects. Dewey's view of the vocations as contexts which provide motivation is also important in terms of this study. It is a concept which was seen to have contemporary support in Taba, Skilbeck and Lawton.

The "core areas of experience" identified by Reynolds and Skilbeck, provide guidance for monitoring the provision of opportunities through which students can develop a broader range of competencies than might be provided through a purely knowledge based curriculum. In this sense they suggest a more student centred approach to curriculum organisation and delivery. It is student-centred approaches to curriculum planning that will be explored in chapter eight.

Chapter Eight

The student and the curriculum

Since references to Plato were used as starting points for the previous chapters, it is perhaps appropriate to begin this chapter in the same way. Plato was primarily concerned with development of the soul which is indisputably, in Plato's terms, the essence of the individual. But there are other aspects to his recognition of the importance of developing the whole person (see *'The Laws Bk. VII'*) and to making the process of learning a good and natural experience. In the following extract from *'The Republic'* he makes it clear that the teacher should make learning a pleasure not a chore.

> "Because, I said, the free man should learn no study under bondage. And while enforced labours do no harm to the body, study forced on the mind will not abide there.... Then my excellent friend, train your children in their studies not by compulsion, but by games, and you will be better able to see the natural abilities of each." (Ibid: *'Book VII'* 536-537)

In acknowledging the importance of educating 'the whole man', Plato recognised that it is not only the intellect that should be developed and nurtured, but also the body and the senses, so that gymnastics, music, ethics and morals should also be addressed (see *'Book II'*, 412, *'Book VI'* 503, *'Book VII'* 521-522).

The student centred approach as idealism

Rousseau is generally regarded as the father figure of the child centred approach to education. Although he might be criticised for his over idealistic even romantic notions concerning the innocence and purity of childhood, and for his advocacy of certain approaches to teaching (see Rousseau's *'Emile'* Foxley 1911: 176,-178, 180), his work did influence others who combined the spirit of his teaching with more 'scientific' approaches to investigating the development of intellect and pedagogy.

Pestalozzi, like Rousseau, was concerned with the important relationship between the teacher and the child. He advocated that the first instruction should appeal to the heart not the head, and that "..it is for a long time (the) business of the woman before it becomes the business of the man." (Pestalozzi translated by Green 1911: 143) Rousseau was particularly concerned with the need for the individual to come to know and understand himself and his feelings before being introduced to the adult world. For Emile the path to adulthood was gradual and natural, a path which Rousseau believed was not permitted by most teachers, who saw only an end product "the man within the boy". Methods of teaching which take no heed of natural progression and maturity were he believed, likely to result in a lack of morality and concern for one's fellow man.

> "I have always observed that young men, corrupted in early youth and addicted to women and debauchery, are inhuman and cruel; their passionate temperament makes them impatient, vindictive and

angry; their imagination fixed on one object only, refuses all others; mercy and pity are alike unknown to them....... A young man, on the other hand, brought up in happy innocence, is drawn by the first stirrings of nature to the tender and affectionate passions; his warm heart is touched by the sufferings of his fellow-creatures."
(Rousseau's *'Emile'* Foxley 1911: 181-182)

Pestalozzi also had fears that as the child comes into contact with the outer world, it is possible for egoism to dominate his relationship with others: "Egoistic feelings and bad examples may now choke the germs of good just stimulated into promising life." (*'The Educational Ideas of Pestalozzi'* Green 1911: 138) The importance of Rousseau's message is the emphasis it places on compatibility between what is taught and the child's own stages of development, and on the learning activities being natural rather than forced. Pestalozzi's approach was influenced by Rousseau and he too built his work on the notion of natural and gradual development, arguing that the most effective method of teaching is "nature's way" (ibid: 105), and that all teaching should be congruent with the child's stages of development.

"Everything which the child has to learn must be proportioned to his strength." (ibid: 106) "If the psychological moment has been found, he will learn in a month what otherwise might take years." (Ibid: 111)

The school was for Pestalozzi, both the source and the testing place of his pedagogical theory. Although Dewey's school in Chicago is probably the best known attempt to establish an 'experimental school', it was Pestalozzi who first realised the need for a more scientific approach to investigating the process of learning and of the importance of psychology. During his time at Burgdorf he applied the principle of observation as the basis for acquiring all knowledge and of developing, not only the powers of observation, but also concentration and memory (ibid: 57). His ideal school was a place where, for both the teacher and the children, education was living (ibid: ch.2). At Stanz he sought to define and apply the fundamental principals of education and instruction which he saw as, structured learning activities taught in a psychologically ordered sequence. A report on his work indicated that the simplicity and effectiveness of his methods was remarkable (ibid: 48). He attached great importance to the link between physical activities and learning and he believed that there is value in linking the learning activities of students with their likely occupations (ibid: 128-129).

Early work on intellectual development and learning through 'activity'
Froebel, like Dewey, had an holistic view of education and, like Rousseau, he had an idealistic love of childhood. The two main themes which ran through his work were the nature of childhood, and idealism. He was also influenced by the work of Pestalozzi (*'Froebel's Chief Writings'* Fletcher & Welton 1912: 17; see also *'Froebel'* translated by Green 1911; 171-172) but although he admired him, he did not find the activities at the school in Yverdun as coherent as he had imagined. Even though he was impressed by Pestalozzi's enthusiasm and the simplicity and naturalness of his methods, he was also aware of deficiencies (ibid: 14). He believed that harnessing the interests of the child through active pursuits such as those inherent in the use of the 'gifts' and 'occupations', was

the way to tackle the problems of interest, motivation and coherence. In Froebel's terms, true education is a "..self directed process" which requires "..unity with all things but particularly with nature." The natural method of instruction in a subject he claimed, "..is to be found within the subject itself". According to Froebel, the purpose of good education and teaching is to enable the individual to find "freedom", "self-determination", "free-will" and "inner love." (see ibid: 16,17,18)

Although he admired him, he did not allow Rousseau's romanticism to detract him from his own doctrine on the need for structure and discipline in the pursuit of learning. Not only did he recognise the importance of active learning, but also the need for the individual to be trained to be resolute and purposeful in his endeavours (ibid: 18-.20, & 31-32). He also believed that learning needs to be stimulated and guided if it is to be effective. His method was to build on the notion of natural progression stimulated by tasks and activities structured and sequenced to harmonise with the child's own stages of physical and intellectual development. In many ways his approach was much like that of Pestalozzi, but he emphasised the inter-connectedness of learning experiences and the relationship between the child and his environment (ibid: 26, see also 49-62, 97, 111). He stressed the importance of nature, which he believed holds the key to learning, and the need for children to understand the laws of nature and the ways in which natural phenomena are inter-dependant and in balance with each other.

His teaching embodied a belief that the study of all subjects, like the study of nature, should first involve a conceptual awareness of the nature and structure of what is to be learned (ibid: 123-127). His philosophy is well illustrated in the following extract from his own work which also reflects his belief that there are many complementary aspects to education: "It must give and take, unite and divide, be directive and adaptable, active and passive, definite and flexible, firm and yielding." (ibid: 34-35) His 'intuitive-experimental' approach has been underpinned by more contemporary studies of the nature of knowledge and of the stages of intellectual development (see Piaget: 1971). Froebel applied this principle to his advocacy of the 'gifts', which employ the same sensual responses as may be applied to natural objects like stone and wood. As he progressed through the 'gifts' and 'occupations', the learner began to associate the objects with perceptions of shape, form and words. This experience he believed, provided the basis for studies in the "three elementary subjects" (see ibid: 84-85).

The beginnings of a more scientific approach to pedagogical development
In 'The Child and the Curriculum' (1902), Dewey echoed the concern of Rousseau about the educator who simply sees the child as an "immature being who is to be matured" (ibid: 8) and who sees it as the duty of the teacher to give and that of the student to receive, through a form of pedagogy which might now be described as subject or teacher centred. He contrasted this with a view of the educator who sees the child as "the centre" or the "starting point", and the student's own development as the principal objective. In such an approach the subjects studied are useful only in so far as they provide one means of organising knowledge, skills and experiences which will enable learning to take place (ibid: 7-9; see also Taba 1962: 391- 392). Dewey pointed to another

danger which arises when the curriculum separates the activities of the school from the world outside. This "dualism" in terms of experience he suggests, is tantamount to the teacher telling the child that "..life is petty" (ibid: 7). The way in which the school curriculum selects, compartmentalises and excludes certain knowledge and experiences, is contrary to everyday living according to Dewey. He was particularly concerned that educators often see the 'disciplines' as being the only means by which knowledge can be organised, and urged that they reconsider the organisation of subject-matter so that it takes on a structure and context which is both integrated and meaningful to the student (ibid: 11).

> "....cease thinking of the child's experience as also something hard and fast; see it as something fluent, embryonic, vital; and we realise that the child and the curriculum are simply two limits which define a single process." (ibid: 11)

He warned of the dangers of objectives which are fixed and may be seen as ultimate goals, thereby dictating the direction of the learning. He contrasted these with objectives which are "an end in view" to guide both teacher and taught through learning experiences that are responsive to the student's needs (ibid: 12-18). In more recent times a similar view has been expressed by Stenhouse (1975: 82-83). Dewey was particularly concerned about the way students are often expected to 'absorb' knowledge. "That education is not an affair of 'telling' and being told, but an active and constructive process, is a principle almost as generally violated in practice as conceded in theory." (Dewey 1916: 46; see also Piaget 1971: 71-72) He gave much thought to the problem of dualism and to the related issues of relevance, interest and motivation, and as is clear from the extract which follows, he recognised the need for knowledge to have a context rather than to be abstract and for the context to be one to which the student could relate. He recognised that problems of structure and sequence are often caused by the presentation of abstract knowledge which in turn, can result in the introduction of concepts at a point in the learning programme which is not congruent with the intellectual development and experience of the student. In such circumstances, content is sometimes missed out or reorganised in such a way as to reduce difficulty. Elimination of content in this way can obscure the conceptual structure of the subject.

> "If, once more the "old education" tended to ignore the dynamic quality, the developing force inherent in the child's present experience, ... the "new education" is in danger of taking the idea of development in altogether too formal and empty a way. The child is expected to "develop" this or that fact or truth out of his own mind. He is told to think things out, or work things out for himself, without being supplied any of the environing conditions which are requisite to start and guide thought. Nothing can be developed from nothing;.... The problem of direction is thus the problem of selecting appropriate stimuli for instincts and impulses which it is desired to employ in the gaining of new experience." (Dewey 1902: 17-18)

Dewey was also aware that when motivation is lacking, the teacher often resorts to even less effective methods (ibid: 22-30). It was through the use of 'occupations' as relevant contexts for learning that, Dewey believed, motivation and interest could be secured (see Dewey 1915: 131-137). Unlike many of those who followed him, Dewey recognised that a planned curriculum is essential and that teachers should think of teaching as a science and not simply as a process of instruction. "Every study or subject has two aspects; one for the scientist as a scientist; the other for the teacher as a teacher." (1902: 22)

Thorndike also believed that education should become a science and that psychology, if it became as rigorous as the physical sciences, could provide information by which the learning processes could be better understood. Like others he wanted to be able to ensure that teaching methods assist rather than hinder the learning process. He also believed that the teaching process itself should be evaluated in order to be improved. However his views on the ways in which a more scientific approach could improve the pedagogical process were substantially different to those of Dewey. Firstly, he believed it would enable the specification of more precise and measurable objectives and secondly, that the study of learning processes would enable the identification of new objectives ('Psychology and the Science of Education: Selected Writings of Edward L. Thorndike' Jonich 1962: 6, 8, 12-13).

Thorndike's interest was in the learning process, particularly the development of intelligence, and more particularly in devising scientific methods by which to analyse individual changes in intelligence and thereby, identify the most effective conditions for learning (ibid: 12-14 see also Skinner 1968: 95). He was not part of the progressive movement in education but his work did have some compatible aspects. He did for example, recommended special provision for children at either end of the ability range (ibid: 20). His work revealed what he believed was the futility of having equal expectations of all students, and that the implementation of pedagogical strategies aimed at achieving such expectations actually increased differences in levels of achievement (ibid: 20). It did however, give strength to the notion of addressing the individual needs of students, in particular of first determining where the student is in terms of intellectual development before commencing a teaching and learning programme.

Stenhouse (1975) made the point that good teachers are perceptive to both what is happening in terms of the learning situation and to the needs of the student, and are able to adapt in order take advantage of learning opportunities which arise either intentionally or unintentionally. This is also a restatement of Dewey's idea of the way in which the good teacher operates. Stenhouse, in a similar way to that which Dewey also envisaged, saw the way of progress in curriculum and pedagogical terms as being through empowering the teacher to become a researcher in the classroom. "It is not enough that teachers' work should be studied, they need to study it themselves." (ibid: 143) He recognised that his idea of research-based teaching may be optimistic and that there are tensions between the two roles of teaching and researching, but he saw the development of a research tradition which informs and feeds the teaching process as essential if education is to be significantly improved.

Motivation and interpretations of 'active learning'

Dewey, like Pestalozzi and Froebel, was interested in how children learn and the ways in which teachers can maximise the individual's capacity and desire to learn. Dewey (1902) believed that the teacher should guide and focus the child's natural instinct to be active, into constructive and purposeful learning activities. The challenge for education he argued, is to guide learning activities in order to give them direction. Education should be an active process involving reconstruction, investigation and discovery. Dewey believed that problems of discipline occur when students are forced into a passive role (1916: ch.13, 14).

Piaget (1971) pointed out that experiments with children have shown that when a learning activity takes the form of a reconstruction carried out by the learner, learning is more effective than when it is a reconstruction carried out by the teacher and simply watched by the learner. He was concerned about interpretations of "active" learning and pointed out that there are two common misconceptions. The first is that activity on the part of the learner has to be physical activity. The second is that physical activity has a low value in terms of intellectual development. In fact there are two kinds of activity, the physical type and the cognitive type, the latter of which includes activities such as reflection (ibid: ch.4, esp 71-72).

Piaget could see no reason why learning activities cannot be active and enjoyable rather than tedious, as in the rote learning of abstract knowledge, nor any reason why activity on the part of the student should threaten the authority of the teacher. However he did recognise that active methods are more demanding than didactic ones: "...the best methods are also the most difficult ones" (ibid: 68-71). He pointed out that for active methods to be effective, the teacher needs to have an understanding of human intellectual development, so that activities are designed to be congruent with the learner's stages of development. Piaget was also very conscious of the need for studies to be relevant to the student's needs and interests, and pointed out the value of sociology in informing the pedagogical process (ibid: 68-71).

Tyler (1949) also emphasised the value of both the psychology and philosophy of education. He defined the learning experience as "..the interaction between the learner and the external conditions in the environment to which he can react", and he endorsed the view that the most effective learning takes place through activity (ibid: 63). There is however, a potential danger that Hemming cautions against, which is that of seeing active learning as the only worthwhile method (Hemming in Skilbeck 1984b). He points out that: "...precision teaching is an element in the learning of any skill." (ibid: 310) However he is equally clear about the value of practical investigation and concerned that much good practice which takes place in primary schools, is lost in the secondary phase.

> "Practical competence grows from the knowledge of how things work, partly gained from explanation and partly from active manipulation of components. A curious anomaly of education as it exists at present is that, whereas putting things together and making them work is a common experience of children at the infant stage, such practices may drop right out of later education. This omission should be remedied." (ibid: 310)

According to Taba, the traditional curriculum based on the disciplines, ran aground in the 1920's. It was attacked by the 'progressives' for failing to motivate students, primarily because of the tendency to encourage the teaching of abstract knowledge and the emphasis it placed on 'training the mind'. She claimed that contributory causes were its neglect of the other aspects of education such as creativity, learner autonomy, and the student's own interests, plus lack of relevance and opportunities to apply knowledge (1962: 387-393). However progressivism was also in part, a reaction to the excesses of behaviourist psychology (for example see Dewey 1916: ch.3) and the nineteenth century view of the purpose of education as being to impart discipline and civilisation (see Lawton in Gordon 1981: 13). This view is clearly indicated in the following extract from *'Matthew Arnold and the Education Of The New Order'*:

"I think I shall get interested in the schools after a little time; their effects on the children are so immense, and their future effects in civilising the next generation of the lower classes, who, as things are going, will have most of the political power of the country in their hands, may be so important." (Smith & Summerfield 1969: 9)

A very generalised over-simplification of progressivism might be that it was a romantic pedagogy, rooted in a belief in the purity and innocence of childhood which, its advocates believed, should be preserved for as long as possible (see Rousseau's *'Emile'*, Foxley 1911: 178). It also embraced the idea that the child is best educated through gentle guidance which supports the natural processes of development and self expression. However it is often this simplistic perception which becomes the stick with which to beat progressivism. In addition, the more extreme notions of curriculum postulated by teachers who purport to be progressive, has often been used out of context by those who would hold teachers to account and is in such circumstances, proposed as the cause of 'falling standards'. Barzun (1959) held a particularly strong view on what he saw as the failure of 'progressive' methods of teaching. In fact the Progressive Education Association was founded in 1919 and by the mid 1920's the more extravagant interpretations of the philosophy were becoming discredited (Tanner & Tanner 1975: 246-247 251).

The importance of psychology in the development of the student centred curriculum

Pedagogical research into the way intelligence and cognitive development takes place. has been rather more fruitful and has explored two particular avenues of interest, cognitive psychology and behavioural psychology, the latter of which was briefly explored in the previous chapter.

Herbart (1776-1841) has been credited with being the first to attempt to organise content so that it was congruent with the child's stages of intellectual development (Williams 1910: 118). He saw the primary purpose of education as the development of morality and was equally clear that it was not for vocational training (ibid: 65). He was as dismissive of passive learning as he was of the value in learning "unrelated facts" (ibid: 68). He valued individuality and was at pains to insist that such qualities should not be lost as a result of what he considered, was the essential need for a breadth of learning experiences. (ibid: 75 see also ibid: 68)   He described learning as the combining of "many-sidedness" and "individuality" which together develop strength of character (ibid: 77). Herbart described balance as encompassing six fields of interest: empirical, speculative, aesthetic, sympathetic, social and religious. He explained the learning process in terms of "formal steps" which are: clearness, association, system and method.   They are sometimes interpreted as: preparation, presentation, comparison, generalisation and application (ibid: 95, 99; see also 114-115, & 116-118; Mulliner 1898: cx-cxii)

Piaget (1971: 147) suggested that the breakthrough in the development of modern methods of pedagogy were a result of the development of "genetic psychology" which took place at the turn of the last century.   He noted particularly, the work of Hall, Baldwin, and the Dewey's in the United States, and the work of their contemporaries in Europe, including Montessori's study of the behaviour patterns of what Piaget called 'backward' children. He pointed to the work of Decroly, the German school of child psychology and pedagogy, and in Switzerland the work of Groos on the importance of play in normal development, an aspect that Piaget also addressed (ibid: 155-157).   Also important was the work of Claparede on progression from learning through physical activity, to the ability to conceptualise (ibid: 146-148, 166-167).   In 'Science of Education and the Psychology of the Child', Piaget explored the value of psychology in experimental pedagogy and came to the conclusion that if the research is concerned with the processes of learning, i.e. the how and why questions, then psychology becomes important (1971: 20-24; see also Bruner 1966: 21).

Bruner's work built on that of Piaget and gave it a practical as well as a theoretical dimension (e.g. MACOS Bruner 1966: 73-101). His investigations into the processes of learning included, as had Piaget's, studies of children with learning difficulties, and like Piaget, he also offers guidance on the stages of intellectual development (1966: 5-6).   Possibly his most telling conclusion regarding learning problems is that they may well be more to do with how students are taught than a lack of 'ability' (1972: 52-58). He blamed such outcomes on a lack of pedagogical skills and failure to apply the outcomes of psychological investigations. Bruner suggested that what is needed is a "theory of instruction" and he provided a model (1966: ch.3). He developed this further and addressed the issue of problem solving, and the value of intuition as a learning strategy, particularly when encountering new experiences (1966: 66-67). It is this schematic which makes Bruner so difficult to place in terms of influence, since on the one hand we have his work on MACOS which presents both teacher and student with a very open ended situation, while the theory outlined briefly above, appears to relate closely to the behaviourist approach to teaching and learning. In 'The Process of Education', (1961: ch.3) he explored the notion of a "spiral curriculum". The spiral curriculum according to Bruner, "respects the ways of thought of the growing child" by providing opportunities to explore the same concepts in different contexts at various stages in his development (ibid: 52-54). Thus, the learner is not only more likely to acquire concepts, but also to have the opportunity to apply them.

Breadth and balance and the development of skills and competencies
Tyler (1949) considered some examples of common types of learning objectives and the characteristics of learning experiences which might address them. The first type of objectives relate to thinking skills, others are associated with personal, social, communication, and information handling skills, etc. He explained in some detail how each can be broken down into specific objectives, the way they inter-relate, and the methods (learning activities) which might be appropriate. These include teaching strategies which are intended to develop learning and other skills, as well those with the objective of bringing about attitudinal change.

Taba (1962) believed that it was necessary to provide greater opportunity for students to achieve "autonomous" and "productive thinking" by focusing attention on the essential principles and key concepts which give structure to the learning, and to the student's modes of thought (see also Hirst in Hooper et al 1971: 244). This she argued, requires teachers to improve their organisation of content and the methods by which they teach it (ibid: 71-72). Taba also made clear how essential she believed it is for students to have greater opportunity for inquiry, discovery and experimentation (ibid: 71; see also Stenhouse 1975: 91-92). Taba re-stated the Deweyan thesis concerning contradictions in what we expect of young people, in particular the dichotomy between the need for creativity and individuality on the one hand, and conformity on the other. This she suggests, puts pressure on the curriculum, the school and the teacher (1962: 71). She called for a better balance between conformity and individuality and warned that when the emphasis is on the former, individuality and creativity are suppressed. A result of this is that students can develop negative attitudes towards their own abilities (ibid: 72-74; see also Hargreaves 1982).

Hargreaves (1982) proposed a curriculum which encourages the development of a broad range of skills and does not focus on cognitive-intellectual development to the exclusion of other abilities (ibid: 55). He stressed the need for a curriculum which values community spirit as highly as individuality (ibid: 134-135; see also Midwinter 1973: chapters 5, 6), and which meets the needs of students from every strata of society (ibid: 128-130). He called for a 'core curriculum' that motivates students and provides a wide range of experiences which are unconstrained by traditional subject boundaries and public examinations (ibid: 128-130), and which keeps options open for as long as possible (ibid: 164). He was concerned about the emphasis on 'subjects' rather than an holistic approach to the curriculum, on 'individuality' at the expense of 'community', and on cognitive intellectual skills at the expense of other important types of skills. He also warned against the dangers of discarding what is good in the search for something better, and against the notion of a curriculum based on working class culture. Hargreaves recommended that we look again at the progressives and their emphasis on caring for all the needs of the individual rather than just the intellectual ones. He called for a curriculum that is more flexible than the subject-based one, and which addresses real life issues and the need for changes in values in order to place community before individuality (ibid: 55, ch. 4, 118-119, 137-143).

Although in many ways they were fields apart in philosophy, it is an interesting thought that Bobbitt shared with Hargreaves, a recognition of the value of 'personal, and social development (as well as vocational' development) which he described as the "major fields of human experience". Within these broad areas of experience, he suggested a programme which should include language and religion, social and health activities, citizenship and parenthood. He also proposed activities which promote physical and mental fitness, and recreational and other non subject specific, or non vocational activities and interests (1924: 8-9, see also Peters C.C. in Patty 1938: 146).

The secondary school curriculum that Hargreaves proposed had three elements: a compulsory core of community studies and expressive arts (ibid: 128) which would account for about 50% of the time (ibid: 163) "remedial" options designed to improve students' access to the core or extend aspects of it, and an element devoted to special interests and studies (ibid: 163-164). The core he proposed, would contain elements of the traditional subjects but not be constrained by them (ibid: 163-164). Courses, he suggested, should cross subject boundaries and be organised in short specific units aimed at improving motivation (ibid: 164). He also argued that not only should all public exams at sixteen-plus be discarded (ibid: 163), but some aspects of the "optional curriculum", such as inter-school sports and residential experience should, because of their personal and social value, become part of the compulsory core (ibid: 158-159).

In Hargreaves' plan, students at fifteen-plus would choose either an academic route to 'A' levels, or a programme of vocationally relevant subjects and courses leading to vocational or academic examinations, or to more specific vocational courses (ibid: 165). The third year of such courses would be geared to preparation for leaving school (ibid: 165). Hargreaves countered the accusation that his plan would lead to falling standards, by suggesting that while cognitive intellectual skills might not reach the same level as in the current system, by the age of fifteen there would probably be an overall improvement in a broader range of skills. He also argued that it was his belief that the three year course to advanced examinations would ensure that standards of 'A' level examinations would not be adversely effected (ibid: 170-174). The real problem of low attainment according to Hargreaves, is not lack of ability but of motivation, which he believed, better curriculum balance would improve (ibid: 171).

Cognitive development - creativity and sensory perception, and the importance of curriculum breadth and balance
Hargreaves' concern, just as Durkheim's had been earlier, was that there was too much emphasis on individuality and not enough on co-operative and community focused learning experiences. Stenhouse on the other hand, described the purpose of education as being to initiate the young person into the culture and to ensure that it supports his individuality and creativity (1967: 10; see also Bantock 1968). Stenhouse, like Hargreaves, also believed that most schools fail to "..generate and transmit a culture which is relevant to the lives of the majority" (ibid: 12). He pointed out that the culture can trap and stifle individuality and creativity as well as enhance it. In stressing the importance of language as a means of internal as well as external

communication, he seems to be very much in tune with Eisner (see Stenhouse 1967: 3; Eisner 1982).

It is the forms which "inner language" takes that produce our individuality and creativity (ibid: 33). Stenhouse argued that it is also the culture which establishes the "critical standards" that help to shape our own creativity. Education's role therefore, is to encourage our "creative impulses" and our "critical reflexes" (ibid: 37) and by doing so it can encourage us to explore, rather than reject, the unfamiliar (ibid: 38-39). Creativity is important because it can influence as well as stimulate and develop our thinking and enable us to shape our subjective responses. It also creates and enriches the culture, as well as communicating it (ibid: 100). Through art for example, we can explore both the real and the unreal from a multiplicity of perspectives (ibid: ch. 4).

Stenhouse considered the practical subjects to be essential, since they provide the means by which the individual can express himself creatively in "concrete forms". Like Hargreaves, Stenhouse pointed out that the expressive arts can encourage co-operation and group activity, and that they are also to be valued for their importance in developing an important range of skills, not least, those associated with creativity and manual dexterity. In addition they give form to our creative impulses and assist in the liberation of our individuality (ibid: 104-105). He rejected the simplistic notion that the non-academically inclined student is automatically more likely to be happy with an education that concentrates on skills rather than concepts, and on technical education rather than on creativity (ibid: 114-121). Stenhouse was very clear about the need for skills to be developed in meaningful contexts, and advocated the use of off-site experience and flexible timetable arrangements, which would support opportunities for curriculum enhancement (ibid: 129, 133,138).

Like Hargreaves, he saw the social interaction, which the curriculum can bring about, as an essential part of the educational experience of all students. He was critical of the 'grammar school curriculum' (ibid: 57; 63) and proposed an alternative concept that of the curriculum as culture rather than knowledge. Such a curriculum, he envisaged, would be explored through learning activities which emphasise group interaction and creativity (ibid: 98-99). Stenhouse believed that creativity is achievable in all areas of the curriculum, but stressed that in order to become creative within the 'academic disciplines', the individual must first reach the highest levels of understanding (ibid: 106).

The complexity of cognition
Cognitive-intellectual skills are complex, and the relationship between creativity and cognition is particularly complex (see Bloom et al 1956, Tanner & Tanner 1975: 122-123). Messick (1976) explored cognitive styles in relation to individuality in learning. Cognitive "styles" refers to the ways in which individuals organise and process information. According to Messick there are two broad styles: field-dependant and field-independent. Field-dependant cognitive preferences are associated with contextual information and social interaction, whereas field-independent cognitive preference is associated with analytical tasks and differentiation between objects and contexts (ibid: 5). Differences in cognitive styles may also manifest themselves in abilities and preferences for certain curriculum disciplines, for example mathematics in the

case of 'field-independent' students, who may be inclined towards "intrinsic motivation" and less inclined towards discovery methods of learning. The opposite may be true of 'field-dependant' students who may also prefer arts subjects.

Messick and his colleagues argue that cognitive styles have implications for both teachers and students (ibid: 60-65) Studies they claim, have shown that teachers and students who share cognitive styles are generally more compatible than opposites (ibid: 63). Wapner suggests that creative and independent thinking is encouraged when teacher and student have opposite cognitive styles (ibid: 78). Messick also believes that cognitive styles influence vocational choices. He differentiates between ability, which he describes as the "content of cognition", i.e. what is understood, and style, which is the process by which by which a "behaviour occurs", i.e. how understanding is achieved (ibid: 7-11).

To Froebel, the development of sensory perception was especially important, not only visual and tactile perception, but the interaction of all the senses with cognitive, manipulative and creative skills. The use of the 'gifts' and 'occupations' was, he believed, the only "true and necessary" means of education. (ibid: 24) They were the means by which he realised the beliefs that shaped his theory and by which he stimulated his charges and united them with their environment. They also provided the vehicles for the children's first 'active' investigations' (ibid: 21-24). The work of Piaget and others, which points to links between sensory perception and cognition, also seems to support the argument in favour of 'active learning' (1971: 33-36).

Within the broad categories of cognitive styles there are a number of what Messick describes as, "cognitive dimensions" which qualify the styles and describe the character and personal qualities of the individual (ibid 6-7, 14-22). He also describes three major sensory modes through which the individual interacts with his environment (see also Eisner 1982). They are the kinaesthetic (i.e. physical / motor responses); the visual (figurative / spatial responses) and the auditory (verbal responses). According to Messick, reliance on a particular mode in childhood, develops into more of a balance between the modes in adulthood, but individuals continue to show marked differences in their leaning towards one or other of the modes. This preference is exhibited in the ways in which they think and learn (ibid: 21-22). There are also two poles associated with thinking processes, these are divergence, often associated with 'creativity', and convergence often associated with 'intelligence' (ibid: 22, see also; 107-109).

The work of Messick and others, underlines the need for caution against adopting simplistic approaches to selecting curriculum content and the kinds of experiences we provide for students, and also to the ways in which we interpret ability. It illustrates that the process of intellectual development and the interaction of abilities and stimuli, is so complex that the exclusion of particular types of learning experience may have unknown and indefinable consequences for the individual. This view is endorsed by Squires (1990) who also, in referring to the work of Messick, points out that cognitive styles, perception, intelligence and personality, are so inextricably interwoven that in any given situation the individual brings a whole range of types of intelligence to bear. He goes on to make the point that if this is the case, we must adopt strategies which support the development of the individual in a multiplicity of ways, each of which should aim to encourage particular aspects of cognitive and other types of development, and that we must consider ability as being multifarious.

Like Messick, Eisner (1982) asserts the belief that the senses are vitally important in the process of conceptualisation, and that since sensibility enables us to communicate with our environment it can be regarded as a form of literacy (ibid: xii; see also Pestalozzi in Green 1911: 87). If one accepts this argument, it follows that literacy is therefore broader than language and numeracy. He explains that although written and spoken language conveys messages through symbols, it is the mental images they stimulate which provide the meaning (ibid: 40-41). Moreover, like Squires, he maintains that cognition cannot be separated from the senses, and that if we neglect certain aspects of human development we cannot be sure of the effect it may have on those aspects which are considered to be 'important' (ibid: 32-33, 68). The forms of representation we use are, to a greater or lesser extent, the most appropriate means through which we communicate our perceptions. But they also depend on our ability to use a particular form, say painting as opposed to writing, and the degree to which we are able to limit the inevitable "reduction" or "abstraction" which takes place in the process of externalising our perceptions (ibid: 49, see also: 40). The ways in which we communicate our ideas and perceptions are, according to Eisner, strongly influenced and limited by the "ways in which we think" (ibid: 47-48-49). He also maintains that the forms of representation we develop, provide us with a range of types of language which vary in the degree to which they can communicate the various forms of information we store through our senses (ibid: 50-51).

In a similar way to Stenhouse, he sees the creative, as well as the critical strand of cognition as important, and argues that education should allow both to be expressed (ibid: 51). The interaction of the individual with his environment is described by Eisner as providing experiences which lead to the formation of concepts, followed by the need to communicate them. It is this need that necessitates a means by which the concepts can be communicated, and the outcomes integrated into the environment. This on-going form of enrichment is limited by our experiences and perceptions (ibid: 54) which is why the development of sensory perception is so important. Eisner described three modes for the forms of representation: the "mimetic mode", which is concerned with imitation; the "expressive mode", concerned with expressive character; and the "conventional mode", which is concerned with signs and symbols etc. (ibid: 56-63). In both the mimetic and expressive modes, the means of communicating an idea is to some extent figurative. The conventional mode is more abstract and requires the receiver to imagine the form of the idea. This implies a need for, and a capability to engage in, the creative or conceptualising process when receiving information. Hence the importance of our ability to both transmit and receive forms of representation in the conventional mode. All three types of representation therefore require sensory perception either in the formulation of the representation, or in the reception of the representation. In the case of the conventional mode, the understanding of the concept depends on our ability to reach into our reservoir of sensory data and locate and retrieve that which is stimulated by the symbols presented to us. Eisner describes cognition in the following way:

> "Cognition is wider than the forms of representation that are common to propositional discourse and simple forms of arithmetic. To apply such solutions to the problems of improving the quality of education is to underestimate seriously the intellectual capacities children posses." (ibid: 68)

Eisner, like Hargreaves and Stenhouse, draws attention to the importance and uniqueness of aesthetic and creative experiences for reasons other than those concerning the development of cognition, which have been briefly examined above. Eisner refers also, to the "syntax" of the forms of representation and points out that, while the creative and expressive arts have rules of organisation, they do not determine what is or is not correct, and they tend to derive from the styles or types of form to which they correspond. Other modes of communication such as mathematics, have "rule governed syntax" (ibid: 63-67). He argued that the imbalance between the conventional mode of representation and the mimetic and expressive modes, which are characteristic of traditional academic curricula, need to be redressed, and that the range of meaning associated with *all* aspects of cognition need to be widened (ibid: 72-73). There is a need for students to have greater access to those aspects of the curriculum which develop sense and sensibility (ibid: 74). Eisner concurs with the notion of 'individualised teaching', but argues that this must address a greater range of variables than simply the speed at which a student progresses through a programme of study. It must be concerned with matching a student's range of abilities with the appropriate modes of representation and presentation, increase the student's range of abilities, and help him or her to find ways in which they can interact and enrich learning (ibid: 79-81).

External constraints on individuality

Finally in this chapter it may be worth pointing again to the limitations which are enforced by the social milieu, and which can undermine the best efforts of educationists to provide an egalitarian and student centred curriculum. Whereas Hargreaves is optimistic that the 'right kind of curriculum' can lead to a better society, others like Bowles and Gintis, see the capitalist system as a perpetual hindrance to progress in this direction.

Bowles and Gintis, like Eisner, Stenhouse and Hargreaves, recognise that full self-realisation requires a breadth of experience and should not be limited to a narrow instrumentalist view of the types of experiences which should be provided.

> "Personal fulfilment depends, in large part, on the extent, direction, and vigour of development of our physical, cognitive, emotional, aesthetic, and other potentials. If the educational system has not spoken to these potentialities by taking individual development as an end in itself, it has failed utterly." (ibid: 21)

They see the meritocratic system as repressive (ibid: 39) and cite as evidence, systems of grading which they believe reward conformists and penalise non-conformists. They argue that the system of rewards and punishments penalises qualities such as creativity (ibid: 42). They also claim that studies have shown that students who rate highest in social terms, are those who exhibit high levels of conformity with the social norms of the school and are seen as possessing "the drive to achieve." These same students, they assert, rate lower on average than other students in terms of creativity and mental flexibility (ibid: 40-41). They also claim that repression and inequality do not originate in the education system but: "..in the structure and functioning of the capitalist economy..." (ibid: 49 see ch. 3). According to Bowles and Gintis, progressive education has been undermined by the values of middle-class capitalist America (see ibid: ch.2, ch.4). They suggest that the kinds of 'qualities' which are valued most highly by employers are cognitive, technical, and operational skills; personal qualities, such as perseverance, motivation, and dexterity; self-preservation skills, such as speech, dress, and the ways in which the individual relates to peers and superiors (ibid: 94-95). The progressive ideals of an integrated, egalitarian and wholly developmental education are, they claim, contradictory to the capitalist system and are therefore bound to fail (ibid: 45).

Summary

In this chapter, the 'student centred curriculum' has been explored, and several different emphases have been highlighted. These have ranged from the romantic idealism of Rousseau and some of his followers, to the more contemporary work of Messick and others, on the development of cognition. The beginnings of an awareness of the interaction of sensory perception and cognition, evident in the work of Froebel, was seen to reach greater fruition in the work of Piaget, Bruner, Eisner, Stenhouse and others. The importance of structuring the learning experience, so important in the work of Pestalozzi, Froebel and Dewey, was contrasted with the most extreme forms of progressivism in which 'natural development' was the overriding concern. In the work of Dewey, Hargreaves, Eisner and Stenhouse, the importance to individual development of: breadth and balance and coherence of content; relevant and stimulating contexts; and active forms of learning experience; were all highlighted. Tyler's definition of a range of objectives relating to personal and social skills (including study skills) is important. Taba's identification of the contradictory expectations concerning conformity and individuality, was echoed in the work of Bowles and Gintis who argue that the capitalist system sets the terms for the forms of behaviour which are seen as acceptable.

The different interpretations of vocational education were explored and the strands of training, motivation, and relevance were examined in both this and the previous chapter. The significance of the work of Pestalozzi, Froebel, Dewey, and Thorndike, in opening the door to a more scientific approach to pedagogy was also acknowledged. Some of the misconceptions concerning 'active learning' were highlighted. Piaget's assertion that activity should be seen as having a cognitive as well as a physical dimension, and that the most effective pedagogy is also often the most demanding, is particularly important in the context of this study. The significance of psychology in understanding intellectual development was also clear. The complexity of cognition was highlighted, as was the danger of assuming that cognitive development can be achieved through the implementation of curricula based on simplistic views of intelligence. The work of Messick and others on cognitive styles was noted as being significant in informing the teaching and learning processes. Also important was the identification of the complex strands of cognitive ability evident in the work of Bloom and others, and in the inter-relationship of cognitive and other skills highlighted by Squires. The work of Hargreaves, Stenhouse, Eisner and Messick et al, was noted as particularly important in providing both a broad rationale for, and methods of ensuring, provision of opportunities for students to develop a wide range of skills and abilities.

In part two I have explored the three main curriculum paradigms, identified some of their principal characteristics, the ways in which they vary and interact, and the educational ideologies which underpin them. I noted some of the more extreme forms of the curriculum and those which are perhaps most relevant in terms of this study, the purpose of which is to attempt to determine the relationship between TVEI and existing education theory. In the third and final part I shall attempt to draw conclusions which will clarify that relationship.

PART THREE

TVEI AND CURRICULUM THEORY: CONCLUSIONS

Chapter Nine

TVEI and the knowledge centred curriculum

The principle objective of this book has been to establish the relationship between TVEI and curriculum theory. There are three questions which now need to be addressed: 1) Does the evidence suggest that TVEI was based on established education theory? 2) If not, is there any evidence to suggest that TVEI would have benefited from the application of education theory to clarify and provide a more sustainable basis for the aspects of curriculum development it supported? 3) Regardless of whether or not TVEI began from a basis of established education theory, to what extent are TVEI developments similar to aspects of it? In the following chapters, drawing on evidence from parts one and two, I will attempt to provide answers to these questions.

Although part two explored curriculum theory under the separate headings of knowledge, society and student centred curricula, in reality these are dynamically interactive elements rather than separate curriculum types. Consequently the conclusions drawn from this study will take account of the tendency of the modern curriculum to draw on all the paradigms, with the emphasis often shifting between them.

Knowledge centred curriculum
The earliest forms of the knowledge centred curriculum, perennial and essentialist studies, the psychology of learning, and the type of pedagogy which they supported would seem to be at odds with the genre of contemporary education in modern societies. The curriculum of Plato, Aristotle and even Comenius would be regarded as somewhat esoteric even in the most traditional of schools. Didactic teaching and purely literature based learning are clearly incompatible with student centredness and practical application of knowledge. Faculty psychology and intellectual elitism, though far from extinction, are at odds with motivation through vocational contexts and the notion of equality of opportunity. A 'permanent' curriculum is likely to become an intolerable obstacle in a society in which knowledge is expanding rapidly. It is hardly surprising, therefore, that there is no evidence to support the notion that TVEI was influenced by the theory which underpins the more extreme forms of the knowledge centred curriculum.

Liberal education
Since liberal education has its roots in classical humanism, one might conclude that it would also be unlikely to provide a theoretical basis for TVEI. Even in its modern form, liberal education, as exemplified in the curriculum of the grammar school, would seem to be at the opposite end of the spectrum. As was pointed out in chapter one, such curricula had during the nineteen seventies, often become models for comprehensive schools and were regarded as unsatisfactory in meeting the needs of both industry and of students. Given that TVEI was at least in part a response to such criticisms, one would hardly expect it to have been much influenced by liberal education philosophy. On the other hand it is distinctly possible that it may have brought about some diminution of the aspects of the curriculum most closely associated with that

philosophy. Indeed that was the case so far as the pilot phase of TVEI was concerned.

Liberal education emphasises the intrinsic value of knowledge, whereas TVEI emphasised the extrinsic / instrumental value of education. There are at least four aspects or strands to such values, the first three of which were identified by Peters, and the fourth by Lawton. Firstly, extrinsic values can be seen in terms of the individual and are primarily concerned with the 'currency' of education. They are associated with obtaining qualifications and gaining accreditation for skills. Secondly, there is a strand which is much more to do with the needs of society and perhaps in particular the needs of industry. The work of Taba and also of Bowles and Gintis, Bernstein, Young and Apple make it clear that there are potential problems in addressing such needs since they are often contradictory.   Society, and industry in particular, needs creativity and individualism but seems much happier with people who are adaptive and conformist and who know their place in the hierarchies into which they are required to fit.

Thirdly, there is a strand which is concerned with the kind of society we live in and is bound up with the role of education in protecting and enhancing the kind of democratic values society shares. The work of Dewey in the early part of this century was mentioned in this context. Fourthly, there is a strand which is associated with changing or shaping attitudes and values in a particular way. This might be through some form of 'social engineering', but more probably, through other subtler ways such as broadening perceptions by expanding the range of experiences which are presented. TVEI would seem to have been particularly concerned with strands one, two and four.

TVEI was not, however, exclusively concerned with extrinsic values. This study has noted the importance of intrinsic values which can be differentiated into three strands. The first, identified by Peters, is 'knowledge for its own sake'. Intrinsic value in this sense is associated with notions of 'cognitive perspective' which includes valuing knowledge because it is intellectually challenging and or rewarding, and for its value in supporting the process of 'becoming educated'. The second strand identified by White is that of personal fulfilment, which in a sense is also associated with the aspect noted above. Intrinsic values in this context might also be associated with personal desires or goals, such as learning to play an instrument or improving one's performance in a particular field. The third strand identified by Stenhouse, is intrinsic value as discovery, i.e. pushing forward the boundaries of human knowledge. This might be connected with expanding or developing the parameters of a chosen field and is often associated with 'high culture', and developments in for example, fine art, music or literature, but could also apply to other aspects of scientific and cultural development.   The TVEI emphasis on learning skills and positive achievement would seem to address aspects of the first of these. However intrinsic and extrinsic values are often interwoven. Extrinsic values can for example, be used as a 'hook' to secure the student's interest in a particular aspect of education which in time may lead to the individual's ability to value the intrinsic worth of other aspects of learning, as exemplified in the philosophy of Kirschensteiner.

There would seem to be a good deal of evidence to support the notion that in the pilot TVEI projects, changes in the curriculum were most supportive of those elements which were traditionally regarded as being low status in the academic curriculum. TVEI enhanced elements such as the technical, the vocational, the personal and social, and possibly to a lesser extent, the aesthetic-creative. The status of teachers in those areas of experience was likewise enhanced. Upgrading the status of these elements was achieved in a number of ways by: (1) providing substantial new and often high-tec resourcing which attracted a more balanced student intake; (2) underpinning this with a contractual requirement for TVEI cohorts to include students across the full ability range; (3) encouraging the elimination of out-dated and gender stereotyped courses; (4) providing development time for teachers of the new courses; (5) drawing to the new courses, teachers from high status subjects such as science and mathematics.

The post-National Curriculum emphasis of TVEI did not detracted from the instrumentalist aims of the project, although in the extension phase developments focused on a much more holistic approach, with aspects such as cross-curricular themes and skills, and records of achievement being developed across the curriculum. In the extension phase of TVEI a number of development 'themes' have been identified most of which are cross-curricular. These can be described as support for: (1) the introduction of the National Curriculum; (2) cross-curricular themes, skills and dimensions; (3) student centred approaches to teaching and learning; (4) the use of real contexts (including work experience); (5) developments in assessment and records of achievement; (6) the development of careers education and guidance; (7) developments in the management of curriculum change; and (8) progression and continuity including careers education. In addition TVEI emphasised the importance of particular subjects, i.e. science, technology and modern foreign languages, and an entitlement curriculum for all students. However the underlying rationale was influenced by instrumentalist arguments, for example, improving the quality of the workforce, rather than intrinsic or liberal education values.

A liberal education is by its very nature meritocratic and hierarchical and thus involves selection processes and may encourage conformist attitudes, all of which according to Bowles and Gintis for example, appear to be highly valued by employers. Unfortunately liberal education does not, as we have seen, value basic skills or other forms of skills training very highly, and it is oriented away from world of work values. Even so one might be tempted to see meritocracy as one aspect of liberal education which TVEI might have developed. Although there was some suggestion of elitism and back-door selection in the early days of the TVEI pilots, there is no evidence to support the notion that there was ever any intention to limit TVEI curricula to students in a particular ability range. There are few examples where the criteria for selection of the TVEI cohort was infringed, resulting in only a narrow band of the ability range being selected. Equality of opportunity and access, one of the main thrusts of TVEI, would therefore seem to be at odds with liberal education values especially if one adopts Hutchins' argument that equality of opportunity means that students should have no option but a literature-based academic education.

If liberal education theory influenced TVEI at all, and there is no evidence to suggest that in policy terms it did, it was a negative rather than a positive influence. TVEI challenged liberal education values, particularly in the pilot phase when it attempted to provide a counter-balance to academic studies. In the extension phase it did, within a subject-based general education framework and with varying degrees of success, draw out and emphasise those aspects most relevant to employment and 'employability'.

Curriculum breadth and balance

The TVEI pilot projects were concerned with particular aspects of curriculum breadth and balance. Firstly, TVEI was influential in broadening the curriculum to include elements of technical and vocational education and with raising the status of technological and vocational courses. Secondly, TVEI was concerned with establishing a better balance between the acquisition and application of knowledge and skills, i.e. between theoretical and procedural knowledge. Thirdly, TVEI placed greater emphasis than had previously been the case on work-related skills and competencies and hence on the extrinsic value of knowledge and skills. In particular, TVEI emphasised the development of personal and social skills and the development of positive attitudes to work.

In the pilot phase the strategy employed was to establish a TVEI core curriculum. I discussed in chapter six, the curriculum model proposed by Squires which has three dynamically interactive dimensions: knowledge, the development of individual abilities, and cultural experiences. It is worth referring to this model in considering the possible forms of a core curriculum. Such a core might be determined by prioritising the dimensions proposed by Squires, or by placing particular emphasis on one of them. A core might therefore be selected on the basis of which is considered to be 'the most important' of the dimensions. Balance on the other hand, might be concerned with achieving parity between all of them. It is clear that the notion of a core of essential activities pre-dates TVEI and indeed, as we have seen, can be traced back to the origins of liberal education. It was evident in the curriculum of the 'Latin school' proposed by Comenius and in the more modern grammar school curriculum, i.e. the 'core plus' model, in which the 'plus' was usually an arts or science emphasis. Contemporary theorists such as White have also proposed a core curriculum. In each of the above instances one could probably argue that the emphasis is very much on the knowledge dimension.

There are however, examples of other core curriculum emphases. Froebel for example, emphasised a core of learning which centres on sensory perception and the skills associated with observation and investigation. In this case the emphasis is on the 'abilities' dimension of the Squires model, although there is no question that Froebel was also concerned with the psychology of learning. The work of Hargreaves provides a contemporary example of the same kind of emphasis.

The third example of a 'core emphasis', that of cultural experiences, is exemplified in the work of both Lawton and Skilbeck although they and Hargreaves, have broader perceptions of the curriculum and should not be thought of only in the context of one particular curriculum stereotype. Indeed both Lawton and Skilbeck are more interested in the concept of an entitlement curriculum in the context of the developing culture than a focused core of essential studies.

It is important therefore, in attempting to view the TVEI core in its correct perspective, that we consider aspects other than the knowledge dimension of the curriculum. In the pilot phase of TVEI the emphasis of the core would seem to have been primarily on the 'abilities' dimension, while in the post National Curriculum extension phase there was a balance between the three dimensions with greater emphasis on contexts and teaching and learning methods. However there is no evidence to suggest that this was the result of a better understanding on the part of policy makers of the theory which underpins these aspects of curriculum.

Breadth in liberal education terms relates principally to the development of a range of cognitive-intellectual abilities through an education in which academic studies dominate the curriculum. Breadth in TVEI pilot terms was concerned with finding ways of including in the curriculum opportunities for students to experience some elements of technical and vocational education as well as a general education core. In the extension phase it was more concerned with the provision of an entitlement curriculum which, using the Squires model, includes the knowledge dimension with emphasis on modern languages, science and technology, plus aspects of the culture and skills dimensions, in particular the personal-social, the aesthetic creative, and the social, economic, communication and technology aspects.

Balance in terms of liberal education would seem to be concerned with balance between a core of essential academic studies and other 'lesser' subjects. In the pre-TVEI curriculum this was a core of English, mathematics and science, plus physical and religious education, and choices from a range of other subjects or areas of experience such as: humanities, arts, modern languages and crafts. The curriculum did cover cognitive, affective and psychomotor skills, but with emphasis on the cognitive. It was concerned with both intrinsic and extrinsic values, but with emphasis on the former. TVEI provided a broader concept of balance. From the evidence in this study it would seem to have addressed the need for balance between: (1) content coverage, learning objectives and teaching and learning methods; (2) intrinsic and extrinsic values including the personal and social aspects; (3) knowledge, culture and abilities and the elements within them; (4) theoretical and practical knowledge; and perhaps most importantly, (5) general and technical and vocational education. Many of these aspects relate also to society and student centred curricula. For example (1 above), would seem to be concerned with student centredness, while (2) also seems to address aspects of society centredness.

It is important to note that TVEI achieved a balance between the academic aspects of the curriculum and the technical and vocational aspects without generally undermining the former. It did this by squeezing out many of the out-of-date craft and commerce courses. Where there was any imbalance in the early pilots, it was at the expense of humanities which were sometimes squeezed between the arts and sciences and the technical and vocational elements. But as the SCRE review revealed, TVEI could be accommodated without serious effect on other aspects of the curriculum. In the extension phase the balance shifted noticeably back towards general education with many of the valuable aspects of TVEI, such as economic and industrial understanding, and personal and social education, becoming elements of the non-statutory cross-curricular themes, skills and dimensions.

The aspects noted above had other spin-off effects also concerned with balance. Firstly, by changing the emphases from: (1) coverage of content to learning outcomes; (2) passive to active learning; (3) whole class teaching to individualised and group activities; (4) teacher directed study to self directed study; (5) those activities which emphasise teacher reconstructions to those which involve students in investigative and reflective activities; (6) the use of traditional learning resources to those which utilise the new technologies; (7) terminal assessment to diagnostic assessment; (8) long-term goals to short-term objectives; and (9) from negative reporting to positive recording.

TVEI pilot projects tackled the dual problems of breadth and balance and an overcrowded curriculum in various often innovative ways. One of the strategies used was modular courses, a strategy familiar in higher education but before TVEI not widely used in the secondary curriculum. The modular curriculum enabled provision of 'tasters' prior to possibly longer term commitment and in so doing proved to be a valuable strategy in addressing preconceptions based on subject and gender stereotypes. It also provided options for broader and more flexible curricula. Another strategy was the provision of a technological core, a feature of many projects. This had the effect of extending the existing core to include technology as part of the entitlement curriculum.

Modular courses, a feature of TVEI, have been shown to have several benefits since they can provide: (1) a possible strategy for addressing curriculum overload; (2) multiple pathways through the curriculum, with the potential to improve the match between the student's needs and the course provision; (3) a wider range of experiences than those which might be available through subject based courses; (4) a strategy for addressing equality of opportunity; and (5) modular courses can encourage a cross-curricular approach. They do however have some possible drawbacks. They may for instance, concentrate too much on breadth and not sufficiently on depth of experience. Greater choice of course options might be confusing rather than helpful to some students. Coherence may also be a problem in modular courses, and they can pose problems in terms of accreditation. In addition, the conceptual structure of modular courses may be difficult to define. However exemplars for modular courses at key stage four of the National Curriculum, which draw together for example, elements of science, technology and mathematics, as recommended in the orders, should have been developed, piloted and evaluated by SCAA.

The use of linked options was another way of broadening the curriculum of TVEI students and of building greater coherence into it by, in some instances, linking the core with particular options. Another strategy aimed at increasing breadth and improving curriculum cohesion was the broad fields approach. This particular method of curriculum organisation also enabled TVEI to be integrated into the entitlement curriculum. It is this approach which the 'original' National Curriculum came closest to implementing. The orders in science and technology for example, encouraged a cross-subject approach to some aspects of the programmes of study. However since the introduction of the National Curriculum, content and assessment overload, which in theory might be expected to force teachers towards a more holistic approach to the curriculum, has arguably had precisely the opposite effect. TVEI extension projects ought to have addressed this issue and should have been supported by SCAA in doing so.

Knowledge and curriculum structure

The value of the forms of knowledge in determining particular aspects of the curriculum has been acknowledged in this study. Equally clear is the fact that such a planning framework can address only that part of the curriculum which is concerned with cognitive-intellectual development. It is doubtful whether such a framework would have been of value in defining the full range of experiences provided by TVEI curricula. Neither Phenix's realms of meaning or Hirst's forms of knowledge would seem to be helpful in placing the technical and vocational aspects of TVEI within the curriculum framework, nor do they help in making decisions which relate to certain aspects of coherence, such as the relative merits of balanced science as opposed to separate sciences, or of creative arts as opposed to art, music and drama. It is also questionable whether they would help in determining the conceptual structure of the new broad design and technology courses or the more specialised high-tec courses highlighted in chapter two.

TVEI was introduced at a time when there was considerable concern that the curriculum was over-crowded. In terms of the knowledge centred curriculum any revision might therefore have been expected to begin with an examination of the existing content to identify 'key concepts' and the knowledge and skills associated with them, across the eight areas of experience identified by HMI. Such an analysis would not on its own have provided all the information required for a full revision of the curriculum. It would not necessarily have highlighted mis-matches between the existing curriculum and the needs of students, industry and society, nor would it necessarily have provided a clear indication of the types of ability students were likely to develop through the existing curriculum, since teaching and learning activities also influence the development of abilities. However it would have provided one of the dimensions for a comprehensive review. Such analysis was never on the formal agenda of TVEI, but one should not be led to believe that because of this, TVEI neither influenced or was influenced by, the knowledge centred curriculum.

In the modern knowledge-centred curriculum, knowledge is represented as dynamic and capable of expansion, but also as having a logical structure which is capable of being defined in ways which have become accepted conventions, such as subjects or disciplines. However knowledge can also be organised in other ways. It can for example be organised as broad areas of experience or multi-discipline courses, both of which can be sub-divided into smaller, more manageable units or modules. This was a pattern familiar in TVEI pilot curricula and to a lesser extent in the extension phase, for example in the creative and expressive arts, in balanced science and in technology.

There is no evidence that TVEI set any clear objectives regarding the structuring of courses or programmes of study, although both units and modules were often used. However it is possible that some of the strategies which were employed in managing the learning process could have addressed this issue. In particular, the formative recording methods, unit accreditation and individual action planning, all features of both pilot and extension projects, required teachers to think more carefully about what they taught, why they were teaching it, and how they would teach it. These criteria are congruent with the notion of the curriculum as content, objectives, and method, a model identified for example in the work of Hirst and Taylor.

The emphasis placed by TVEI on empowering students to take greater responsibility for their own learning, to become involved in the assessment process and to apply the knowledge and skills gained in new situations, clearly had a positive effect on the way in which content was structured. The unit accreditation process alone requires the identification of concepts, knowledge, and skills outcomes, and while the emphasis it places on measurable outcomes may be questionable, the process itself does provide a potential basis for a clearer sequencing of learning experiences and in particular the identification of 'key concepts'. Effective use of flexible learning strategies requires the same clarity of purpose since a clear and progressive structure is needed to enable students to both understand the conceptual structure of units of study and progress through them.

It is interesting to note that both Hirst and Peters refer to 'modes of thinking' which relate to the logical structures of the forms of knowledge, and to the importance of enabling students to acquire the appropriate modes of thinking. In the case of technology this might be described as 'thinking technology'. If the ability to acquire the appropriate modes of thinking depends on conveying to students the conceptual structure of the subject, it could be that modular pathways make it difficult or perhaps even impossible for students to acquire the appropriate modes of thinking. Perhaps that is why the emphasis in many of the TVEI pilot courses, particularly the broad fields modular courses (as opposed to the more focused ones, such as electronics and business education), was on skills rather than concepts. The rationale is of course, that these are the aspects of learning which TVEI was intended to develop and that the content was essentially a vehicle for their development. This rationale was genuine and the skills emphasis was not seen by teachers as 'the easy option'. However building coherence into courses which draw from several disciplines may present problems, and where there is little existing commonalty (such as there clearly is in the very successful balanced science courses) there may be some fundamental problems concerning structure and coherence. This may have been one of the reasons why so many of the new and innovative courses which were developed in the pilot phase of TVEI had problems with accreditation, and so disappeared in the extension phase. Application of theory concerning the structure of knowledge would undoubtedly have benefited the development of new courses and the current problems with technology in particular could almost certainly have been avoided if developments had been based on established education theory and good practice.

Another aspect of the knowledge centred curriculum which was explored was the differentiation of knowledge content into two broad types: (1) theoretical knowledge (knowing that), and (2) procedural knowledge (knowing how). Liberal education would seem to emphasise the former, while TVEI placed emphasis on the latter. TVEI also added a third emphasis - competence, i.e. the ability to select and apply appropriate knowledge, concepts and skills in real contexts. There would seem to be at least three ways in which contexts can potentially enhance the learning process: (1) by aiding the management of content, (contexts can help in setting manageable parameters); (2) by providing a mechanism through which the same concepts can be explored at various levels (the notion of the spiral curriculum); (3) by providing relevance and motivation (they can help to demonstrate the extrinsic / instrumental value of the learning). In TVEI the emphasis was primarily on the last of these but it is not entirely exclusive of the other aspects. However, there is no evidence to support the notion that any congruence with theory is more than coincidence.

It was pointed out in chapter three, that TVEI emphasised the application of knowledge and skills through problem solving activities. In addition, it is clear that many of the new TVEI curriculum elements, including work experience and careers education and guidance, are concerned with the development of work-related skills and competencies. Even where direct application of knowledge and skills is not possible, raising students' awareness of the potential for application in 'world of work' situations has been and still is, an important consideration both in terms of what is taught, how it is taught, and also in the range of achievements which are to be recorded. The last of these has posed problems in respect of accreditation since, as was pointed out in chapter four, subject focused examinations were not geared to accrediting generic skills and competencies. This undoubtedly highlighted a gap in the English system of examinations and accreditation pre-sixteen. The educational system in Scotland was slightly more responsive, and the introduction of SCOTVEC clearly had an impact in the area of skills accreditation. The record of achievement and unit accreditation has provided a form of accreditation but it is debatable how widely they are understood, accepted and valued by end-users.

The new subjects and courses introduced by TVEI such as: technology and balanced science, (both of which are now elements of the National Curriculum); the vocationally oriented pilot courses; personal and social education; information technology (which now has statutory status as a cross-curricular skill); work experience; and economic and industrial understanding; all provide examples of the attempt to achieve a better balance between theory and application. This is a process which was encouraged by TVEI. It is perhaps a measure of the influence of classical humanism on the modern curriculum that the importance of applied knowledge and skills, stressed earlier this century by Thorndike and more recently by Reynolds and Skilbeck for example, was understated before TVEI.

Chapter Ten

TVEI and the society centred curriculum

In chapter seven I explored the society centred curriculum as reconstructionism and noted that it has three strands the first of which is utopianism, the second is social reconstructionism and the third is democratic reconstructionism. In respect of the first of these it is interesting to note that even in Plato's perfect society in which knowledge is true riches, extrinsic values are not altogether excluded. This was evident in aspects of arithmetic, logic and astronomy, each of which had some practical application. TVEI would seem to have had little, if anything, in common with utopianism, except perhaps a lack of realism in terms of the immensity of its task.

Social reconstructionism

The second strand of reconstructionism, social reconstructionism, is worth exploring a little further. In chapter one I highlighted a number of issues which arose at the time of the 'great debate' and appeared to suggest that there may be in our society, a deep cultural problem which has an adverse effect on the way in which our value system relates to industry. In chapter seven I noted that Lawton's cultural analysis also showed up faults in the existing curriculum provision which resulted in a serious mis-match between the curriculum and the needs of society. There is clearly an issue over whether or not the mismatch was a result of an anti-industry emphasis perpetuated by the education system. TVEI was part of a strategy aimed at changing the value system in some fundamental way so that over time society's attitudes to industry become more positive. Compacts, education business partnerships and other initiatives such as the use of industry tutors, and teacher secondments to industry, are examples of other elements in the strategy. This being the case, it may be that some of the aspects of the TVEI programmes have implications which go beyond the parameters of this study.

The process which TVEI began seems to be one of ensuring that business and industry has a 'stake' in education. As a strategy to avoid future criticism of education for being out of touch with industry's needs, this would seem to make sense. However it is not without dangers, as has been clearly indicated. A curriculum increasingly based on instrumental values may be one which excludes important areas of experience such as, for example, the creative and expressive arts. It will therefore be important for educators to keep a protective eye on the entitlement curriculum in the years ahead.

TVEI developed numerous strategies specifically aimed at improving student attitudes to work and industry and bridging the divide between school and work. These included an emphasis on personal and social education, and the development of work related knowledge and skills such as economic and industrial understanding, enterprise activities, and work experience. TVEI enhanced careers programmes, encouraged the use of industrial tutors and real contexts for learning, and supported various kinds of industry-related off-site experiences. TVEI would seem to have been successful in addressing many of the criticisms of industry regarding the abilities of school-leavers, in particular the perceived lack of young people with the skills needed by the new industries, poor attitudes and a lack of basic communication skills.

In areas where heavy industry was run down, the established patterns of employment and skills requirements changed swiftly and brought with them social traumas. There was a need in such situations, for some short-term remedial action as well as long term reconstruction programmes. TVEI (and the youth training programmes) could be regarded as elements of both. The pilot projects had a brief to respond to local employment trends and circumstances and the extension programmes were expected to provide a 'bridge' between education training and work.

In the pilot phase of TVEI there was a definite emphasis on the development of vocationally oriented courses. There are however, very few examples of instances where the TVEI pilot programmes were closely related to the skills needs of particular industries, and I have found no examples of specific training for jobs. In general, the main thrust of the TVEI pilot programmes was in awareness-raising. This included encouraging people from industry to become involved in education, and teachers and students undertaking activities which made them more aware of local industry and its needs. Secondly, it involved the development of programmes which included a core of generic work-related skills. Thirdly, it emphasised qualities such as self-reliance, enterprise and business skills in order to change attitudes which could be described as dependence on others. This might relate to an expectation of being channelled into a particular job (possibly for life) or being dependant on government to 'mop-up' local economic problems such as unemployment. Fourthly, TVEI emphasised the 'usefulness' of knowledge and skills so that students were encouraged to see education and training in a positive way. It did this by employing strategies which were intended to show students the relevance of their studies, through the use of real contexts, off-site experience, and other strategies which extended the parameters of the classroom. All of these initiatives were continued in the extension of TVEI and are in the spirit of reconstructionist theory. They are aspects of development in which genuine curriculum innovation has occurred by pragmatic development rather than theoretical approaches.

TVEI also employed strategies which were intended to regenerate the desire to learn by, for example, encouraging the use of information technology and by making the learning experience a positive and 'grown-up' activity. It advocated student centred approaches to teaching, positive recording of achievement, individual action planning and in some instances negotiated learning activities. While there is no evidence of outcomes of psychological research being applied, the success of these strategies should be noted and good practice highlighted nationally.

The extension phase became closely associated with implementation of the National Curriculum which has very specific objectives that relate to knowledge, skills and attitudes. TVEI extension also placed emphasis on science, technology and modern foreign languages, all of which have in the past had problems in terms of gender stereotyping and negative student attitudes. In the case of modern languages, there has been a further problem which might be associated with our having an insular rather than outward looking culture, and perhaps even a lack of respect for other cultures. The National Curriculum orders for modern languages, technology and the humanities subjects in particular, have addressed this issue and have been supported by TVEI in so doing. There is no doubt that meeting the challenge of foreign industrial competition has been a factor in determining the new emphases which TVEI supported.

In chapter seven I explored the issue of political pressure on reconstructionism and noted in particular the work of Apple, Bernstein, Bowles, Gintis and Young. However it is worth recalling the main thrust of their argument concerning equality of opportunity which is that: (a) it is not achievable; (b) it is actually the last thing that those most influential in a capitalist economy really want; and (c) it is 'wasted human potential' which might, if properly channelled, help to maximise investment in expensive new technologies, that is the main concern. In TVEI, equality of opportunity was a main objective from the first pilots, so one might justifiably ask: Is it to do with a serious attempt to implement egalitarian values in the education system or is it the implementation of capitalist values associated with 'wasted potential', and maximising industrial capacity and investment? Two other issues also need to be addressed in the context of equality of opportunity and both are closely associated with the previous question. The first relates to Bantock's argument that a common curriculum is not guaranteed to maximise the individual's potential, nor are egalitarian approaches which lead to the establishment of a common curriculum in the best interests of students from working class backgrounds, because the resulting curriculum invariably reflects predominantly middle class values. The second issue relates to the extent to which TVEI was: (1) a genuine attempt to underpin the legislation relating to equality of opportunity, or (2) simply paying lip-service to it in an attempt to ameliorate criticism that profound social problems were not being addressed. It is of course extremely difficult to reach firm conclusions and in truth there is probably a little of the egalitarian, the instrumental and the political incorporated into the motives behind the emphasis on equality of opportunity.

Another interesting question concerns the 'cultural' emphasis of TVEI, and whether TVEI came closer than the pre-TVEI curriculum to the notion of a 'working class curriculum'. It is worth reminding ourselves of some of the points raised in connection with Bantock's theory. Firstly, he pointed out the value of applied knowledge and of applying knowledge through problem solving activities. Secondly, like Dewey, he refuted the need for studies to be separated from life. Thirdly, he advocated improved technical education and specialist technical schools for those who would benefit from such an education. If this really is in part at least, a rationale for a working class curriculum, one has to conclude that TVEI (particularly in the pilot phase) came close to implementing it. However Bantock also advocated an academic curriculum for those suited to it. This kind of 'dualism' was not encouraged in TVEI, but the recent availability of GNVQ and NVQ units pre-sixteen, which might owe something to the success of vocationally oriented pilot TVEI courses, may mean that it will become the norm in the future.

This study has shown that even advocates of systematic approaches to curriculum development and methods often associated with social engineering had a broader view of the purposes of education than their stereotypes suggest. Skinner's writings on problem solving as a learning experience indicates approaches which TVEI, with its strong emphasis on problem solving, could profitably have drawn on. Bobbitt proposed a curriculum which included many objectives relating to aspects of personal and social education. Tyler also endorsed the use of objectives associated with development of personal, social, and study skills, all of which were important aspects of TVEI. There is no question that TVEI utilised the objectives approach to curriculum planning through modular courses and unit accreditation, but not to the exclusion of other models of curriculum development. What is not clear is how it became a TVEI strategy. It seems likely that it was introduced via the MSC's skills training programmes rather than as a consequence of planning based on curriculum theory. In terms of 'social engineering' there appears to be no substantive evidence of TVEI producing a 'particular kind of product'. If anything, considering TVEI's accent on student centredness and individualised learning programmes, the emphasis might be expected to be precisely the opposite.

Democratic reconstructionism

Finally in this chapter I want to turn to the form of the ideology Lawton describes as 'democratic reconstructionism' and which the evidence would suggest can be more closely associated with TVEI than either of the other forms. There are several reasons why this is so. Firstly as was indicated in chapter seven, there are good reasons why education is closely associated with cultural change. Changes in the culture affect the purpose, content and processes of learning in fundamental ways. These changes, as has been indicated in the earlier chapters, are brought about by a variety of factors including political and economic changes, and technological developments. They can effect any of the cultural systems identified by Lawton, and they can impact on our perceptions, priorities and relationships with each other and with our environment. We can respond to them in various ways, for example by attempting to reject or react against them either as individuals, as groups, or as a whole society. This might be a Utopian strategy realised by for example, 'opting-out of society' and establishing a 'sub-culture', or by imposing a doctrinaire political regime. Alternatively we might seek to channel or direct them in a particular way or to absorb them with as little change as possible to our established ways of living. This is perhaps the way in which the classical humanist ideology survives so effectively. We can also respond to them in positive ways and try our best to benefit from them. This would seem to have been the response immediately post 'great debate'.

To do this we need to monitor the elements of the curriculum periodically to make sure that they reflect the culture. This approach might involve the kind of cultural analysis described by Lawton and Skilbeck. We know from the writings of Tyler, Taba, Lawton, and Skilbeck that sometimes the changes in modern industrial societies like ours can be very rapid and that the content of the curriculum can get 'left behind'. This 'cultural lag' as Lawton calls it, clearly existed in the curricula of the nineteen seventies and eighties. We know this to be the case not simply because Lawton's analysis showed it to be true, but because DES and HMI reports, as indicated in chapter one, all highlighted similar concerns. Those concerns have already been explored at length in this study and there is a reasonably high level of congruence between them. The cultural analysis which took place was never undertaken systematically and there is no indication that the outcomes of the various studies resulted from similar methods being employed. Nevertheless, some kind of analysis must have taken place in order for the particular outcomes to have been reached. They relate to the whole curriculum, to problems of content, method, and purpose, and clearly reflect a desire to address the issues. They also relate to the kind of society we live in and indicate clearly a programme for change. TVEI, as is particularly evident in "Better Schools", was part of that strategy.

TVEI addressed some of the main criticisms of the existing curriculum which emerged as a result of Lawton's analysis, in particular the need for real contexts. But TVEI was concerned with: (1) enhancing the status of technology; (2) establishing it as part of the entitlement curriculum; (3) the notion of entitlement itself; (4) establishing use of information technology as a cross-curricular skill; and (5) enhancing the status of the creative and expressive arts; (although there is no substantive evidence that it has necessarily helped establish them as part of the entitlement curriculum). Given the pressures which still exist on curriculum time, the TVEI developments in 'combined arts courses' and the establishment of GCSE examinations for such courses may help in ensuring some aesthetic / creative experience for most students at key stage four of the National Curriculum. As far as technology is concerned, there are still some major problems as was indicated in chapter two. The attitudes of students revealed in the TVEI extension survey, clearly indicate that the quality of experience is at best variable. The evidence supports Hemming's view that not enough attention is paid in secondary schools to encouraging students to undertake practical investigations concerning how and why things work, and to acquire and apply 'key concepts'. On the other hand, through TVEI, information technology has become a valuable motivating and learning tool, a view supported by HMI.

Chapter Eleven

TVEI and the student centred curriculum

The emphasis which TVEI placed on procedural knowledge and its application in 'real contexts' has, as was pointed out in chapter three, had important implications for teaching and learning methods. The 'liberal arts' curriculum places great emphasis on coverage of content, teacher direction and didactic methods. Such methods are inappropriate where the emphasis is on application of knowledge in real contexts through for example, problem solving activities, nor are they appropriate in learning situations which attempt to offer individualised progression through programmes of study. One of the strategies employed by TVEI projects to encourage individualised programmes, was flexible learning an element of which, is supported self-study. However supported self-study has two polarities. When it is confined to academic or theoretical knowledge, self-study might be possible through an entirely literature based course such as that advocated by Hutchins. At the other extreme, self study in the context of some of the more esoteric forms of progressivism, might provide an entirely open learning situation where the student is merely pointed in the direction of a range of resources and left to find his or her own way. TVEI would seem to occupy the middle-ground, with students being gradually encouraged to take greater responsibility for their own learning. This approach has value in preparing students for further and higher education and life-long learning.

Learning and development
In chapter eight, I explored the student centred curriculum and noted that in the work of Rousseau, and also to some extent that of Pestalozzi and Froebel, there was a romantic idealism attached to the development of teaching and learning processes. Both Froebel and Pestalozzi were aware that learning activities which were active and which took account of the student's stage of intellectual development were the most effective. There was perhaps, something of the romantic and the experimental about the student centred developments in the early TVEI pilot projects. Any evidence that they were based on scientific research or principles is certainly hard to find. It is debatable whether even in some of the major developments such as recording achievement, which has had a significant effect on pedagogical development, there was even a pragmatic approach. Evidence supports the view that in the early TVEI projects, developments in teaching and learning began with identification of problems (in the case of recording achievement it was probably the difficulty in accrediting transferable skills) solutions were then generated and tested on an ad-hoc basis and where there was a degree of success, the theory, if it existed at all, followed and underpinned the development in either a conscious or unconscious way.

In TVEI there were a host of developments concerned with student-centred approaches to teaching and learning which appear to reflect previously documented approaches to similar issues. For example, the arguments of Dewey and more recently of Hargreaves and Stenhouse, that there is no reason why content should always be organised as disciplines, is reflected in many of the curriculum models described in chapter two. Similarly the concern expressed by Dewey, Thorndike, Taba, and more recently Lawton and Skilbeck regarding relevance, motivation, interest, and the sequence and structure of learning, is also evident in TVEI developments, as was shown in chapters three and four. In some of the early pilot projects there were examples of activities such as business and enterprise simulations, where the notion of learning through 'occupations' was an objective. In terms of active learning, it would appear that amongst senior managers and teachers there was an awareness of the potential value of making learning, in Dewey's terms, an active and constructive process, and like Piaget, an understanding that the best methods are also the most difficult. Stenhouse's notion of the teacher as classroom researcher is not too distant from that of the original purpose of the TVEI pilots. Of course the main difference is the level of consciousness attached to the processes and the emphasis, which in the case of TVEI was perhaps more concerned with curriculum organisation than the learning process. However TRIST in particular, would seem to have been very concerned with classroom review and evaluation and with classroom based development.

There was, as explained in chapter four, a considerable emphasis in TVEI on student motivation. Various strategies were employed. Real contexts for example, were encouraged, as was the establishment of greater balance between: (1) passive and active learning; (2) (negative) reporting and recording achievement; (3) long-term goals (terminal examinations) and short term objectives (unit or module outcomes). There are, doubtless, aspects of the work of Thorndike and Bobbitt as well as of Tyler, Taba, and Hargreaves reflected in the development of modular courses and unit accreditation. The change of emphasis from content coverage to learning outcomes has had a lasting effect as can be seen in the organisation of the programmes of study in the National Curriculum. When handled sensibly and sensitively, objectives can be of great value in terms of motivation, particularly where they are clearly connected, in the student's understanding, with assessment criteria. Giving students access to such criteria, better still, giving them an opportunity to input into them, is surely one of main strategies in empowering students to take greater responsibility for their own learning. Unfortunately there is little hard evidence to suggest that in general, TVEI teachers were substantially more skilful in using such strategies, or that students were any better prepared to handle their newly found autonomy when they had it.

Thorndike's notion of establishing where the individual student is and progressing from there through individually structured programmes, is still 'light-years' away from the actuality, even within student centred programmes like the flexible learning projects supported by TVEI. What is often provided currently by teachers is more akin to a variety of pre-planned routes rather than individualised learning programmes negotiated with the students. Given the pressures on curriculum time and on teachers, it is likely that even where there is a genuine desire to move in the direction of individualised learning programmes, progress will be restricted. What can be achieved is greater variety of learning experiences across the curriculum, better structure and sequence, improved access and extension opportunities, better communication of assessment criteria to students, and much greater time, status, and student participation in the assessment process. These are areas where it would seem that TVEI and flexible learning have had a significant impact.

TVEI did, consciously or unconsciously, address some of Taba's criticisms concerning the traditional curriculum, in particular its neglect of creativity and learner autonomy, lack of relevance and the opportunity to apply knowledge. The strategy she proposed for achieving what she calls 'learning autonomy' and 'productive thinking', is to focus on key concepts which provide the structure for learning. This is being encouraged through projects such as flexible learning. Unit accreditation, introduced to support TVEI curriculum developments, also requires that the main concepts are identified as well as knowledge, skills and experiences. It is also one way in which TVEI addressed another of Taba's criticisms, that of the need for teachers to organise their ideas better. Tyler's objectives: learning skills, personal, social, communication and information handling, could describe the objectives of almost any pilot core curriculum, and are very much in tune with the cross-curricular skills encouraged in extension projects. They also reflect the GNVQ core skills. What Tyler describes are objectives which not only address skills development, but also attitudinal change, which again would seem to be reflected in TVEI strategies such as work experience and other off-site activities intended to encourage positive attitudes to work and industry.

The importance and complexity of cognitive development has been explored in terms of entitlement and would seem to be closely related to the abilities and culture dimensions, as well as the knowledge dimension of the Squires model. There is a need for education to develop both our critical and creative instincts and encourage exploration rather than rejection of the unfamiliar. TVEI strategies which addressed this need included the implementation of an entitlement curriculum and developments in student centred teaching. Although TVEI emphasised certain previously undervalued elements of the curriculum, including the creative and aesthetic ones, it did not generally reduced the range of experiences available to students and it has sought to improve balance between the three dimensions. There have been few instances noted in pilot project case studies, of skills rather than concept-based courses especially for non-academic students, and there is no indication that TVEI encouraged such an approach. However there is also no substantive evidence of TVEI having encouraged any form of differentiation other than by outcomes.

There is no indication of any direct reference to the interaction of sensory perception, intelligence, personality and cognition, even in terms of a rationale for curriculum breadth and balance, though this may be encouraged as the scope for options at key stage four of the National Curriculum opens up. It has certainly become an issue for headteachers in two of the Humberside consortia, who are revisiting the notion of an agreed entitlement at key stage four in the context of the new vocational opportunities now emerging. The pressures on certain elements of the National Curriculum, and issues such as the status of art, music and drama, ought to prompt greater consideration of the contribution all areas of experience make to the intellectual development of the student.

Student centredness
In chapter eight a number of points made by Hargreaves were highlighted concerning: (1) the lack of value attached to community spirit in the traditional curriculum; (2) the under-use of curriculum organisation which is not based on

subjects; and (3) the lack of attention given to personal and social education. In terms of TVEI curricula there was a deliberate attempt to extend learning beyond the classroom, this was noted especially in chapter three. The use of both modular pathways and broad courses has also been highlighted. Hargreaves talks about units as a strategy, not only to break down subject boundaries, but also to deal with disaffection for particular subjects, a strategy very similar to that employed in TVEI to introduce students to courses which, because of problems of stereotyping, they might not normally choose. Off-site experience and courses such as "personal and community services", are also examples of aspects of Hargreaves' philosophy in practice. Personal and social education, encouraged in TVEI extension projects as a cross-curricular element, was shown in chapter one to have been a major part of the compulsory core in many pilot projects.

Even Hargreaves' notion of abolishing public examinations at sixteen may not be entirely ruled out in the future. There are two reasons why this is so. The first is hypothetical and concerns problems of alignment of National Curriculum levels of attainment with GCSE grades and the questionable need for both. A related factor is the cost of GCSE examinations, which in the context of LMS is significant. In addition the level four threshold for GCSE grading may in some instances, also become the threshold for examination entries. The second more concrete reason is the introduction of GNVQ 'part one' and units pre-sixteen, with the option to continue and extend studies post-sixteen. It may not affect great numbers of students initially, but with the emphasis in GCSE shifting from course-work and teacher assessment to externally set and marked examinations, it could eventually be the majority rather than the minority of students who choose this route. If the fourteen to eighteen continuum becomes a reality, the profiling, recording achievement and action planning processes which have been pioneered in secondary education by TVEI, will become even more important than they already are.

As this study has made clear, recording achievement has been a major factor in developing student centred approaches to teaching and learning but the processes it involves are only understood and properly valued when they are an integral part of the management of the whole learning process. It is debatable whether the majority of teachers have the kind of holistic over-view advocated for example by Taba, or fully understand the dynamic interaction of the formative processes of teaching, learning and assessment. It is doubtful whether any curriculum development project could have the kind of permeating influence required to achieve such objectives.

Chapter Twelve

Conclusion

TVEI has had a major and largely positive effect on the secondary curriculum and there are many outcomes which reflect a much improved balance between knowledge-centredness, society-centredness and student-centredness. It has encouraged balance between content, methods and outcomes, and has influenced all of them. It has encouraged developments in teaching and learning by emphasising practical activity and application of knowledge and skills. In best practice it has encouraged teachers to be more aware of congruence between content and methods. TVEI also emphasised a fourth element, that of context / relevance. The effects of TVEI on managing the learning process, in particular on assessment and recording achievement, have produced many important outcomes. It is debatable whether policy makers are aware of them. They need to be made aware since the outcomes can influence greatly, the student's learning potential. Teachers also need to be made more aware that the 'formative processes' are as much about teaching as learning, and that as Bruner pointed out, low student achievement can be more to do with teaching than student ability.

TVEI has also had a very significant effect on enhancing the work-related aspects of the curriculum in both pilot and extension phases. Off-site experience for both students and teachers is becoming established as an integral element in many courses and is being supported through compact extensions and the developing education business partnerships. These are healthy developments and should continue to be encouraged, but industry should, if it really values them, be prepared to resource them.

There are some aspects of curriculum development brought about by TVEI which do appear to have been undermined by erratic changes in government policy on education, including the re-focused GCSE emphasis on terminal assessment and the 'falling standards' argument. The non-statutory status of most of the National Curriculum cross-curricular elements, combined with the pressures noted above, has effectively down-graded the themes and core-skills in the eyes of many teachers, and often re-scheduled them in the order of priorities of teachers who value them, but feel that other pressures take precedence. The cross-curricular themes, skills and dimensions should be made part of the statutory requirements of the National Curriculum.

Finally, in returning to the three questions posed at the beginning of this chapter, one has to conclude that there is no evidence to support the notion that the policy makers who proposed TVEI ever consulted academics for advice or guidance based on established education theory. However there is evidence that TVEI implemented aspects of curriculum development which HMI identified as necessary following the 'great debate'. There is also some evidence to suggest that the balance which TVEI sought to achieve between knowledge, society, and student centredness (now to some extent undermined by the National Curriculum) was deliberate, and that the TVEI emphasis was largely on the culture and abilities dimensions.

The second question related to the potential value of curriculum theory in clarifying aspects of TVEI developments. It is important to stress that all aspects of theory are potentially valuable to any major curriculum development initiative and although I may have been rather dismissive of the earlier forms of the knowledge centred curriculum in terms of their direct value to TVEI, they are important in the sense that we need to be aware of them and their limitations in order to move forward. It is equally important to be mindful that even the most idealistic philosophies of education may have important lessons we can learn from. For example, it is the interpretation and compartmentalisation of certain aspects of Plato's philosophy (e.g. the classical curriculum) which is perhaps outmoded in the modern world, not necessarily the means by which he arrived at it, or indeed all the purposes of it. Plato's curriculum was right for his time and his society, he had a clear perception of the whole purpose of education in that context and a 'thought through rationale' to underpin it. In the contemporary context, some kind of over-view of education based on established education theory and good practice, might have prevented the lurching from one 'good idea' to another which has characterised education policy making in Britain over the last twenty years.

TVEI could then have benefited greatly from a stronger theoretical underpinning. I have provided several examples of instances where the knowledge centred approach is potentially of great value to the organisational aspects of curriculum content. Particularly important is the need for curriculum developers to be aware of the 'conceptual structure' of courses and units of study, in order to ensure a clarity and organisation which facilitates the student's acquisition of the appropriate 'modes' of thinking. Also important is an awareness of the need for compatibility between 'the broad fields of knowledge', i.e. theoretical and procedural knowledge, and teaching and learning methods, and the relationship between concepts and contexts. In teaching some forms of knowledge it is appropriate to use a context as a means, not only of providing relevance for content, but also of determining the level at which concepts are to be explored and to provide manageable parameters for the content. The National Curriculum, which TVEI extension supported, has seemingly attempted to do this. What it has failed to do and what TVEI attempted to do with varying degrees of success, is to link this approach to student centred teaching, so that contexts are chosen for their congruence with the student's stages of intellectual development. No project-led research into the psychologies of learning has been evident. Had theory been applied to the student-centred developments in TVEI, the links between the structure of knowledge and the management of learning would have been clearer to teachers.

Other aspects of TVEI developments which would have benefited from the application of theory have been highlighted in part three and include the value of awareness raising amongst teachers, of the problems of 'cultural lag' and the need to periodically realign the curriculum with the culture. Teachers would almost certainly have responded more positively to change had they fully understood the need for it. Similarly a greater awareness of the complexity of cognitive development and its relationship with, for example, sensory perception, would have provided further support for the notion of an 'entitlement curriculum'.

There are many similarities between TVEI developments and aspects of curriculum theory, but they tend to be fragmented and ad hoc, and the theory has probably come after rather than before the event. Such similarities are to be found principally in the society and student-centred paradigms, and in the part that TVEI played in providing what Jones described as, 'the other legs of the curriculum stool'.

What is clear is that TVEI was a 'good idea' of policy makers that was remarkably successful in promoting and supporting curriculum change. But teachers have, generally speaking, had enough 'good ideas' thrust upon them over the last twenty years. Sir Ron Dearing's promise of a period of stability is welcome, but change will continue because it has to if the curriculum and the methods of teaching used are to keep pace with the demands of a modern technological society. What we have to ensure is that in the future all proposed change is underpinned by sound theory and good practice. If it is, teachers, policy makers and support agencies will be able to progress with confidence.

BIBLIOGRAPHY

Abbott J. (1989)
   From Teaching to Learning (A first consultation).
   TVEI Training agency & Education 2000
   Moorfoot, Sheffield: The Training Agency.

Ainley P. (1990)
   Vocational Education and Training
   London: Cassel Educational Ltd.

Apple M.W. (1982)
   Education and Power
   Boston: Ark Paperbacks 1982.

Arnold Matthew edited by Wilson J.D. (1932)
   Culture and Anarchy
   Cambridge: University Press.

Arnold Matthew edited by Smith P. & Summerfield G. (1969)
   Matthew Arnold and the Education of the New Order
   Cambridge: University Press.

Bain J. (1988)
   'Biotechnology Means Business in Merseyside'
   Insight Digest (3) 3,4.
   Moorfoot, Sheffield: The Employment Dept.

Bander P. (1968)
   Looking forward to the Seventies: a blueprint for education in the
   next decade.
   Gerrards Cross: Colin Smythe Ltd.

Bantock G.H. (1963)
   Education in an Industrial Society
   London: Faber & Faber.

Bantock G.H. (1968)
   Culture, Industrialisation and Education.
   London: Routledge & Kegan Paul.

Barnes D., Johnson G., Jordan S., Layton D., Medway P. and
Yeomans D. (1987)
   The TVEI Curriculum 14-16: An interim Report Based on Case
   Studies in Twelve Schools
   Moorfoot, Sheffield: MSC.

Barzun J.M. (1959)
    The House of Intellect
    London: Secker & Warburg.

Belth M. (1965)
    Education as a Discipline
    Boston: Allyn & Bacon Inc.

Black H. et al (1988)
    The Gift Horse: the management of change and resource
    implications in TVEI pilot projects.
    Scottish Council for Research in Education
    Moorfoot, Sheffield: Training Agency.

Black H. et al (1990b)
    TVEI: The Teachers' View
    Scottish Council for Research in Education.
    Moorfoot, Sheffield: Training Agency.

Black H. et al(1990c)
    The Impact of TVEI: a summary of three reports to the Training
    Agency by the Scottish Council for Research in Education.
    Moorfoot, Sheffield: Training Agency.

Black H. et al(1991)
    Changing Teaching, Changing Learning: a review of teaching
    and learning methods in secondary schools.
    Scottish Council for Research in Education
    Moorfoot, Sheffield: Training Agency.

Bloom B.J. et al (1956)
    Taxonomy of Educational Objectives: handbook 1: cognitive
    domain.
    London: Longman Group Ltd.

Bobbitt F. (1924)
    How to Make a Curriculum.
    Boston: Houghton Mifflin Co.

Bowles S. and Gintis A. (1976)
    Schooling in Capitalist America: educational reform and the
    contradictions of economic life
    New York: Basic Books Inc.

Boyson R. (1975)
    The Crisis in Education
    London: The Woburn Press.

Braine T. (1988)
'A TVEI Taster Programme in Sutton'.
Insight (14) 24-25.

Bridgwood A. (1988)
"TVEI's First Graduates Deliver Their Verdict"
Transition Sept. 1988: 18-20.

Broudy H.S. (1954)
Building a Philosophy of Education
New York: Prentice Hall.

Bruner J.S. (1960)
The Process of Education
Cambridge Mass: Harvard University Press.

Bruner J.S. (1966)
Towards a Theory of Instruction
Cambridge Mass: The Belknap Press of 1966; Harvard Univ.
Press.

Bruner J.S. (1971)
The Relevance of Education
London: George Allen & Unwin Ltd.

Burgess T. (1964)
A Guide to English Schools.
Harmondsworth: Penguin.

Clough P. and Nixon J. (1989)
The New Learning: contexts and futures for curriculum reform.
Basingstoke: Macmillan.

Cohen G. "Managing Change in Education Long term Strategy"
International Journal of Educational Management 1989 (3) 3;
13-18.

Comenius translated by Keatinge (1910)
The Great Didactic of Comenius
London: Adam & Charles Black.

Cook R. (1989)
Evaluation Working Paper No. 3: education-industry links, an
overview of evaluation findings.
Moorfoot, Sheffield: Training Agency.

Cox C.B. and Dyson A.E. (1971)
The Black Papers on Education
London: Davis-Poynter Ltd.

Crittenden B.S. (1982)
Cultural pluralism and common curriculum.
Carlton: Melbourne University Press.

Cross J. (1988a ed.)
Developments 1
Moorfoot, Sheffield: Training Agency.

Cross J. (1988b ed.)
Developments 2
Moorfoot, Sheffield: Training Agency.

Cross J. (1988c ed.)
Developments 3
Moorfoot, Sheffield: Training Agency.

Cross J. (1988d ed.)
Developments 4.
Moorfoot, Sheffield: Training Agency.

Cross J. (1988e ed.)
Developments 5
Moorfoot, Sheffield: Training Agency.

Cross J. (1988f ed.)
Developments 6
Moorfoot, Sheffield: Training Agency.

Cross J. (1988h ed.)
Development 8
Moorfoot, Sheffi`eld: Training Agency.

Cross J. (1989 ed.)
Developments 9.
Moorfoot, Sheffield: Training Agency.

Cross J. (1990 ed.)
Developments 11
Moorfoot, Sheffield: Training Agency.

Cross J. (1990b ed.)
Developments 13.
Moorfoot, Sheffield: Training Agency.

Cross J. (1991 ed.)
Developments 14
Moorfoot, Sheffield: Training Agency.

Dale R. (1989 ed.)
  The State and Education Policy
  Milton Keynes: Open University Press.

Dale R. (1985 ed.)
  Education Training and Employment: towards a new
  vocationalism.
  Oxford: Pergamon Press.

Dale et al (1990)
  The TVEI Story: policy practice and preparation for the workforce.
  Milton Keynes: Open University.

DES (1972)
  Education: a framework for expansion
  London: HMSO.

DES (1977)
  Circular 14/77
  DES Circulars & Administrative Memoranda: issued 1977
  London: HMSO.

DES (1977)
  Education in Schools a Consultative Document.
  London: HMSO.

DES (1977b)
  Curriculum 11-16: working papers by HM Inspectorate: a
  contribution to current debate.
  London: HMSO.

DES (1981)
  Curriculum 11-16: a review of progress: a joint study by HMI and
  five LEA's.
  London: HMSO.

DES (1983)
  Curriculum 11-16: towards a statement of entitlement.
  London: HMSO.

DES (1985)
  Better Schools.
  London: HMSO.

DES (Hargreaves D.H. et al) (1989)
  Planning for School Development: advice to governors
  headteachers and teachers.
  London: HMSO.

DES (1990)
   Statutory Instruments: National Curriculum: technology
   Circular 3/90
   London; HMSO.

DES (1991)
   Statutory Instruments: National Curriculum: science order.
   London: HMSO.

Dewey J. (1902)
   The Child and the Curriculum
   Chicago: University of Chicago Press.

Dewey J. (1915)
   The School and Society (revised edition)
   Chicago: University of Chicago Press.

Dewey J. (1916)
   Democracy and Education: an introduction to the philosophy of
   education.
   New York: the Macmillan Co.

Dobinson C.H. (1963)
   Schooling 1963-1970
   London: G. Harrap & Co. Ltd.

Duncan J. (1987)
   "Important, Relevant and New"
   Insight Digest (2) 5-8; 32-33
   London: MSC.

Dunham D.B. (1983)
   The Transition from Technical and Vocational Schools to Work.
   Paris: UNESCO.

Dunkerton J. (1988)
   "Encouraging Equal Opportunities within the Science National
   Curriculum".
   Insight (17) 7.

Durkheim E. translated by Fox S.D. (1956)
   Education and Sociology
   Glencoe, Illinois: The Free Press.

Edwards R. (1960)
   The Secondary Technical School.
   London: University of London Press.

Eisner E.W. (1971)
  Confronting Curriculum Reform
  Boston: Little Brown & Co.

Eisner E.W. (1985)
  Learning and Teaching the Ways of Knowing: eighty-fourth year
  book of the National Society for the Study of Education.
  Chicago: University of Chicago Press.

Eisner E.W. (1982)
  Cognition and Curriculum.
  New York: Longman.

Elliot G. (1981 ed.)
  The School Curriculum in the 1980's
  Aspects of Education
  Journal of the Institute of Education - University of Hull
  Hull: The University of Hull.

Emmerson C. and Goddard I. (1989)
  All About the National Curriculum: what you need to know and
  why you need to know it.
  Oxford: Heinemann Educational.

Employment Dept. (1990)
  Industry-Education Policy Strategies: broadsheets for teachers
   with case studies (No. 3. Modern Languages in the Work-related
  Curriculum).
  Moorfoot, Sheffield: Training Agency.

Employment Dept. (1991)
  Technical and Vocational Education Initiative - Review 1990.
  Moorfoot, Sheffield: Employment Dept.

The British Market Research Bureau Ltd. London. (1991b)
  Into Work: An initial study of the recruitment and performance of
  school leavers from the first 11 extension programmes.
  n.p: Employment Dept.

Employment Dept. (1991c)
  This is TVEI: Technical and Vocational Initiative what it means
  to local education.
  Nottingham: Meads.

Employment Dept. (Nov. 1991)
  A Strategy for Skills Executive Summary: guidance from the
  Secretary of State for Employment, on training, vocational
  education and enterprise.
  n.p: Employment Dept.

Employment Dept. (1992)
   TVEI Performance Indicators Progress Report 1988-90.
   n.p: Employment Dept.

Eraut M., Nash C., Fielding M. and Attard P. (1991)
   The Effective Management of Flexible Learning in Schools.
   University of Sussex Institute of Continuing and Professional
   Development.
   n.p: Employment Dept.

Evans A. (1991)
(for the National Symposium on Partnerships in Education).
   Partnerships in America "A Radical Agenda".
   Moorfoot, Sheffield: Employment Dept.

Fennel E. (1991 ed.)
   "Partnerships Take the Credit".
   Insight (21) 4-7.

Fennel E (1991 ed.)
   "Education and Training for the 21st Century -
   White Papers Published".
   Insight (22) 6-7.

Fennel E (1992 ed.)
   "News on Qualifications: GNVQ's Now Underway"
   Insight (25) 16.

FEU   (May 1989)
   Extending TVEI Bulletin 1
   n.p: FEU.

Finch H. (for Employment Dept., SKILL, SCPR)(1992)
   TVEI The Technical and Vocational Initiative: a study of the
   impact of TVEI on young people with special educational
   needs.
   Nottingham: Meads.

Froebel translated by Fletcher S.S.F. and Welton J. (1912)
   Froebel's Chief Writings on Education.
   London: Edward Arnold & Co.

Gagne R.M. (1966)
   The Conditions of Learning.
   New York: Rinehart & Winston Inc.

Gagne R.M. (1975)
   Essentials of Learning for Instruction (expanded edition).   ●
   Hinsdale Illinois: The Dryden Press.

Galton M. (1982)
> The Lessons of a Decade.
> Leicester: Leicester University Press.

Gleeson D. (1987)
> Curriculum Change.
> Leicester: Leicester University Press.

Glenn M. (1991)
> "Ten out of Ten for TVEI!"
> Science and Technology January (516) 34.

Gordon P. (1981 ed.)
> The Study of the Curriculum
> London: Batsford Academic & Educational Ltd.

Green. J.A. (1911)
> The Educational Ideas of Pestalozzi.
> London; University Tutorial Press.

Grego J. and Lane I. (1991)
> Flexible Learning in Modern Languages: case studies from
> Brackenhoe School and George Stephenson Community High
> School.
> North Shields: Flexible Learning North East.

Hall G. (1992 ed.)
> Themes and Dimensions of the National Curriculum: implications
> for policy and practice.
> London: Kogan Page Ltd.

Hamilton D. (1977)
> Beyond the Numbers Game: a reader in educational evaluation.
> Basingstoke: Macmillan Education.

Hargreaves D.H. (1982)
> The Challenge for the Comprehensive School: culture, curriculum
> and community
> London: Routledge & Kegan Paul Ltd.

Harrison G. et al (1988)
> Developments 7
> Moorfoot, Sheffield: Training Agency.

Harrison G. (1989 ed.)
> Curricular Changes 1982-1987 (14-16 Age Group): a report on the
> TVEI pilot schools in England & Wales, from the TVEI Database
> Trent Polytechnic.
> London: Training Agency.

Havelock R.G and Huberman A.M. (1978)
Solving Educational Problems: the theory and reality of innovation in developing countries.
Paris: UNESCO.

Hayes C., Anderson A. and Fonda N. (1984)
Competence and Competition: training and education in the Federal Republic of Germany, the United States and Japan.
A report prepared by the Institute of Manpower Studies for the National Economic Development Council and the Manpower Services Commission.
London: NEDO.

Hazelwood R.D., Fitzgibbon C. and McCabe C. (1988)
"Student Perceptions of Teaching and Learning Styles in TVEI"
Evaluation and Research in Education (2) 2; 61-68.

Herbart J.F. translated and edited by Mulliner BC. (1898)
The Application of Psychology to the Science of Education.
London: Swann Sonnenschein & Co. Ltd.

Hewitson J.N. (1969)
The Grammar School Tradition in a Comprehensive World
London: Routledge & Kegan Paul.

Hirst P.H. (1974)
Knowledge and the Curriculum: a collection of philosophical papers.
London: Routledge & Kegan Paul Ltd.

Hirst P.H. and Peters R.S. (1970)
The Logic of Education.
London: Routledge & Kegan Paul Ltd.

Hitchcock G. (1988)
Education and Training 14-18: a survey of major initiatives.
London: Longman Group Ltd.

Hopkins D. ed. (1990)
TVEI at the Change of Life
Clevedon, Avon: Multilingual Matters Ltd.

HMI   (1986)
Education in the Federal Republic of Germany: aspects of curriculum and assessment.
London: HMSO.

HMI   (1990)
Aspects of education in the USA: vocational and continuing education: a commentary.
London: HMSO.

HMI   (1991)
Technical and Vocational Education Initiative (TVEI) - England and Wales 1983-1990)
London: HMSO.

HMI   (1991b)
Aspects of Vocational Education and Training in the Federal Republic of Germany.
London: HMSO.

HMI   (August 1992)
Curriculum Issues 14-19: a discussion paper prepared by HM Inspectorate.
London: HMSO.

Holt M. (1979)
Regenerating the Curriculum
London: Routledge & Kegan Paul Ltd.

Holt M. (1980)
Schools and Curriculum Change.
Maidenhead, England: McGraw-Hill Book Co. U.K. Ltd.

Hooper R. (1971)
The Curriculum: context, design and development.
Edinburgh: Oliver & Boyd in association with the Open University Press.

Horton T. and Raggatt P. (1982)
Challenge and Change in the Curriculum.
Sevenoaks, Kent: Hodder & Stoughton Educational.

House of Commons Education, Science and Arts Committee (1982)
Education and Training 14-19 Year Olds: minutes of evidence 20th Dec
London: HMSO.

House of Commons Education, Science and Arts Committee (1982)
Education and Training 14-19 Year Olds: minutes of evidence Thursday 27th Jan. 1983
London: HMSO.

House of Commons Education, Science and Arts Committee (1982)
Education and Training 14-19 Year Olds: minutes of evidence
Monday 18th April 1983.
London: HMSO.

House R.H. (1974)
The Politics of Educational Innovation.
Berkeley, California: McCutchan Publishing Corp.

Hughes J. (1979)
"Education, Work and Unemployment in the 1980's
Educational Research (22)1; 3-14.

Hutchins R.M. (1952)
The Great Conversation: the substance of a liberal education.
Chicago: William Benton.

Jamieson I and Lightfoot M. (1982)
Schools and Industry: derivations from the Schools Council
Industry Project.
London: Methuen for the Schools Council.

Jenkins D. and Shipman M.D. (1976)
Curriculum: an introduction.
London: Open Books.

Jones A. (1988)
"The Real Aims of TVEI"
Education (173)15; 351-352.

Jones A. (1989)
"Talking to the Director"
Insight (15) 2-3.

Jones A . (1989)
"Training for Change a Training Agency Perspective"
NUT Education Review Spring 1989 (3)1; 48-53.

Kelly A.V. (1980 ed.)
Curriculum Context
London: Harper & Row.

Kelly A.V. (1982)
The Curriculum: theory and practice (second edition)
London: Harper & Row.

Keppel D.C. Duchess of Albermarle (1962)
The Adolescent Worker and Society: the twenty-eighth memorial
lecture, Birkbeck College London.
London: Birkbeck College.

Larkin J.C. (1959)
    The Main School Curriculum in the Grammar School.
    Sheffield: Institute of Education.

Lawton D. (1980)
    The Politics of the School Curriculum.
    London: Routledge & Kegan Paul Ltd.

Lawton D. (1983)
    Curriculum Studies and Educational Planning.
    Sevenoaks, Kent: Hodder & Stoughton Educational.

Lawton D. (1986 ed.)
    School Curriculum Planning.
    London: Hodder & Stoughton.

Lawton D., Gordon P., Ing M., Gibby B., Pring R. and Moore T. (1978)
    Theory and Practice of Curriculum Studies.
    London: Routledge & Kegan Paul Ltd.

Lawton D and Chitty C. (1988)
    The National Curriculum.
    London: Institute of Education University of London.

Lines A. and Stoney S. (1989)
    Managing TVEI in Schools: four years on: an evaluation report
    prepared for the Training Agency by NFER
    Moorfoot, Sheffield: Training Agency.

Lloyd G.E.R. (1968)
    Aristotle: the growth and structure of his thoughts.
    Cambridge: University Press.

Luck A. (1991)
    "The TVEI Revolution"
    Employment Gazette October 1991: 543-544.

Lyon M., Black H. and Thorpe G. (1990)
    Pupils and the Curriculum
    Scottish Council for Research in Education
    Moorfoot, Sheffield: Training Agency.

MacDonald B. and Walker R. (1976)
    Changing the Curriculum.
    London: Open Books Publishing Ltd.

Magnussen O. (1977)
    Education Employment: the problems of early school leavers.
    Paris: Institute of Education, European Cultural Foundation.

McCabe. (1986 ed.)
    TVEI: the organisation of the early years of the technical and
    vocational education initiative.
    Clevedon: Multilingual Matters.

McIntyre T. (1987)
    Evaluation Working Paper: equal opportunities for boys and girls.
    Moorfoot, Sheffield: Training Agency.

McIntyre T. and Coombes H. (1988)
    Evaluation Working Paper: TVEI work experience an overview of
    evaluation findings.
    Moorfoot, Sheffield: Training Agency.

Medway P. and Yeomans D. (1988)
(University of Leeds School of Education)
    Technology Projects in the Fifth Year.
    London: MSC.

Messick S. and Associates. (1976)
    Individuality in Learning.
    San Francisco: Jossey-Bass.

Michell M. (1987)
    Better Science: key proposals.
    London: Heineman Books / Association for Science Education for
    the School Curriculum Development Committee.

Midwinter E. (1973)
    Patterns of Community Education.
    London: Ward Lock Educational.

Moon B (1988 ed.)
    Modular Curriculum.
    London: Paul Chapman Publishing.

Morris M. (1992 ed.)
(NFER for the Employment Dept.)
    Pathways to Implementation: pathways to 14-19 provision:
    managing progression.
    n.p.: Employment Dept.

MSC (1984)
    The Technical and Vocational Education Initiative. (leaflet)
    Moorfoot, Sheffield; MSC.

MSC (1985)
    TVEI Review 85
    Moorfoot, Sheffield: MSC.

MSC   (1987)
      TVEI Changing Education 14-19.
      London: MSC.

Munro N. (1990)
      "TVEI Enters the Mainstream"
      Times Scottish Educational Supplement (1214) A8.

Murray K. et al (1991)
(NFER for the Employment Dept.)
      Pathways to Implementation: equality of opportunity?
      (Managing educational entitlement)
      n.p: NFER for the Employment Dept.

National Curriculum Council (1989)
      Circular Number 6: the National Curriculum and whole
      curriculum planning: preliminary guidance.
      York: National Curriculum Council.

Newsom J. (1963)
      Half Our Future: a report of the Central Advisory Council for
      Education (England).
      London: HMSO.

NFER (1992)
      Experiencing TVEI Extension 14-16 Overview Report: cohort
      study of TVEI extension students: 1991 survey.
      Moorfoot, Sheffield: Employment Dept.

NFER (1992)
      Experiencing TVEI Extension 14-16 Summary Report.
      Moorfoot, Sheffield: Employment Dept.

Nichol A. (1987)
      "Talking Together"
      Insight Digest (2) 33-34.
      London: MSC.

Norwood (1929)
      The English Tradition of Education
      London: John Murray.

NPRA (1989)
      Cross-curricular Approaches in Schools (1988-89): an NPRA
      investigation.
      Northern Examining Association & the Training Agency.
      Moorfoot, Sheffield: Training Agency.

OECD (1970)
    Education Policies for the 1970's
    Paris: OECD.

OECD (1983)
    The Future of Vocational Education and Training
    Paris: OECD.

Orlosky D.E. and Smith B.O. (1978 eds.)
    Curriculum Development: issues and insights.
    Chicago: Rand McNally.

Parker T. (1988)
    "Cross-Gender Options in Birmingham"
    Insight Digest (3) 18-19;
    Moorfoot, Sheffield: Employment Dept.

Parry J.P. (1971)
    The Provision of Education in England and Wales: an introduction.
    London: George Allen & Unwin Ltd.

Passow A.H. (1961)
    Secondary Education for All: the English approach.
    Columbus: Ohio State University Press.

Patrick D. and Cross J. (1990a eds.)
    Developments 12: technology for all across the curriculum.
    Moorfoot, Sheffield: Employment Dept.

Patty W.L. (1983)
    A Study of Mechanism in Education: an examination of the
    curriculum making devices of Franklin Bobbitt, W.W. Charters and
    C.C. Peters, from the point of view of relative pragmatism.
    New York: Teachers College Columbia University.

Pedley F.H. (1964)
    Guide to The Educational System in England and Wales.
    Oxford: Pergamon Press Ltd.

Peters R.S. (1966)
    Ethics and Education.
    London: George Allen & Unwin.

Peters R.S. (1973 ed.)
    The Philosophy of Education.
    Oxford: Oxford University Press.

Peters R.S. (1977)
    Education and the Education of Teachers.
    London: Routledge & Kegan Paul.

Phenix P.H. (1964)
    Realms of Meaning: a philosophy of the curriculum for general
    education.
    New York: McGraw-Hill Book Co.

Piaget J. (1971)
    Science of Education and Psychology of the Child.
    London: Longman Group Ltd.

Pierson D. (1990)
    "Shampoo formulae proves a winner"
    Insight (19) 4-5.

Plato translated by Taylor A.E. (1934)
    The Laws.
    London: J.M.Dent & Sons Ltd.

Plato translated by Lindsay A.D. (1935)
    The Republic of Plato.
    London: J.M.Dent & Sons Ltd.

Poinant R. (1970)
    Education in the Industrialised Countries.
    The Hague: Martinu Nijhoff.

Pollard A., Purvis J. and Walford G. (1988 eds.)
    Education Training and the New Vocationalism: experience and
    policy.
    Milton Keynes: Open University Press.

Popham J.W. and Baker E.I. (1970)
    Instructional Objectives.
    Chicago: Rand McNally & Co.

Preedy M. (1989 ed.)
    Approaches to Curriculum Management.
    Milton Keynes: Open University Press.

Price J. and Thompson A. (1988)
    "Staffordshire School Shares Business Experience with Mr
    Kipling"
    Insight (13) 7-10.

Pring R. (1989)
    The New Curriculum.
    London: Cassell.

Rajan A. (1991)
    1992 A Zero Sum Game.
    London: Industrial Society Press.

Rajan A. (1992)
(for The National Training Task Force)
National Targets for Education and Training: the case for targets
Rotherham: TAR Publications.

Rée H.A. (1956)
The Essential Grammar School.
London: George Harrap & Co. Ltd.

Reynolds J. and Skilbeck M. (1976)
Culture in the Classroom.
London: Open Books Ltd.

Richardson W. (1992 ed.)
(University of Warwick in association with the DTI)
Work-Related Teaching and Learning in Schools: education and
business in partnership: a report and commentary from the
Centre for Education and Industry.
Warwick: Warwick Printing Co. Ltd.

Roderick G. and Stephens M. (1982)
The British Malaise.
Barcombe, Lewes, Sussex: The Falmer Press.

Rousseau J.J. translated by Foxley B. (1911)
'Emile'
London: J.M.Dent & Sons.

Sanderson T. (1988)
"TVEI Horticulture in Wirral"
Insight (3) 64-65.

Saunders L. and Stradling B. (1991 eds.)
(NFER for the Employment Dept.)
Pathways to Implementation: clusters and consortia:
co-ordinating educational change in the 1990's.
n.p: Employment Dept.

Schools Council (1968)
Enquiry 1 Young School Leavers: report of an enquiry carried out
for the Schools Council by the Government Social Survey.
London: HMSO.

Schools Council (1973)
Evaluation in Curriculum Development: twelve case studies.
n.p: Schools Council Publications.

Sims D. (1989)
Project Management in TVEI: continuity and change.
Moorfoot, Sheffield: Training Agency.

Simon B. (1960)
    <u>Studies in the History of Education</u>.
    London: Lawrence & Wishart.

Simons D. (1966)
    <u>Georg Kirschensteiner</u>
    London: Methuen & Co. Ltd.

Skilbeck M. (1984)
    <u>School-Based Curriculum Development</u>.
    London: Harper Row Ltd.

Skilbeck M. (1984b ed.)
    <u>Readings in School-Based Curriculum Development</u>.
    London: Harper Row Ltd.

Skinner B.F. (1968)
    <u>The Technology of Teaching</u>
    New York: Appleton-Century-Crofts.

Smith G. (1988)
    "Staff Development and the Core TVEI Update"
    <u>NATFE Journal</u> (13) 2; 28-30.

Socket H. (1976)
    <u>Designing the Curriculum</u>.
    London: Open Books.

Squires G. (1987)
    <u>The Curriculum Beyond School</u>.
    Sevenoaks: Hodder & Stoughton Educational.

Squires G. (1990)
    <u>First Degree</u>.
    Milton Keynes: Open University Press.

Stafford E.M. Jackson P.R. (1982)
    "School and Work: A Technique to Help Bridge the Gap".
    <u>Educational Research</u> (24) 4; 243-249.

Stake R.E. (1976)
    <u>Evaluating Educational Programmes: the need and the response</u>
    <u>a collection of resource materials</u>.
    Paris: CERI.

Stenhouse L. (1967)
    <u>Culture and Education</u>.
    London: Thomas Nelson & Sons Ltd.

Stenhouse L. (1975)
> An Introduction to Curriculum Research and Development.
> London: Heinemann.

Stenhouse L. (1980)
> Curriculum Research and Development in Action.
> London: Heinemann Educational Books Ltd.

Still H. (1988)
> "TVEI its Aims as a Learning Programme and its Role in the
> Wider Curriculum"
> Educational Change and Development (9) 10-15.

Swann (Lord) (1985)
> Education for All: a brief guide to the main issues of the report.
> London: HMSO.

Taba H. (1962)
> Curriculum Theory and Development: theory and practice.
> New York: Harcourt Brace & World Inc.

Tanner D. and Tanner L.N. (1975)
> Curriculum Development: theory into practice.
> New York: Macmillan Publishing Co. Inc.

Tanner D. and Tanner L.N. (1980)
> Curriculum Development: theory into practice.
> New York: Macmillan Publishing Co. Inc.

Training Agency (1989)
> Papers of National Interest 6:
> TRIST regional network - new approaches to teaching and
> learning.
> Moorfoot, Sheffield: The Training Agency.

Taylor P.H. (1966)
> Purpose and Structure in the Curriculum: an inaugural lecture
> delivered in the University of Birmingham on 3rd Nov. 1966.
> Birmingham: Birmingham University Press.

TEED (1992)
> Flexible Learning a Framework for Education and Training in the
> Skills Decade.
> Moorfoot, Sheffield: Employment Dept.

Tenne R. (1989)
> TVEI Students and Studies: 14-16 students: a third report of the
> student / teacher database.
> Moorfoot, Sheffield: Training Agency.

The North West Record of Achievement Group (1992)
Borland L., Dale M., Deamer P., Godfrey N., Kirby R. and Thomas S.
(1992 eds.)
Achievement: assessing, recording and reporting achievement
and individual development in education and training.
Manchester: TVEI North West.

Thorndike E.L. edited by Jonich GM. (1962)
Psychology and the Science Education: selected writings of
Edward L. Thorndike.
New York: Bureau of Publications, Teachers College Columbia
University.

Tomlinson T. and Kilner S. (1991)
The Flexible Approach to Learning: a guide
Employment Dept.
Nottingham: Meads.

Tomlinson T. and Kilner S. (1992)
Flexible Learning Flexible Teaching: the flexible learning
framework and current educational theory.
Moorfoot, Sheffield: Employment Dept.

The Training Agency & the National Curriculum Council (1989)
"TVEI and the National Curriculum."
Insight (16) 3.

Trayers M. et al (1989)
Developments 10: flexible learning.
Moorfoot, Sheffield: Training Agency.

Tyler R.W. (1949)
Basic Principles of Curriculum and Instruction.
Chicago: University of Chicago Press.

Versey J (1989)
"The National Curriculum and TVEI"
Education in Science (134) 21-23.

Wallace R.G. (1987)
"From Concept to Reality - A Working Partnership"
Insight Digest (1) 3-5.
London: MSC.

Wardman M. (1989)
(NFER for the Training Agency)
Making the Grade: views of higher education institutions,
examining bodies and professional associations on TVEI.
Moorfoot, Sheffield: Training Agency.

Watson K. (1983)
   Youth Education and Unemployment : International Perspectives.
   London: Croom Helm.

Watts A.G.(1983)
   Education Unemployment and the Future of Work.
   Milton Keynes: Open University Press.

WEA (1962)
   15 t0 18: a summary of the major recommendations of the report
   of the Central Advisory Council for Education (England) on the
   education of boys and girls from 15-18.
   n.p: WEA.

Wheeler S. (1989)
   "Training for Change Some School-focused TRIST Activities"
   Educational Management & Administration (17) 4; 176-182.

White J.P. (1973)
   Towards a Compulsory Curriculum.
   London: Routledge & Kegan Paul.

Weiner M.J. (1981)
   English Culture and the Decline of the Industrial Spirit 1850-1980
   London: Penguin Books.

Williams A.M. (1911)
   Johann Friedrick Herbart: a study in pedagogics.
   London; Blackie & Sons Ltd.

Williams R. (1961)
   The Long Revolution.
   London: Chatto & Windis.

Woodhouse J. (1987)
   "Broad, Balanced, Liberal and Modern."
   Insight Digest (2) 40-41.
   London: MSC.

Worswick G.D.N. (1985)
   Education and Economic Performance.
   Aldershot, Hants: Gower Publishing Co. Ltd.

Wells M.M. and Taylor P.S. (1949)
   The New Law of Education.
   Sevenoaks: L. Butterworth & Co.

Young D. (1982)
"Technical Schools: Mailed Fist and Velvet Glove from
Mr. David Young".
Education (160) 21; 385-386.

Young M.F.D. (1971 ed.)
Knowledge and Control.
London: Collier-Macmillan Publishers.

INDEX